The Soul's Journey nourishes mind, heart, and "real life" through classic and contemporary spiritual quotes, meditations, deeply personal spreads, and concise card meanings. Ricklef's inclusion of the Minor Arcana honors our everyday life as a portal to the eternal. A beautiful, restorative tarot text!

— James Wells, author of *Tarot for Manifestation*

———

With this essential guide, Tarot earns its place at the grownup table of spiritual thought. Ricklef effortlessly distills the wisdom of the Universe and shares it with us.

— Christiana Gaudet, author of *Tarot Tour Guide*

———

Power packed with spiritual inspiration and mystical insight, *The Soul's Journey* is an invaluable book of tarot wisdom. As well as offering practical tools to learn how to use the tarot, Ricklef's magic with words invokes a "Higher" understanding of the significance of the cards and a longing to take the mystical path.

— Kooch Daniels, lead author of
Tarot D'Amour: *Find Love, Sex, and Romance in the Cards*

———

The Soul's Journey

About the Author

James Ricklef is a Tarot reader, lecturer, and writer. He has been a frequent workshop presenter at Tarot conferences and symposia from Los Angeles to New York. He is the author of several Tarot books, including *Tarot Tells the Tale* which was first runner up in the General Interest category for the 2004 Coalition of Visionary Resources (COVR) Awards. He is also the creator of the acclaimed *Tarot of the Masters* deck.

THE SOUL'S JOURNEY

Finding Spiritual Messages in the Tarot

JAMES RICKLEF

2013
CreateSpace.com
A *KnightHawk Books* Production

The intention of this book is solely informational and educational. The material in it is not intended as medical, psychological, psychiatric, financial, or legal advice. For such advice, please consult a qualified professional. The author assumes no legal liability for any damages, losses, or other consequences of any decisions or actions, subsequent to, or based on, the material in this book.

Also by James Ricklef

KnightHawk's Tarot Readings
(Writers Club Press)

Tarot Tells the Tale
(Llewellyn Publications)

Tarot: Get the Whole Story
(Llewellyn Publications)

Tarot of the Masters deck
(Self-published)

Uncovering the Tarot of the Masters
(KnightHawk Books)

Tarot Affirmations
(KnightHawk Books)

Tarot Reading Explained
(KnightHawk Books)

CB ED

This book is dedicated to Wil,
as always.

Table of Contents

CB BO

"I'm not a teacher, only a fellow traveler of whom you asked the way. I pointed ahead — ahead of myself as well as you."
— *George Bernard Shaw*

Foreword

Tarot illuminates our spiritual journey, the soulful journey of enlightenment.

Simply expressed, to be enlightened is to be one with the light. This is the most powerful teaching and modeling of the Tarot, our individual and communal journey of light and love. The seventy-eight cards we hold in our hands (or access through the wonders of modern technology) are a visual, symbolic, book of wisdom. As such, we are invited to study the lesson of each card by entering the archive so richly illustrated on each page of these sacred transcripts. Then, their lessons can be combined and rearranged to access multiple dimensions of meaning and message as we explore the layered complexity of this tried and true oracle.

Over time, these sweet and sometimes bitter lessons taught through our growing friendship and respect for our mentor, the Tarot, shape us to fulfill the deep potential we each carry within us to be our highest spiritual selves. Thus, the Tarot initiates us into our greatest adventure, our *Soul's Journey*.

Tarot as a sacred journey is intertwined with the history of the development of the deck of cards, forming the sacred fabric of our lives in which we are woven together. It was mythologist, Joseph Campbell, who charted the pathway of *The Hero's Journey* compiled from his cross-cultural studies of creation stories, the "In the Beginning" motif from ancient peoples and civilizations, as he discovered the essential theme that they hold in common—our collective spiritual journey.

Often called *The Fool's Journey* in the Tarot world, and what I have taught as *The Sacred Journey of the Soul*, the major trumps display the four-fold adventure in the tradition of all great stories: (1) the *Opening* where the stage and characters are set, (2) the *Mounting Action* when things begin to happen, (3) the *Crisis Point*, and (4) *Resolution*, when a momentary conclusion is established.

Each trump of the major arcana is a stepping stone to the next in what appears as an orderly sequence in the Fool's story, while the minor arcana's pips, the numbered cards, emanate the essential color of the major laws through the hues of their subsequent suits. For example, all four Aces carry the potential for manifestation imbued by trump I The Magician, yet each takes this essential energy into a different area of life. The people, or court cards appear as the living embodiment of these spiritual principles.

"Tarot *is* Life." This classic set of seventy-eight templates attempts to carry representations of every aspect of what we experience in our physical, emotional, mental, and spiritual lives. We observe these intertwined and layered themes in and among the cards, allowing the reader to tap into varying reflections of their querent's journey in life.

James Ricklef has dedicated this work to highlighting the subtle, yet very important spiritual impetus within each Tarot card, allowing us easy access to the divine communication at our fingertips. In so doing, we are inspired to open our minds and hearts to universal consciousness, enabling us to tap into our greatest potential.

Mindfulness, shifting our focus, and developing a daily practice of conscious awareness are all tools promoted in this essential volume for fostering our most spiritual selves. We walk hand-in-hand with James's thoughtful words as our guide to exploring many aspects of the mindset and practice needed to develop our realization of unity—the alpha and omega of the Tarot's ultimate message— our return to universal love and divine unity.

Drawing from the spiritual wisdom of the ages, *The Soul's Journey* is a masterful resource for accessing the many faces of God. What a beautiful marriage of the sagacious voices of our spiritual teachers and the cosmic template of the Tarot. Allow this book to be your guide on your spiritual adventure, this soulful journey called *Life*.

Katrina Wynne, M.A.
September, 2013, Yachats, Oregon, USA

Introduction

Why did I write this book?

"We are all on the journey towards enlightenment and at each stage must share what has been discovered with those who will listen. The sharing is part of the work. The listening is part of the work. We are all on the path." — Ram Dass

My initial reason for writing the material in this book was for the process itself—to explore the spiritual side of the cards. And so this book sprang from my research and explorations into spirituality and the Tarot—both applying spiritual truths that I found to the cards and discovering what the cards themselves were saying about our sacred journey. This process took me on an incredible journey of awakening, which I found to be valuable beyond words. Then in the midst of the process, I came to realize that I needed to share what I was discovering. So the second reason I wrote this book was to help other people along their spiritual path through the facility of the Tarot cards and Tarot readings.

Historically, Tarot readings have addressed matters of the material plane while generally ignoring the spiritual aspects of the questions at hand. The essential truth, however, is that every question has an unseen spiritual foundation, as does every authentic answer. We have but to look for those hidden aspects.

As Tarot readers, it can be our work and our privilege to help people investigate the spiritual aspects of their lives if they agree to have their readings delve into that level of exploration. And, of course, we can also use the cards to illuminate our own spiritual path. My hope, then, is that this book will help others bring the light of spiritual awareness into their Tarot readings by expanding their understanding of the cards to include spiritual layers. This book also suggests a few spreads that have spiritual components, and that too can facilitate the process of doing readings that are more enlightening.

How did I write this book?

The Tarot cards themselves were not the only source of wisdom for this book; sometimes they were the receptacle of and then vehicle for divine insights.

The fact is that I have drawn heavily upon a wide variety of spiritual sources ranging from the teachings of the Buddha to the poetry of Rumi to the philosophy of Plato and finally to contemporary books by authors such as Eckhart Tolle, Ram Dass, and Marianne Williamson.[1] Whenever I found a notable spiritual message in such sources, I sought to relate it to whatever card intuitively came to mind.

But the Tarot is (among other things) an esoteric system itself that has incorporated a wealth of spiritual wisdom over the centuries from such sources as Alchemy, Astrology, and the Kabbalah. Consequently, it is not surprising that the messages of its cards would be in strong accord with the wisdom of the sources mentioned above. Indeed, as I discovered sacred insights in such sources, I realized that there were cards that conveyed similar wisdom, so I considered what explanations or expansions they could provide about the pearls of wisdom I was finding. The result is this book's compilation of spiritual messages associated with the Tarot cards—messages that were often brought forth from the spiritual wisdom of the ages and then further explained by the wisdom of the cards.

There is one caveat about these reflections that I want to make at this point. These spiritual insights have, of course, been discovered, interpreted, and recorded through the filter of my own understanding of spirituality. They suit my philosophy well, and they work for me at this point in my spiritual journey. But am I presenting them as ultimate truths? To answer that question, let me present a little fable.

There is a parable in several eastern religions about a group of blind men who touch an elephant to learn what it is like. Each one feels a different part, but only one part—the trunk, a leg, the tusk, etcetera. They then compare notes and discover to their great annoyance that they are in complete disagreement as to what an elephant is. The reality unknown to them, however, is that each one is providing a valuable piece of the overall description.

Likewise, the Divine is beyond the scope of our limited, human comprehension. Consequently, although any spiritual revelation may be valuable, it will also be incomplete. But as we listen to all sorts of teachers, we can piece together our own understanding of the Divine. With a sincerity of seeking, that understanding will improve with time, but we should know it will never be perfect or complete.

---

[1] *See the Bibliography at the end of this book for more source material.*

Thus, to paraphrase George Bernard Shaw, I am a fellow traveler who is pointing the way ahead of both of us, myself as well as you. You may agree with some of the material in this book, and some you may not. Some of it will resonate for you; some will not. That is okay either way. I am not trying to impose my beliefs on you, so take from this book what you will. Feel free to adjust the card meanings here as you see fit. My hope is that this material will cause you to think about the topic of spiritual enlightenment in an open and heartfelt way and that you will continue your own search for truth guided always by your heart and soul, and perhaps also, in at least some small way, by this book.

How might you use this book?

Perhaps the most basic use of this book is as a resource to illuminate a "card of the day" draw. At the start of each day, you might pull one Tarot card and look it up in this book. Then consider one of the messages for the card as a lesson or insight to keep in mind throughout the day.

The card meanings in this book are also a great resource for interpreting the cards in spiritually-oriented spreads. (See *Part 3: Spreads for Spiritual Readings*.) Thus, for example, when a card comes up in a position defined as "How can I address the problem I am facing in a way that is spiritually awakened?" its meanings in this book will be more appropriate and useful than the worldly interpretations common in Tarot books. Of course, you might also use these spiritual meanings to infuse your ordinary Tarot readings with a more extraordinary, sacred content.

You can also use this book as a sort of daybook, or you can use it for bibliomancy. As a daybook, you would read it sequentially, considering one entry per day. For bibliomancy, open it at random and read the entry on that page for inspiration or even for an answer to a specific question. In either case, you may also want to pull the indicated card and carry it with you during the day as a reminder of its message.

Additionally, this book can help you deepen your knowledge of the cards as you explore them from a spiritual versus worldly point of view. However, you don't have to know about, or even care about the Tarot to find spiritual advice and inspiration in this book. Thus, you can read this book as an exploration of its spiritual messages, regardless of the card associations. In that way too, this book will help you find deeper spiritual wisdom in your journey through life.

How can you discover your own spiritual meanings for the cards?

As previously noted, you should feel free to adjust the card meanings in this book as you see fit. Or you may want to add to them. But how might you do that? How can you explore and discover your own spiritual meanings for the cards?

First, you can meditate on a card. There are several ways to do this. You might just sit in quiet contemplation of the card image or in thoughtful reflection upon your understanding of the card's various meanings. You can also do a guided visualization into the scene of the card where you can interact with the people there and talk to them about spiritual questions. Briefly, the following are the basic steps for doing a guided visualization into a card.

- ONE: Enter a meditative state in whatever way works best for you. Perhaps you want to relax by focusing on deep, slow breaths.
- TWO: Explore the card. Describe its physical details, then the mood, atmosphere, and feeling of it. This step will bring you further into the spirit of the scene and imprint it in your mind.
- THREE: Enter the card. Close your eyes and visualize it as clearly and in as much detail as you can. See the card grow in size until it becomes life-sized, or even a bit larger than life. Imagine the borders around the card as a doorway leading into its scenery, and then visualize yourself stepping through that doorway and into the card itself.
- FOUR: Experience the card. As you find yourself in the card, look around and notice all that your five senses are taking in. Engaging your senses as much as possible will put you deeply into the experience of the card.
- FIVE: Interact with the card. Approach a person in the card with whom you want to interact and engage him or her in a dialogue. You might want to ask this person to tell you what the card means, either in general or as it specifically applies to your spiritual journey.
- SIX: Exit the card. Thank the person with whom you have interacted, and then turn back toward the borders of the card and step out through that doorway, leaving the imaginary landscape of the card behind. Watch the card shrink back down to its normal size until it once again becomes just a Tarot card. Take three deep breaths, and on the exhalation of each, silently say your own name. When you are ready, open your eyes.
- SEVEN: Assimilate the experience. It is important that you immediately write down as much about this experience as you can, including your thoughts about what it means to you. This is because a guided visualization is similar

to a dream, and like a dream, if you do not write it down quickly, it will soon begin to evaporate, forever to elude your conscious grasp of it. Write a narrative of the experience, including a description of your interaction with the figure in the card and what you think this experience means to you.

Another method involves relating non-Tarot sources of wisdom to the cards, which is how I developed many of the spiritual meanings in this book. As you read other spiritual resources (for suggestions, see the bibliography at the end of this book) or listen to spiritual teachers, you will discover new insights that you can relate to specific Tarot cards. When that happens, allow that association to rest within your consciousness for a while. Consider how the meanings of the card that you already have may further illuminate the spiritual insight, and vice versa.

Finally, you may want to keep a journal chronicling your unfolding appreciation of the cards on a spiritual level, which will serve as an excellent resource to supplement the contents of this book.

Card meanings

I have opened the chapter for each card with a short introduction to common meanings for it. If you would like to explore traditional meanings for the cards further, there are many books on the topic. Probably the best one is Rachel Pollack's *Seventy-Eight Degrees of Wisdom*.

CB SO

Part 1: The Major Arcana

"We are spiritual beings having a human experience."
— *Teilhard de Chardin*

The cards of the Tarot's Major Arcana are sometimes considered to populate a metaphor called The Fool's Journey that represents a soul progressing along a spiritual path. In that fable, the Fool represents our manifestation into the world as a soul in search of experience. The subsequent twenty cards (Magician through Judgment) represent those experiences, and the final card, the World card, represents our goal, mission, or purpose in life: the realization of our divine nature, which is sometimes called our return to "God consciousness."

0. Fool

"Every man is a divinity in disguise, a god playing the fool." — Ralph Waldo Emerson

The Fool is an innocent who lacks the fetters of an ego. Thus, he takes a leap of faith and discovers his full potential, not yet having forgotten his divine Self. And being the number Zero, i.e., nothing, he possesses the pure potential to become anything he wants to be.

Nothing about the Fool

We are souls born into this world, yet not truly of it, as in the popular saying, "in the world, but not of the world."[2] This state of being is reflected in the traditional Tarot allegory called "The Fool's Journey" in which the Fool travels through the other Major Arcana cards, experiencing and learning from each along the way. And so we see that although this card is placed in the Major Arcana, it is also separate from it. Consider also this card's curious and unique assignment of the number zero. So again, the Fool is *in* the Major Arcana but not *of* the Major Arcana just as we are to be in the world but not of it.

We may also consider that we, like the number zero, are nothing. This is not meant as a put down. It means that our essential Self is not a thing (no-thing) of the material world. For example, you may be a student, but that's not really what you are; you may be a parent, but that's not really what you are; and so on. All those roles that we play in the material world aren't who we really are. Again, our true identity lies outside of the world; we are souls living a material life for a while in search of learning experiences.

Think about all the ideas we have of who we are, which we have accumulated through our experiences and assimilated through the labels that other people have put upon us and that we have put upon ourselves. These ideas and labels are illusions that define us only if we let them. They are just garments we have put on and that we can also take off when we choose to do so, but only if we remember that we are always pure spiritual potential.

So every day is a blank slate upon which we can write a new story of who we are. We typically don't see it that way, thinking that we are defined by all that

---

[2] *This saying is commonly considered to be a biblical quote, but technically it is not. It is a paraphrase of a New Testament passage (John 17:13-16). It is also attributed to Sufi teachings.*

has come before. But that is not true if we decide to recognize and access our unlimited potential and if we decide to march to the beat of whatever drummer we choose to hear.

Nothing, something, and everything

As just noted, the Fool is unique in that it is the only card numbered zero, which means "nothing" but also indicates the potential to be anything since it is not yet something. There is, however, more that we may consider about this nothingness of the Fool.

Our egos would like us to think that nothingness (i.e., begin no thing) means unworthiness or insignificance, but that portrayal cannot possibly describe us. The problem is that the ego suspects the truth, which is that our sacred nothingness transcends our mundane "somethingness," and this truth means that on a higher level, it is the ego that is not real. This, the ego desperately wants to hide from us, and it has been quite adept at that.

Thus, accepting the Fool's message about our sacred nothingness brings liberation from all the constricting beliefs about ourselves that we have accumulated in life. And from that realization of our nothingness we can discover our connection with everything, which we may call our "everythingness." The irony is that the ego wants everything (although it does not understand everythingness), but it fears nothingness, not realizing that we can't have the one without the other.

Achieving nothing

So far we've seen that the Fool is nothing and thus everything, so now let's see how we can achieve nothing and realize everything.

In Zen Buddhism, there is a circular symbol called *ensō* which looks like the number zero that delineates the Fool card. It also relates to the Fool in that it symbolizes a quality of emptiness of thought in which the spirit is free to create without the chattering interference of the mind. Similarly, in *The Power of Now*, Eckhart Tolle defines the term "no-mind" as "consciousness without thought." Tolle says that in our rare moments of no-mind, we are able to reconnect with our true, essential being, and in that state, we are able to experience authentic love, joy, and peace. This reflects our higher awareness of our oneness with the

Divine.

But how do we achieve this no-mind state of consciousness? First, we need to accept that our thoughts and desires are illusions that distract us from our higher awareness of our oneness with the Divine. Then there are some practices that can lead us to this no-mind state of consciousness.

The best known is the practice of meditation, which is defined as the art of quieting the mind. There are many different practices, though, so you may want to look around to find one that suits you. It also helps to become an observer of your thoughts and feelings. Be aware of your thought process. When a thought arises, acknowledge it but don't think about it or judge it. Just be objectively aware of it. Then you can dismiss it without getting caught up in it.

Something else that is effective is the practice of mindfulness, which means focusing your attention on whatever it is that you are doing at the moment. Don't think about what you're doing; just be aware of yourself doing it, almost as if you were watching yourself in a movie.

In any case, don't expect immediate results. It takes time. It's a long journey, this Fool's journey, but for now, setting forth on it—taking a leap of faith—is a start.

Beginner's luck

"Beginner's Luck" seems like a pretty good thing, but by definition, it's also ephemeral. We can, however, have a sort of Beginner's Luck in our lives whenever we have an open mind and act from a place of trust and humility. We can manifest this in several ways.

A beginner believes in luck because at that point, what else is there to trust? Similarly, we can trust that the Divine will support us, and when we do, we gain access to the vast creative power of the Universe.

A beginner is humble, but when we become adept at something, our pride may tell us that we already know everything we need to know. Similarly, we tend to think that we already know everything about the game of life so we don't need to be open to learning more about it. And our pride certainly does not want to entertain the possibility that our preconceptions may be wrong. But when we have the humility to be open to learning new things, when we gently move our ego out of the way of the window to the wisdom of our soul, we become open to amazing new possibilities in life.

A beginner also is able to play the game in a relaxed manner because he is free from the pressures of expectations and doesn't have an attachment to success. In *Be Here Now*, Ram Dass said:

The mindless quality of total involvement ... comes only when the ego is quiet and there is no attachment.

Typically, however, we attach to the results of our actions, and as a result we suffer fear of failure, which sets up an inhibiting tension within us. But when we trust the Divine, we can stop attaching to the results of our actions. Whether we win or lose at the game we have chosen for ourselves is not really important. What matters is that we will be safely led to winning the game that the Divine has chosen for us.

The way to do this is to remember the Fool's advice to be "in the world, but not of the world." We can be actively involved in the world, but at the same time remember that in truth we are of Spirit, not of flesh, and thus remain unattached to the results of our efforts. In other words, although it's important that we do the right thing, we should not attach to the results of our actions since our material life is but a shadow of our Spirit. We do the right thing to manifest our divine nature, but we detach from the results in recognition of that nature.

Assume innocence

This is such a simple suggestion, so clear and succinct. So why is it so hard for us to do this? Whenever someone does something we don't like or understand, we jump to conclusions and think the worst of them instead of giving them the benefit of the doubt.

She didn't call when she said she would? She is so inconsiderate.

He cut ahead of me in line? What a jerk.

Sometimes the other person has a good reason or excuse for doing what they did, but all too often we assume they don't. We think ill of them. Yes, sometimes the person actually is being a jerk, but often they really aren't, and typically, we don't know which is the case. And even if they are being a jerk, we don't know what wounds or burdens they may bear. So remember, appearances can be deceiving, and good explanations usually are not right at hand. The following are a couple of examples of this.

One time a friend was supposed to come over, but he did not show up. He did not even call to cancel. What a jerk, right? Boy, did I ever cuss him out in my head! As it turns out, though, he had been in an accident on the way over to my place, and this was back before cell phones so he couldn't call. When I finally found out what had happened (and after expending a lot of energy uselessly reviling my friend) I discovered who the real jerk was.

Another time, I was in line to get a ticket at an event, but there was a problem when I got to the cashier. He told me to go somewhere else to resolve that problem, and then when I came back, I was supposed to return directly to him to get my ticket without getting back in line. When I came back and did just that, a woman nearby observed this and loudly proclaimed, "Some people must think they don't have to obey the rules." She was quite indignant and spiteful. But besides hurting me, she caused herself agitation, which she would not have felt if she had assumed innocence.

So if we have to assume something, let's assume innocence. It's the best place to start.

Seize the day!

"If a man does not keep pace with his companions, perhaps it is because he hears a different drummer. Let him step to the music which he hears, however measured or far away." — Henry David Thoreau

The Fool tells us to go out there and live. Seize the day! Don't worry about what other people think. Go where your soul leads you, and do what your heart tells you to do. Don't be afraid to be a "wild and crazy guy" now and then. Go ahead and march to the beat of a different drummer.

Conventional thinking and fear of embarrassment should not hold you back when you hear a calling to do something different from the norm. It is only when you are willing to risk looking like a fool that you can be your authentic self, and allowing your true spirit to manifest in your physical life is a very spiritual act. The following quote from Mark Twain expresses this sentiment beautifully:

Twenty years from now you will be more disappointed by the things you didn't do than by the ones you did do. So throw off the bowlines. Sail away from the safe harbor. Catch the trade winds in your sails. Explore. Dream. Discover.

Leap of Faith

In the section on the Fool card in *Rachel Pollack's Tarot Wisdom*, the author tells of a Native American belief that "each of us has a spirit child inside of us, and this child is the part of us that can fly if only we know and accept it." This account calls to mind a saying (which is attributed to John Burroughs) that is often associated with this card: "Leap and the net will appear."

The idea that sometimes we must take a leap of faith to achieve something of value is so important that it has been expressed repeatedly by sages of all cultures. What follows is but a sampling of quotes that express this wisdom from a few of our more contemporary pundits:

"A bit of advice given to a young Native American at the time of his initiation: 'As you go the way of life, you will see a great chasm. Jump. It is not as wide as you think.'" — Joseph Campbell

"We must walk consciously only part way toward our goal, and then leap in the dark to our success." — Henry David Thoreau

"To love is to risk not being loved in return.
To hope is to risk pain.
To try is to risk failure,
But risk must be taken,
Because the greatest hazard in life is to risk nothing."
— Leo Buscaglia

"All growth is a leap in the dark, a spontaneous unpremeditated act without benefit of experience." — Henry Miller

"The Universe will reward you for taking risks on its behalf." — Shakti Gawain

That final quote takes things an interesting step further than the rest. What does it mean that we are taking risks on behalf of the Universe? It refers to those actions, those leaps of faith, through which we co-create with the Divine. In other words, what's important is not just that we take risks, but that the risks we take are for endeavors that serve a high purpose. It may not always be easy to know if we are serving that purpose, but we do get better at it as we travel along our spiritual path and become more familiar with a feeling of rightness that we can't put into words but that we can recognize nevertheless.

So when should you take that leap of faith? That's a crucial question. The answer is that you should take that leap when you feel in your heart of hearts the tug of your soul urging you in a new direction. However, you have to be willing to rest in silence now and then to be able to hear and recognize that call.

For all its power, a spiritual call is often but a whisper, and the din of errant desires can easily drown it out. Experience will help you know the difference, but in the meantime, a way to help differentiate between the two—the call of your soul versus that of your ego—is to consider if this new direction is merely of benefit to you or if it also serves the good of the world around you.

1. Magician

Based on its title, this card is obviously about magic and miracles. More generally, though, it is also about our creativity. Its numerological association also relates it to both our uniqueness and our oneness with the Divine.

What is a miracle?

Besides providing answers, the Tarot cards also pose questions that lead us to think about the deeper aspects of life. The Magician asks us to consider the question, "What is a miracle?" Is it just a trick and an illusion, or is it real? And if it is real, where does it come from?

To examine this question, let's begin by considering the perspective of two of humanity's greatest minds, one from antiquity and one from modern times. Despite the fact that they are separated by a couple of millennia, the following quotes are remarkably similar. The first is from an ancient philosopher, Aristotle, and the other is from a modern scientist, Albert Einstein.

"In everything natural there is something marvelous." — Aristotle

"There are two ways to live your life. One is as though nothing is a miracle. The other is as though everything is a miracle." — Albert Einstein

From these insights we may consider the miraculous nature of existence to be a matter of perception. In fact, in her book *A Return to Love*, Marianne Williamson describes a miracle this way:

"[A Miracle is] a decision to see love where we had seen fear before. It's a shift in perception, a return to love. "

Similarly, *A Course in Miracles* says:

"Miracles arise from a miraculous state of mind, or a state of miracle-readiness."

What all this tells us is that we realize the miracles of life through our openness and willingness to perceive them. Also, when we view the world through the eyes of love, which is our highest mode of perception, we reawaken to our divine nature and we begin to see the miraculous nature of the world around us. At that point, we are able to see miracles unfolding everywhere and in every little circumstance of life. In fact, life itself is the original miracle. We only have to choose to see it as such and all the other miracles will begin to appear.

We are all divinely creative

"Our duty, as men and women, is to proceed as if limits to our ability did not exist. We are collaborators in creation." — *Pierre Teilhard De Chardin*

During a discussion in one of my Tarot classes about how this card relates to our creativity, I mentioned that many of the world's greatest artists have said that they don't create their art; they just "transcribe" what they are inspired to do. Divine inspiration flows down through them from the heavens, which is what we see in the Magician's "lightning rod" stance in many versions of this card. At that point a student asked, "What did those people do differently from what we do? How can the rest of us ordinary people access that sort of creative power?"

There are several answers to that question. The first (and least helpful) is that many such people are extraordinarily gifted. For example, Mozart was a musical prodigy, already performing and composing when still a child. Related to that is a somewhat more helpful answer, which is that we are all born with the ability to channel creative power from a divine source. The problem is that our creativity is then beaten out of most of us as we grow to adulthood. (It's notable that Mozart's father nurtured his son's creativity rather than stifling it.) We are told that we have more important things to learn and that we have to give up our silly, childish creative endeavors. Well, that's half true: we do have many important things to learn, but that does not mean we can't continue to be creative too.

In support of this, here is a story I once heard in a recorded lecture by Leo Buscaglia. He said that when he asks a room filled with children a question like, "How many of you are artists?" or "How many of you can sing?" every hand in the room will shoot up along with a shouted chorus of offers to prove their talent. When he asks that same question of a group of adults, however, he gets a very different result. Perhaps a few hands will go up timidly. What we need to realize is that the Magician is someone who raises his hand enthusiastically to Leo Buscaglia's questions, and we can all be that Magician.

There is another answer to my student's question that can help every one of us, even those of us who steadfastly refuse to raise our hands when the Universe asks us if we are creative. One way of stating this answer is expressed through this quote:

> *"When you look upon what you do or where you are as the main purpose of your life ... your* doing *then becomes a channel through which [Divine] consciousness enters this world." — Eckhart Tolle*

Another way to find an answer is by considering the subsequent card in the Major Arcana, the High Priestess, in comparison with this one. The Magician represents our ability to work miracles when we are open to the miraculous nature of the Universe, but how do we do that? The High Priestess holds the answer. She tells us that the entire Universe is oracular, filled with omens that will guide us truly when we are open to seeing the sacred meaning of everything around us. And while the Magician urges us to act with soulful intent as we travel along our spiritual path, the High Priestess instructs us to listen to the soft voice within our hearts so that we may better see our way along that path. The messages of both cards are equally important, each depending on the other. It is through a proper balance of right action and sincere contemplation that we achieve our creative purpose here on Earth.

Channeling creativity

"God is the doer and we are his instruments." — Swami Prabhavananda

Another way to look at the preceding messages about creativity is to consider the symbolic imagery common to many modern versions of the Magician card. A table with the four Tarot suit icons is set before the Magician, which implies that the material world sits manifest in front of him, although he is set apart from it. In other words, he can operate upon it, but his essential being and miraculous nature are distinct from it.

Similarly, we can consider the Magician's stance—one hand held up and the other down—as a metaphor. We may consider him to be like a television set where his raised hand is an antenna and his lowered hand projects an image like a television does. Of course, a television does not create images; it just receives and manifests them. In the same way, divine power is channeled through the Magician so that as he acts, he manifests what the Divine has "broadcast" to him.

Consequently, the message of this card is that we don't create magic in this world so much as we are a channel for divine creativity. Divine Will is the source and the essence of the magic that we do. However, this should not be a matter of sadness or disappointment. Indeed, it is the miracle of our lives. To realize that we are not an actor separate from the Divine is to allow the Divine to act through us. We thereby realize our role as co-creators of our lives and of the world.

Our miraculous uniqueness

The Magician, with its numerological association with the number one, suggests the question: "How are you wonderfully unique?" The answers that we find for this question bring us into a world of the miraculous, for living our uniqueness leads us to our soulful purpose in life. We are all here to discover our divine Self, and in that, we all have a common cause, but each of us has a different path to our oneness with the Divine. Each of us is unique in some way, and that way leads us along our path.

The requisite beginning of this process is the discovery of our uniqueness. This requires a bit of heartfelt introspection, and it also takes an open mind and a bit of humility. For a few notable individuals (Mozart, for example) that uniqueness can be obvious to see and magnificent in its manifestation, but for most of us, it is more modest and subtle than that. It may be something as seemingly simple as a lovely smile that brings joy into the lives of others. This may seem trivial when compared to the grand uniqueness of a Mozart or Einstein, but there is no order of magnitude in the world of the miraculous. We are all here to contribute our essential piece of the divine puzzle.

The next step is to turn our attention ever toward our uniqueness. After all, our focus of attention defines and creates us. So if we dwell on our unique beauty rather than on our problems, mistakes, and wounds, we will draw ever closer to being the distinctly brilliant individuals we are meant to be, and our souls will unfold perfectly.

2. High Priestess

"The only tyrant I accept in this world is the still voice within." — Mahatma Gandhi

The High Priestess is the archetype of the oracles of myth and legend, and as such, she represents the quiet, intuitive voice within that reveals and expresses the ineffable secrets of life. She also represents and comments on duality by her numerological association.

The still voice within

"They understand but a little who understand only what can be explained." — Marie von Ebner-Eschenbach

There are many things we can neither understand nor explain in a rational way, from the mystique of a lovely painting to the deep mysteries of life and love. As Lao Tzu said in the *Tao Te Ching*, "The Tao that can be explained with words is not the Tao." In time, though, we may intuitively gain an inexpressible sense of knowing about these ineffable mysteries even though logic-based explanations of them are fated to be merely the proverbial finger pointing at the Moon.[3] Despite being so veiled, however, these mysteries, when intuitively received, reveal the truest and most profound realities of life. Unfortunately, we rarely hear our intuitive voice because our chattering thoughts drown it out. And even if we do happen to hear it, we typically don't pay it any mind because its wisdom runs counter to the dictates of our ego, which always seeks to protect itself by casting doubt and aspersions upon spiritual truth.

And so we spend our lives looking for answers in the outside world. And yes, there are many answers there, but they are only of worldly things. If we are to find the deep, spiritual answers that bring beauty and meaning into our lives, we need to look within. We need to listen to the quiet whisper of knowing that dwells inside every one of us. But to do this, we have to quiet the mental chatter that constantly fills our heads. As the prominent Zen Buddhist, Hakuun Yasutani, said, "The quieter you become, the more you can hear." This is not only good advice for our interpersonal communications; it is the essential advice for tuning in to our intuitive connection to the sacred mysteries of life. We also have to

---

[3] *This fable is related in the section of the Hierophant titled "The finger and the Moon." See page 28.*

learn to accept the wisdom that comes from our intuition, even when it runs counter to our ego's desires, even when it runs counter to the dictates of society and tradition, and even when it seems irrational. Such wisdom, when truly realized, transcends this world and connects us to the Divine.

The Oracle

The High Priestess may be seen as the archetypal Oracle, such as Cassandra of ancient Troy, Tiresias, the blind seer in the Oedipus myth, and the priestesses of the Delphic oracle who offered oracular pronouncements to the ancient Greeks and Romans for over a thousand years. Besides indicating prophetic individuals, however, this card also represents the more general fact that the whole universe is oracular. It's not just the cards we deal or the runes we cast; everything has the potential to express the voice of the Divine. In this way, the Universe is constantly talking to us; we just have to be willing to stop and listen. And so the High Priestess represents the sacred ability to hear the soft whisperings of the Universe. People often think that she (or someone like her) must be special and that they themselves cannot do this, but that's not true. We all can; it just takes practice and patience.

The Divine always wants to speak to us. The Tarot is one particular tool to help us hear the voice of the Divine, but it certainly is not the only one. In ancient times, for example, people saw portents in things like the flight of migrating birds. But again, Deity's voice can use any vehicle, and if we listen, we will hear the sacred whisper of the universe in everything. To hone this ability, spend a moment in silent contemplation of the world around you. Breathe deeply, calm your mind, and get centered. Then look around you and consider what the message may be behind whatever catches your attention. As Lon DuQuette says, "When you actually know the question, the answer is everywhere, and you can see it in anything you observe."[4]

Duality and Polarity

In numerology, the number two represents (among other things) duality and

---

[4] *For more about this, I refer you to Lon DuQuette's* Book of Ordinary Oracles *wherein he demonstrates how to use ordinary items around the house—from pocket change to your television remote control—to divine answer to everyday questions.*

polarity, which consequently associates these meanings with the Major Arcana card assigned this number: the High Priestess. However, the High Priestess is typically depicted sitting between light and dark pillars, so this card can represent a balance or middle ground between opposites. It also indicates the concept of *unity within duality* that is represented by the Yin Yang symbol. This means that polar opposites are interconnected and only exist in relation to each other. A couple of simple examples of this include the fact that "hot" only exists in relation to "cold" and the fact that defining the inside of a circle also defines the area outside of it. In other words, you can't talk about the one without implicitly discussing the other.

This concept of the interconnectedness of polar opposites can lead to a deeper understanding of life and the world around us. As an exercise, think of two opposing forces or factions in an area of your life where you feel stressed by the resulting polarization. This may be in any area—your family, religion, politics, etcetera—and its scope may range from the personal to global. For example, you may be experiencing tension because you and your spouse have widely divergent ideas about how to raise your children, or you may feel that your vision of a peaceful world is challenged and threatened by political factions that support war.

Now consider these polar extremes and try to discover their inherent unity. What do they have in common and how do they depend upon one another? For example, how are the anti-war movement and the country's war efforts related? Or how might you and your spouse find common ground in your child-rearing efforts? It's also important to realize that in such polarizing conflicts, railing against the opposition strengthens it and creates more of it. Try to see how that might be the case in your situation.

This exercise will probably be uncomfortable at first since our egos want to separate our position and that of our opponents to create a false dichotomy of "right versus wrong" or "good versus evil." However, doing this will bring you to a place where you can begin to see how everything is interrelated and how everything is a mixture of what we think of as good and evil. You will begin to see the oneness in everything and your illusions of duality will begin to dissolve. Then you will be able to dispel the ultimate dualities of your separation from others as well as your separation from the Divine.

3. Empress

The Empress represents both motherhood and Mother Nature. Consequently, this card can have a range of meanings including nature and creativity, motherhood and nurturing, and beauty and luxury.

The springtime of renewal

"Measure your health by your sympathy with morning and spring. If there is no response in you to the awakening of nature, if the prospect of an early morning walk does not banish sleep, if the warble of the first bluebird does not thrill you, know that the morning and spring of your life are past." — Henry David Thoreau

The Empress, a card of creativity, fertility, and generative powers, is often associated with springtime. An important implication of this vernal association is the reminder that there is always a springtime of spiritual renewal waiting to blossom forth from the barren depths of our every winter of discontent. We just have to be eager to welcome it.

When we are in a dark and dismal period, however, we tend to believe that there will never be a time of revitalization, or at least it seems only a distant prospect. But rather than waiting for a metaphorical spring to come, we can manifest this card's archetypal energy and become the spring we wish to see, and in so doing, we can co-create the time of renewal that we seek.

So whenever you feel depleted, consider how you can nurture yourself and your creative efforts in order to become more productive and abundant, and explore how you can express your compassionate nature in order to find more love in your life. Also, you can follow Thoreau's advice and take an early morning walk or listen for the warble of the first bluebird. Embrace Nature's awakening in all its forms and you will discover a similar awakening within yourself.

Beauty

An interesting meaning for the Empress card is beauty, a concept that is all too often twisted in our culture. The glossy images of celebrities that we see in our media are generally manipulated by airbrush or Photoshop to make them seem like perfect, flawless people, turning them into ideals that no real human can possibly attain. Thus, our concept of beauty has become unrealistic and superficial, which is something that the Empress would disdain.

True beauty in nature and in our lives comes from an inner radiance, and it always has outer "flaws." But those flaws give it character, not defect. This authentic beauty shines through in things like the wrinkled smile of an old woman or a child's scrawled drawing posted on a refrigerator. It is also revealed in the hint of eternity we may see in fleeting moments such as that of a dazzling sunset or a crimson leaf quivering in a chill autumn breeze.

Profound beauty shines brightest in such things, and when we look for it, we can find it everywhere. And as we become increasingly aware of this sacred splendor of the world, it seeps into our lives and we begin to manifest our own unique part of it.

Motherly wisdom

The fact that the Empress is the archetypal mother suggests all the well-known aphorisms of wisdom and advice that our mothers gave us when we were children. It's almost as if there is a *Handbook of Motherly Advice* that women are given upon the birth of their first child, so ubiquitous is this sort of advice. Things like:

Say please and thank you.

Honesty is the best policy.

Play nice; don't fight.

Share your toys.

Go outside and get some fresh air.

For some reason, though, as we grow up and set out on our own lives, we tend to forget, discount, or ignore the things our mothers told us. We stop saying please and thank you. We tell lies. We fight with other people. We don't share. And we stay inside too much, even when a walk outside would refresh our souls.

So this card's advice is to think of some words of wisdom your mother (or a surrogate mother figure, if that is more appropriate to your situation) imparted to you. You can use some of the above bits of advice or come up with others from your own memory. Then take them to heart and put them into practice. As you do that, you will bring some motherly (and divine) wisdom into your life.

Motherly love

This card can imply a mother's unconditional love, from which we may infer a few spiritual messages. The first is an assurance of the love that the Divine has for us. After all, if a mother can love her child so totally and unselfishly, how much more must we be loved by Deity?

The next message is that treating everyone with unconditional love and compassion brings peace and joy into our lives. So much of the sorrow and turmoil of life comes from judging others and putting them out of our hearts. To see the benefits of unconditional love, consider the look of bliss on the face of a loving mother of a newborn child. She looks with eyes of love and sees only the sacred beauty of her child.

Another message is that loving others is a way to bring the Divine into our lives. The practice of seeing with love and acting with compassion is a way to express our devotion for the Divine. When we look with love, we see the Divine everywhere, and when we act with compassion, we manifest our own innate divinity.

Luxury and spirituality

A couple of notable meanings for the Empress card are luxury and comfort, which are typically seen as obstacles to a spiritual path, both in terms of our popular notions (remember the stereotype of an ascetic guru sleeping on a bed of nails) and as explained by many religions (consider the well-known biblical adage that compares a rich man's chances of getting into heaven with those of a camel going through the eye of a needle). Consequently, some people are daunted by a spiritual path, thinking that they have to abandon all of their comforts in order to find their sacred calling. They give up before they start because they are not ready, as is the case for most of us, to go live in a hut somewhere. However, in the book *Religion in Practice*, Swami Prabhavananda wisely states, "It is possible to live in a most uncomfortable way and think lustful thoughts, and it is possible to live in comfort and think of God."

Of course, this is not to say that materialism is compatible with spirituality. Luxury certainly can be an obstacle to a spiritual path, or at least a distraction from it, but this comes from an attachment to possessions and from giving them undue attention and importance. As we may infer from the preceding quote from Swami Prabhavananda, a poor person can be materialistic and a wealthy person can be spiritual. It is not luxury per se that is in conflict with spirituality; it is giving wealth a higher priority or focus than spiritual pursuits that holds us back. In other words, spirituality is not hampered by material things, it is hampered by materialism. It is imperative that we consider where our thoughts dwell, what our desires yearn for, and where our efforts lead us. And so the question is, do the comforts of your life support your spiritual pursuits, or do you let them get in the way?

4. Emperor

The Emperor card has a variety of meanings that one might infer from its name, such as secular authority and power, control and leadership, laws and society, plans and goals, analysis and logic, order and structure. The Emperor is also the archetypal father.

Take a "staycation" from your plans

"Life is what happens to you while you're busy making other plans." — *John Lennon*

Do you have big plans for your life? Do you have set ideas about what should and should not be happening in your life? Well, all those plans can keep you from experiencing your life just as it is in this eternal moment of Now. This is not to say that you need to throw out your plans for your life or that you shouldn't make such plans. But plans should be kept in perspective; they are the servant, not the master. Unfortunately, we often let our preparations and arrangements control our life, so they keep us from experiencing our authentic life and block us from being true to our soul's journey.

To find a way out of this self-made trap, here is a suggestion. Try this for just one day: live without plans to see what it's like. Take a vacation from the oppressive *Empire of Should*. You can think of it as a mini-staycation. (You probably don't want to choose a work day to do this.) Just do whatever comes up instead of what you think you should do. This doesn't mean you need to lounge around all day in your pajamas doing nothing, although if that's what you feel like doing, go for it. What it does mean is letting you heart and intuition tell you what to do for a day instead of being a slave to the clock, to convention, and to your plans. Eat when you're hungry, not when it's the "right" time to eat. Give yourself permission to make a meal of pancakes and scrambled eggs in the evening instead of in the morning. Wear socks with your sandals if you want to. Skip the nightly news and watch a cartoon instead. Play fetch with your dog (or cat!). Be spontaneous. Spend the day doing what you feel like doing and (here's the really important part) live in the moment. Then remember what this experience was like as you return to your normal life.

Escape from the *Empire of Should*

As mentioned in the previous section, there is a sad place called the *Empire of Should*. Its terrain includes all the things society tells us we should be, all the things we tell ourselves we should have, and all the things we tell other people they should do. These are the dark forests, the swamp lands, and the deserts that make up this empire.

Try examining the *shoulds* in your life. Some may be right and some wrong, but they all can use a bit of close examination. Are they outdated, obsolete artifacts of a past phase of your life? Are they valid for some people, but not for you? Do they reflect your (or someone else's) notions of what life is all about? Are they things that would be "good to do" but aren't necessarily things you "have to do"?

Here is a suggestion: In brainstorming mode write up a list of *shoulds* in your life. They can be things you think society says you should do, things your parents said you should not do, or things you tell yourself you should have or be. Then examine these *shoulds* to see how valid or useful they are in your life. You may want to keep some of them, modify others, and toss out a few. In any case, once you examine them, you transform them into possibilities instead of *shoulds*, and this is how you can escape from the stifling *Empire of Should*.

Release control

The Emperor signifies control issues, and this is one of the areas where many of us hit a roadblock on our spiritual path. We want—need, even—to control the people around us, the conditions of our lives, and the results and outcomes of our actions. Although at times there may be some short-term satisfaction to be gained from this course of action, in the long run and at a deep level, our attachment to controlling things causes us a great deal of distress because there are always limits to what and how much we can control. And since we think we should be able to control things that we cannot, we get frustrated and suffer from a sense of loss.

But when we release our need for control and allow the Divine be the Emperor of our lives instead, we find our way toward peace. This does not mean we should never make plans; it just means we should not worry about them. It doesn't mean we should not work toward our goals; it just means that we should do what we can and then realize that the results will unfold as they are meant to. This is how we can evade the pain of dissatisfaction. This also means we cannot control what other people do or what kind of person they are. We may, perhaps, offer suggestions or help, but, as the saying goes, "you can lead a horse to water but you can't make it drink." Everyone is going through their own life's lessons, and we have to allow that.

Finally, the message here is that power and control are as much an illusion as the material world is. Since the ultimate reality is at a spiritual level, the ultimate power and control lie on that plane also. In other words, when we try to control life here in the material world, it can be like trying to control shadows without realizing where they come from.

A pigeonhole for the Divine

Our minds constantly try to force a sense of order and structure onto our experiences. If we cannot fit something into a known pigeonhole, we refuse to acknowledge it or we reject its true meaning. And contrary to what we tell ourselves, we are not attempting to bring our understanding into alignment with *what is*; we are making a misguided attempt to bring *what is* into alignment with our understanding.

We can see how this need for structure and order will conflict with a search for spiritual meaning within our experiences. When we try to impose our own meanings and interpretations on our experiences, we imprison them within the limited framework of human thought. And so we try to force the round peg of our spiritual life into the square hole of our limited concepts of the material world. In doing this, we also miss out on living our experiences in a way that is authentic and profound. We end up with a rigid, mechanical life.

Fortunately, there are things we can do to avoid this sort of life if it has overtaken us. We can become more flexible by letting uncertainty and ambiguity enter into our understanding of things. We can allow "maybe" and "I'm not sure" into our vocabulary. Also of use is a meditative practice of spending quiet time in thoughtful observation of the things around us without trying to define any of them. We can also open up to the irrational side of life and engage in creative, right-brain activities such as painting, playing the piano, or writing poetry. It also helps to just do something silly, absurd, or ridiculous now and then—just for fun. And finally, we can take the advice of the High Priestess and meditate, look within, and quiet our mental chatter.

An unexamined faith

Although the preceding sections for the Emperor use terms like control, order, and planning more as warnings than as good examples, certainly they are not necessarily obstacles to spirituality. In fact, when used appropriately they can serve us well along our spiritual path. Specifically, although faith is essential to a spiritual journey and intuition is a guiding light along the way, reason is an indispensable factor as well. We must carefully examine the spiritual teachings we have received in order to choose our true path. To paraphrase one of Socrates' famous sayings, "The unexamined faith is not worth believing."[5]

5. Hierophant

"God has no boundaries, including those of religion." — Reb Yakov Leib HaKohain

The most common interpretations for the Hierophant are about religion. In addition, this card is also about teaching, education, belief, faith, tradition, and hierarchies.

The true House of God

"While God waits for his temple to be built of love, men bring stones." — Rabindranath Tagore

The true House of God is not made of brick and mortar; it is not a temple, church, or mosque. It is made of blades of grass, gusts of wind, and drops of rain.

---

[5] *Socrates said, "The unexamined life is not worth living."*

Its choir is composed of larks and whales, its hymns, the chirp of crickets and the howl of wolves. Its stained glass windows are sparkling lakes, painted sunsets, and starry skies on cool, clear nights. Its statues are majestic redwoods, towering mountains, and gnarled stalagmites in deep, dark caverns. Its sacred works of art are the iridescent throats of hummingbirds, flashes of gold in a koi pond, and the fathomless depths in a baby's eyes.

We sit in the pews of this temple every moment of our lives, whether we realize it or not. But how do we act in this temple? Our every thought is a prayer of devotion to the Divine ... or not. Our every word is a hymn to the Divine ... or not. And everything we do is an act of service to the Divine ... or not. The choice is always ours to make.

Religiosity

"And whosoever shall exalt himself shall be abased; and he that shall humble himself shall be exalted." — Matthew 23:12

The Hierophant card typically indicates religion, which can mean the external, cultural aspect of spirituality. However, a dark side of this card is its implication of religiosity, i.e., the affected show of piety and religious devotion. Sometimes under the guise of spirituality, we complain about other people's sins and condemn them for their lack of spiritual awakening. At other times, we crave recognition, praise, and admiration for our own efforts and progress along our spiritual path. But this all comes from the ego and not from our soul.

Spirituality is not about what we do in a church or temple, but what we do in our everyday lives, and in large part, it's also about how we treat each other. So one suggestion from this card is to think of and commit to doing an act of compassion or charity that cannot result in any recognition for yourself. It's even better if you can do this for someone who you have criticized for their lack of spiritual awakening.

The finger and the Moon

"I don't believe that my tradition defines God. It only points me to God." — *Bishop John Shelby Spong*

There is a Zen proverb about a student who asked his teacher, "What is this thing I've heard of called 'The Moon'?" In answer, the teacher pointed up into the sky, but rather than looking up into the heavens, the student stared at his teacher's finger and thereby mistook it for the Moon. Religion is often like that: people mistake the finger (the religion and its teachings) for the Moon (the Divine).

Many paths up the mountain

"One should not think, 'My religion alone is the right path and other religions are false.' God can be realized by means of all paths." — Sri Ramakrishna

Although religion is intended to facilitate, nurture, and guide our spiritual journey, often it does the opposite. Stultifying dogmas, ego-laden hierarchies, and contentious internal politics can obscure this sacred purpose, and the resulting suffering and confusion a person may experience at the hands of a specific religious tradition can turn them off to spirituality in general. They then assume that all paths up the mountain are as impassable as the one they originally encountered, and throwing the baby out with the bath water, they may turn away from other valuable spiritual sources.

Fortunately, there are many different paths up the mountain of spirituality. Anyone who has a viscerally negative reaction to one particular religion may choose from among a variety of contemporary spiritual teachers of differing backgrounds who point the way. What follows are but a few suggestions of books that present such alternatives.[6] First, there are a few contemporary sources, then some from antiquity.

A Course in Miracles (and Marianne Williamson's *A Return to Love* which is based on *ACIM*) uses Judeo-Christian terminology, but it certainly does not employ traditional Christian dogma.

Be Here Now, by Ram Dass, draws upon the author's Hindu-based spiritual journey although he has "translated" that philosophy somewhat into more Western terms, albeit with a distinctively Hippie jargon and appearance that now may seem rather quaint.

For a fascinating synthesis of Christian and Hindu spirituality, I recommend *The Sermon on the Mount According to Vedanta*.

---

[6] *For more references, see the Bibliography at the end of this book.*

Thich Nhat Hanh is a Buddhist monk and peace activist. His book *Call me by My True Names* is but one of over 100 of his books that have influenced Western understanding of Buddhism.

Eckhart Tolle, the author of *The Power of Now* and *A New Earth*, is the most non-denominational of these writers, and his books read more like philosophy than religion.

For works from ancient Greek and Roman paganism, there are *Plato's Republic* and *Meditations* by Marcus Aurelius, the second century Roman "philosopher-king."

If you are interested in Sufism, you might like a powerfully beautiful book called *The Rumi Collection*. Rumi was a thirteenth century Persian poet and mystic who wrote the following poem, which wonderfully illustrates the point of this section:

> *I tried to find Him on the Christian cross, but He was not there;*
> *I went to the temple of the Hindus and to the old pagodas,*
> *but I could not find a trace of Him anywhere...*
> *I searched on the mountains and in the valleys*
> *but neither in the heights nor in the depths was I able to find Him.*
> *I went to the Ka'bah in Mecca, but He was not there either...*
> *I questioned the scholars and philosophers but He was beyond their understanding...*
> *Then I looked into my heart and it was there*
> *where He dwelled that I saw Him,*
> *He was nowhere else to be found.*

What is a true religion?

This question, "What is true religion?" is a logical corollary to the discussion in the previous section. Beyond the superficial trappings of rites, rituals, and dogma, there is a truer essence of religion which many spiritual leaders have tried to articulate. For example, a very pithy explanation may be seen in a simple statement attributed to the 14th Dalai Lama: "My religion is kindness." We may add to this what Roger Housden said about Kabir, a fifteenth century spiritual leader, in his book *Ten Poems to Change Your Life*: "Any religion without genuine personal devotion was worthless to him." Consider also this quote from Rumi: "Asleep or awake, writing or reading, whatever you do, you must never be without the remembrance of God." Similarly, when asked which is the greatest of the Ten Commandments, Jesus said:

> *Thou shalt love the Lord thy God with all thy heart, and with all thy soul, and with all thy mind. This is the first and greatest commandment. And the second is like unto it, Thou shalt love thy neighbour as thyself. On these two commandments hang all the law and the prophets.*[7]

It is significant also that these two essentials (kindness to others and devotion to the Divine) are two of the primary spiritual disciplines described in the Bhagavad Gita: Karma yoga (the path of selfless work) and Bhakti yoga (the path of devotion). Indeed, compassion and devotion are the basis of the teachings of all of history's greatest religious leaders. When we combine these sentiments, we find we have a wonderfully effective litmus test for any religion or religious leader, which is this: Any religion is authentic only to the extent that it is primarily based on love and kindness to others and on devotion to the Divine. In fact, all other religious dogma that does not serve and support those two things is basically just window dressing or an issue of that religion's collective ego.

This seems simple enough, but it is worth elaborating on one of these points. Kindness to others is generally well understood, but devotion to the Divine is often misunderstood. Contrary to common belief, Deity does not need our adoration. Rather, we need to practice that devotion in order to reunite with the Divine. As stated in the Bhagavad Gita:

> *"Being completely absorbed in Me, surely you will come to Me."*

The cynic and dogmatic

The cynic and the dogmatic both rightly criticize the other, but wrongly exalt themselves. They both indulge in a false belief that these are the only two alternatives regarding religion, but in reality, they are polar opposites on a broad spectrum. Both tend to be egotistical and blind in their rigid belief, and neither sees the true essence of the Divine. One denies it totally while the other is fooled by a caricature of the Divine. Thus, both suffer in their separation from divinity.

In matters of spiritual belief, a humble and open mind leads us to a sacred middle ground where the seeds of Truth may be found, where an ecstatic experience of divine union takes root, and where a profound serenity will flourish.

---

[7] *Matthew 22:37-40*

Priest, prophet, and avatar

We may see this card as indicating one of three levels of intermediaries with the Divine: priest, prophet, and avatar. These have been common roles described by religions for thousands of years, but the time is at hand when we will realize that we don't need someone to intercede with the Divine on our behalf.

In addition to the now common realization that we don't need priests to intercede in our communication with the divine, we are awakening to the fact that we are all prophets when we walk a spiritual path. And even more profoundly, we are all avatars of the Divine; we just have not yet awakened to the conscious realization of our own divinity.

A living sermon

"There is no royal road except through living the creed in your own life, which must be a living sermon." — Mahatma Gandhi

Many people think that religion is a club to be joined, and then merely through the joining, they will gain salvation. Of course, like any club, there are dues to be paid (i.e., tithing), and a certain minimum attendance record necessary, or at least, strongly suggested (such as Sunday services). But outside of those superficial obligations, there is very little required, or so it is commonly (and erroneously) believed.

However, a religion that stays behind in the church when we walk out on Sunday morning (for example) is hollow. For our faith to be meaningful, we must practice spiritual living in everything we do. The highest spiritual practice is one that suffuses our every thought and action, but of course this is an ideal that lies beyond of our ability at the outset. It is, however, sufficient that we keep this goal in mind and strive toward it, as in the following advice from Swami Prabhavananda.

The goal is the important thing. If God is your goal, and you are on a path with that intention, it will lead you to Him.

Consequently, whenever we are in doubt about the spiritual aspect of an act or about the path we are on, we should ask ourselves questions like these: "Is this in accord with my desire to reunite with the Divine? Does it help me realize my innate divinity? Is it an act of love for another person? Does it reflect my devotion to Deity?" In this way we can become loving, kindhearted people, we can realize our divinity, and we can become what we believe in. This is the greatest testament to our spirituality that we can give. This is how we can become a "living sermon."

Keys to understanding

On many versions of this card we see two crossed keys, one silver and the other gold. This symbol echoes the keys displayed on the Vatican Coat of Arms, which are a symbol of "binding and loosing," which refers to the papal authority to declare what is forbidden and what is permitted.

There are, however, other ways to interpret these keys without locking them into meanings related to Christian iconography. One is that the teachings of religion should be keys to open the doors of both physical reality and spirituality. Another meaning we may infer is that both internal and external teachers have their own wisdom to impart; they each have their own domain and time. These two teachers are tradition (external), and our own intuitive connection to the Divine (internal). Comparing and evaluating the relative wisdom of these two teachers is of crucial importance on a spiritual path and will be discussed in the following chapter on the Lovers card.

6. Lovers

"The path of relationships leads us through the veil of separation to a realization of our ultimate oneness." — Rick Fields

This card's most obvious connotations are about love and romantic relationships. However, it is also about important, life-changing choices.

Choose your own path

It is instructive to consider why this card may have been positioned between the Hierophant (representing orthodox, traditional ways of doing things) and the Chariot (forging ahead on your own path). This placement implies that the Lovers card can be about questioning established thinking, choosing between tradition and new ways, and deciding what you want to take from tradition and what you need to discard from it as you discover your path in life.

Certainly we should consider the traditional wisdom that religion has accumulated over the centuries, but the motives of religious teachers (both historical and current) are not always pure, and being human, their abilities aren't perfect. Also, changing circumstances sometimes require new and unorthodox approaches. This is not to say that there inevitably comes a time when we must reject the beliefs and mores with which we were raised, but if we never question them, we will, by default, end up with someone else's beliefs, which may be as ill-fitting as a hand-me-down coat.

Consequently, this card can be about rejecting the religious dogma you were taught as a child and finding a spiritual path that now resonates with the truth of your being. Ultimately, this may turn out to be one of the most important decisions you will ever make.

Life choices at the crossroads

Pre-Twentieth Century Tarot decks typically depicted Cupid hovering over three people, although interpretations of the identities of those three people varies. Some see them as a man and a woman standing before a priest who is about to marry them, while others see them as a man choosing between two women who represent virtue and vice. (This discrepancy may be because the gender of one of the figures is sometimes rather ambiguous.) The latter interpretation seems more likely, though, since that motif was common in classic works of art, and the development of the Major Arcana illustrations was greatly influenced by contemporary artwork.

On one level, this card is about arriving at a moral or ethical crossroads in life. At such times, we are faced with important choices that can be defining moments in our lives, changing them forever. We may be called upon to choose between temptation and respectability, or perhaps one choice will lead us onto a spiritual path while the other will keep us on a material one.

At a deeper level, we may consider the three people typically seen on early versions of the Lovers card as differing facets of ourselves. Everyone is part virtue and part vice, and we are constantly called upon to choose which aspect to express in ways both big and small. These everyday decisions have profound effects on our lives beyond the obvious implications of which alternative we manifest. They also shape our character since we feed one or the other aspect of ourselves through those choices. Thus one aspect grows while the other withers.

Similarly, since everyone has both aspects within them, we are also constantly called upon to choose which one we want to see in the people around us. Do we see the sacred in them or the mundane, the sinner or the saint? Perhaps, however, a higher choice is to recognize both aspects in people, but to love them anyway. This is a non-judgmental love, and it is the truest way to love other people.

Choose love

"None love, but they who wish to love." — Jean Baptiste Racine

Valentine's Day, with its celebration of romantic love, has an obvious association with the Lovers card. That day, however, has a somewhat dual personality. For those who are in a happy relationship, it is a romantic day filled with celebrations and reaffirmations of love. For them, this card has a message about celebrating, reaffirming, and strengthening that relationship. It also says that for our relationships to succeed, we must choose love over and over again, which is not always easy to do. Often in our relationships we are faced with circumstances where we might choose things like judgment, fear, or rejection instead of love, compassion, and understanding. For example, when a spouse makes a mistake or does something hurtful, we can choose anger or we can choose love. Similarly, when we are confronted with temptations, we can choose either fidelity or betrayal. When we are faced with such choices, our relationship gives us the chance to practice choosing love in our lives, which also means (whether we realize it or not) choosing to manifest our sacred nature over our mundane one.

For those who are not in a relationship, however, Valentine's Day can be a bitter occasion filled with reminders of love's disappointments. For those people, this card suggests a couple of helpful affirmations:

I am ready for love.
I deserve to be loved.

These affirmations may seem to state the obvious, but deep down, many of us are not as ready for love as we think, and not being ready means that we doubt that we deserve to be loved. The way out of this loveless state is to choose love. But in this case the advice is to choose to love ourselves, for if we have not made that choice, we are not really looking to love another person; we are looking to find someone to complete us through their love of us, which can lead to a dysfunctional, or at least inequitable relationship.

<u>Love versus desire</u>

"You can't love something that can't love you back."

When I was a child, my mother used to tell me, "You can't love something that can't love you back," if I said something like, "I love ice cream." I would roll my eyes, thinking this was just another one of Mom's silly sayings, but as I grew up, I came to realize the deep truth of this simple maxim, which points out that we tend to abuse and dishonor the word "love." We turn it into a synonym for simple desires and trivial cravings. But words have meaning and power, so when we say "I love ice cream," we are diluting a word that should describe our feelings for other people and our compassionate dealings with them. In so doing, are we not trivializing love and making it disposable?

Perhaps this is why we have come to use this word in our relationships so quickly and easily, but without really meaning it in its deepest and truest sense. What happens when "I love you" begins to mean "I desire you for the moment and merely for my own self-gratification"? True love involves caring about someone in a selfless way, which we don't do for things like ice cream. Unfortunately, we don't always do that for other people either. Our "love" for them is often a matter of our own needs and desires. Perhaps, however, if we stop using the word love when we mean words such as like, want, or desire, we will start loving people in ways that are kind and selfless, which is what love should be.

Finally, notice that the saying is not "You can't love *someone* who *doesn't* love you back." While a romantic relationship does require reciprocity of love, we can (and should) love people who do not love us. Of course, it is much easier to love those who love us and are kind to us, while it is not nearly as easy to love someone who has harmed us or rejected us. However, a persistent effort to love someone who does not love us back is a valuable practice of our ability to love universally and unconditionally.

<u>Finding someone special is an inside job</u>

"We become dependent on other people to make us feel totally and permanently loved. This expectation ... will always be defeated. ... The cause [of our relationship problems] is an inability to develop an unshakable relationship with ourselves. The Higher Self is the source of love." — *Deepak Chopra*

Although it may be a stereotype that the most common question asked of a Tarot reader is "When will I meet my soul mate," there is some validity in that stereotype since this (or variations on it) is such a frequent question. When it is asked, the Lovers is a very welcome card in the reading because to the uninitiated eye, it seems to be a simple, direct promise of a new romance coming into the picture. Of course (as is the case with every Tarot card) the Lovers card is much more complex than that.

One bit of advice here is that the best way to find a wonderful relationship with someone else is by first developing a positive relationship with yourself. In other words, seek to love and accept who you are. In fact, when you are able to love yourself and to love how you are living your life (which comes from discovering and pursuing your deep, soul-inspired passions), you will begin to see love all around you. And when you cultivate love in your heart, your external relationships will become more aligned with the greater good and higher purpose of everyone involved.

An important aspect of this card to consider here is its inclusion of a divine figure hovering above the people on it. As noted previously, in antique decks, this was usually Cupid, the God of Love, while in modern decks, we often see an angel.[8] The message we may infer from this is that to find a fulfilling external relationship, it helps to recognize and develop our inner relationship with the Divine. With this sacred foundation in our lives, the people who are right for us will begin to appear, and we will be able to recognize and appreciate them when they do. That last point is of vital importance. The problem for many of us is not that the right person doesn't come along. It is that when they do, we don't realize that they are the right person since we are busy evaluating potential partners with materialistic or self-indulgent criteria. With a higher spiritual connection, however, we remove such blinders and see clearly.

Finally, this card says that when we do find a satisfying relationship, it is

---

[8] *In the RWS deck, this angel is generally regarded to be Raphael, the angel of healing.*

crucial that we realize that it is not the source of love in our lives; it is a means for us to practice and express our ability to love. (See the quote from Deepak Chopra at the beginning of this section.) With that practice, two people may use their relationship as a vehicle for spiritual awakening. As Ram Dass wrote in *Grist for the Mill*, "The reason that you form a conscious marriage on the physical plane with a partner is in order to do the work of coming to God together."

7. Chariot

The Chariot indicates setting out on your own path and achieving victory and success. On a higher level, though, it is also about the alignment of your personal will with that of the Divine.

The dancer and the dance

In many versions of the Chariot card, the charioteer seems to be an integral part of the chariot, almost as if he has melded with it. This suggests a line from a poem called *Among School Children* by William Butler Yeats:

How can we know the dancer from the dance?

Indeed, we cannot tell the dancer from the dance because the person and the movements are integrated in the performance. How can there be a dance without the person? And how can the person be a dancer if not for the dance? And so this suggests a question: "Is there a difference between what we do and who we are?"

Do we act bravely because we are courageous, or do we become courageous through acts of bravery? Do we perform charitable works because we are generous, or is it the other way around? It is both, and it also involves a positive feedback loop, so to speak. The more we act out of compassion, for example, the more we become a compassionate person, and as a result, the more we want to act compassionately. This is how the chariot carries us along. But just as the proverbial journey of a thousand miles begins with a single step, it also is taken one step at a time.

So this card has a suggestion. Today, take a step, just one little step, in the direction that you believe your Higher Self want your life to take—take a step toward manifesting your divinity. For example, if you want to be a more generous person, do something charitable. Don't wait to take such action until you feel like generous. The being is the doing; the doing is the being.

Running roughshod over yourself

Sometimes the chariot on this card looks like it's ready to run roughshod over someone, which can indicate the aggression of one person trampling the rights of another. However, a subtler implication is that our own aggression can run over us if we don't control it. It can change us into something we do not (or should not) want to be.

One example of this danger is the way that some of us change when we get behind the wheel of our cars. When we are safely protected within the steel cocoon and anonymity of a car, our Mr. Hyde persona may come out and replace our public, Dr. Jekyll face. (This Jekyll and Hyde phenomenon may be inferred from the symbol of the comedy and tragedy masks often seen on this card.)

The risk of doing harm to ourselves and others that is inherent in uncontrolled aggression is obvious. What is less obvious, though, is the fact that when we act aggressively, we harm ourselves subtly in that this makes us a bit more belligerent every time we do it. It moves us away from our true identity—our divine Self—and it keeps us locked in our ego-illusion of a world of lack and struggle.

So how do we escape this pattern? How do we avoid this dark aspect of the Chariot card? One step on this journey is to understand some possible causes of this pattern of behavior and to recognize when we are acting this way so we can stop ourselves. Aggressive behavior can be, at least in part, the result of an adrenaline addiction, and if you understand that, then you can recognize the signs. When you feel a surge of excitement, that can be an adrenaline rush. This isn't always a sign of aggression, of course. You can get that feeling when you do fun and exciting things too, but when you also feel like you are acting out of control while in conflict with someone else, that's a warning sign that Mr. Hyde has taken over. Stop and take a few deep breaths then, and remind yourself that you, not your anger, are in control of your actions.

Another case of our passions controlling us instead of the other way around is when our drive for success controls our lives. This problem is superbly illustrated in the following quote from the book, *The Book of Awakening*, by Mark Nepo: "We think that accomplishing things will complete us, when it is experiencing life that will." This quote also suggests a treatment, which is to realize that what really matters is our sense of fulfillment in what we do and our enjoyment of life, not our material achievements.

For example, consider this: are you working hard to be successful in your career because you love what you are doing, or are you doing it out of fear of being a failure, or even just the fear of not being as successful as someone else, such as a parent, a neighbor, or a friend? It's also helpful to reflect upon what kind of life you are living right now as the result of your career. And finally, it's not only important that you are living in joy; it's also important that the people in your life are joyous too. After all, if you're not spreading joy, how much of a joyful person are you?

The masks we wear

In the previous section, I mentioned how the Tragedy and Comedy masks seen on the Chariot card can indicate our Jekyll and Hyde dual nature. However, they have another symbolic meaning that we can also examine, which is that we all wear various masks in our lives—i.e., we play different roles—that we often struggle to reconcile and behind which our authentic selves are hidden.

For example, the dictates of a career may be in conflict with the requirements of being a parent or a spouse, and some people even have a secret part of themselves that they try to conceal from the world at large. So these masks represent the disguises we often wear (metaphorically speaking) in our lives, often to succeed and get ahead. They may have value on our material level of being, but it's important to consider sometimes if perhaps we have become lost in any of them. Have we forgotten that a mask is not who we really are? And can we live an authentic life while wearing that mask? We also may ask ourselves, "What masks am I wearing in order to succeed, and is worldly victory worth having to disguise or suppress my spiritual identity?" The answers to these questions require an awareness that the obstacle to living authentically lies not in wearing a mask, but in letting it define and restrict us, for every mask is of the world and not of Spirit.

The passions that drive us

"If your life is in harmony with your part in the Life Pattern, and if you are obedient to the laws which govern this universe, then your life is full and good but not overcrowded." — Peace Pilgrim

This card, with its typical image of two horses (or another animal such as a sphinx, depending on the Tarot deck) pulling a chariot can represent the desires and passions that carry us along through life. There is a saying, however, that a man cannot ride two horses, and we might consider that those proverbial horses could represent the conflicting passions of materialism and spirituality.

Certainly, for most of us, there is a conflict between our earthly desires for fame and fortune versus our spiritual passion for enlightenment and divine union. But are the two totally incompatible? For instance, does a spiritual path require a vow of poverty? There are some who have made that severe choice, but is it necessary?

Consider first the fact that the "two horses" metaphor applies to riding them, not to having them pull a chariot. Of course, those two horses must be pulling the chariot in the same direction and not working at cross purposes. So we can have two different horses—our spiritual pursuits and our worldly ones—pulling the chariot of our lives, but we have to make sure they are pulling together. In other words, we must make a choice as to what we believe is truly important to us—our worldly goals or our spirituality. Which is the higher purpose of our life, and which the subordinate one? With that decision made, then, we have to reconcile and coordinate these two passions so that they both pull us in the same direction.

As a related point, this card is also about our personal will and the true victory in life that comes when it serves divine will. As Paul Foster Case says about the Chariot card in *The Tarot: A Key to the Wisdom of the Ages*:

> *The more perfectly we understand that the office of human personality is to serve as a vehicle for cosmic forces, the more freely does the Primal Will behind all manifestation find expression through us.*

When our desires and passions are in alignment with our purpose in life, then solutions to our problems appear and we are empowered to succeed. And when that is the case, our spiritual life and our worldly life will advance together. Consequently, a sign that we are on the correct path in life is when those two aspects of ourselves are working together and not against each other.

Finally, let's return to the original question of this section: "Are our worldly and spiritual passions incompatible?" The answer is that when we align our activities in our material life with our spiritual pursuits, and when our personal will aligns with that of the Divine, then there is no incompatibility between them.

8. Strength

This card indicates inner strength such as courage, fortitude, and passion. The lady and the lion on it may also represent our good and bad sides, much like the old cartoon representation of a little angel and a little devil sitting on a person's shoulders presenting their respective advice.

The lion within and the lion in others

The image on the Strength card in most decks is of a woman gently calming or subduing a lion, and both figures have important symbolic reference to our lives. We may hope to identify with the lady, or we may fear identification with the lion, but we are both; the lady and the lion are two aspects of ourselves. The lady represents our connection to a Higher Power and our divine nature, while the lion symbolizes our powerful weaknesses such as anger, jealousy, and aggression. This visual motif of a lady and a lion also begs a comparison with the classic tale, *The Beauty and the Beast*. That tale illustrates how a deep level of compassion will enable us to see goodness in others, especially where we may be tempted to see ugliness, wickedness, or malice instead.

We may see the lion as symbolizing the people who we feel have attacked us or angered us. When someone angers us, the roar of their lion calls to our own inner one, which usually roars back. Of course, this works in the other direction as well, which is why our anger usually elicits an angry response in other people. This suggests that anger is a rather dysfunctional use of our energy.

In his book *Call Me by My True Names* Thich Nhat Hanh tells us, "The only thing worthy of you is compassion... Hatred will never let you face the beast in man." Similarly, in *A Return to Love*, Marianne Williamson says, "Whether we choose to focus on the guilt in people's personality or the innocence in their soul is up to us." Thich Nhat Hanh is talking about the lady and the lion within us while Marianne Williamson is referring to those aspects in other people, but there is no substantial difference.

Your lion and that of another person are kindred spirits, and how you handle one of them both reflects and affects how you handle the other. Dealing compassionately with your own inner beast helps you become more like the lady and less like the lion. As a result, you will become more compassionate with other people and thus call to their lady instead of to their lion. This transition takes time and practice. It is not easy, but we must learn to deal with difficult people compassionately, because to do otherwise keeps us in the role of our own internal lion. It keeps us from rediscovering and manifesting our divine nature.

And so the people who challenge us the most are really our best teachers. They show us how far we still are from being in touch with our own divinity and how far we are from seeing divinity within other people. They also give us an opportunity to work on tolerance and forgiveness, and that work leads us back to our divine nature.

One thing that can help us awaken is to pray for the courage and wisdom to change the focus of our attention, to look for the lady in others, rather than the lion. This is a valuable approach instead of hoping or praying for the other person to change, which is what we usually do.

Passions — master or slave?

This card asks, "Are you the master of your passions or are you their slave?" Momentary pleasures come from the latter while true, deep, and abiding fulfillment come from the former. Note, however, that this control does not mean sublimation or eradication of our passions. It means that we should not let our desires control our awareness, judgment, and actions.

The woman on the card has tamed the beast, which indicates that she is controlling her passions and desires through understanding and compassion. However, she has not repressed, destroyed, or hidden them, for it is only when we embrace the beast within that we can tame it and use its power positively and constructively. We should not try to beat it into submission, for that which we resist, persists.

Good wolf / Bad wolf

Jesus said: "Blessed is the lion which the man shall eat, and the lion become man; and cursed is the man whom the lion shall eat, and the lion become man." — The Gospel of Thomas

This verse from the *Gospel of Thomas* talks about the bestial soul (the lion) and the divine soul (the man), and their struggle within us for supremacy. It says that we are all struggling to live according to our divine nature, but the important difference between people lies in the extent to which we let our bestial soul dominate us versus the extent to which we let our divine soul rule instead.

We find a similar illustration in the Cherokee legend of "Two Wolves." In that story, an old Cherokee tells his grandson that there is a fight going on between two wolves inside every one of us. One wolf is bad (anger, greed, arrogance, false pride, ego, etcetera) and the other one good (joy, peace, love, humility, generosity, compassion, etcetera). When the boy asks, "Which wolf will win?" the wise old man replies, "The one you feed."

The first step toward the actualization of our divinity and subjugation of our bestial nature comes with our dawning awareness of this conflict. So listen carefully to what's going on inside when you react to a problem or provocation. Which wolf do you hear, the bad one or the good one? Use that realization to decide if that is the wolf you want to feed (i.e., if it's the one you want to reward with your attention), and then act accordingly. If you feed the good wolf more and the bad wolf less, the good one will become stronger and the bad one weaker. Correspondingly, the voice of the good one will begin to prevail inside of you, and you will find more peace and less agitation in your life.

Release the lion

The Strength card is commonly thought of as advice to cage or control our inner beast, but there is another way of looking at it. It may also suggest that we should find and release that beast, for if the lion represents our passions, it also offers us a great deal of power. Thus this card may say, "Stop being afraid to live your life to its fullest. Find your passion. Discover what makes your heart race, what gives you a reason for living. Does it come from an artistic or athletic endeavor? Do you find it in music? Whatever it is, do it, and thereby bring enthusiasm and vitality back into your life." This is an exciting approach to this card's spiritual message that we will explore here.

The lady and the lion may represent enthusiasm and vitality in both our spiritual and our physical worlds. This may seem like an irreconcilable conjunction, just as it may seem that a woman and a beast could not possibly coexist, although strangely enough, we do see them here in this card in a harmonious relationship. This indicates that unifying our spiritual yearning and our physical passion is possible too. In fact, such a union gives us the courage to take the challenging first step on a spiritual path as well as the strength to continue that journey whenever the going gets tough. But how do we bring about this union?

First, we must allow our enthusiasm and aspirations to emerge. Although this is easy for some of us, many of us are fearful of facing or releasing our passions. Perhaps we fear public disapproval of acting outside the staid, social norms, or maybe we are afraid of what the lion of our passions will do once released from the dungeons of our inhibitions. It is true that throwing open that door can take a great deal of courage. It's dangerous, but that's what life is all about. We aren't here to play it safe. What's the point of that since no one gets out of this life alive anyway? So set the lion free in realization that your passion for union with the Divine is limited as long as the animal in you is imprisoned. Caged, its energy is stifled, and so is yours. Released, it brings forth immense power to transform your life.

Once the lion is free, however, we must guide it in order to channel its energy. In other words, we must direct our passions into productive, not destructive pursuits, and we must transform them to be in accord with our spiritual passion. It is our love for others and for ourselves that allows us to do that. This is because our heart beats not only in the body of our higher self, but in the beast as well. So as we make our hearts more loving—as we exercise and expand our love—the lion's heart will become a loving one, and our passion and compassion will intertwine and meld together. The vitality of our life will empower our spiritual quest, and our higher self will take loving control of the energy of our life. This is the true union of the lady and the lion.

9. Hermit

"If you light a lamp for somebody, it will also brighten your path." — Buddhist Saying

The Hermit can represent a guru, an unorthodox or even iconoclastic teacher or guide to help you along your soul's journey. Thus, a spiritual quest is also a typical meaning for this card, as well as withdrawal, solitude, and seclusion. Considering the characteristics of asceticism and austerity attributed to the hermit archetype, this card also indicates turning away from worldly concerns to those of the soul.

<u>When the student is ready...</u>

In contrast to the conventional teacher we see in the Hierophant card, a

Hermit is often considered to be a wise, unorthodox guru living in seclusion somewhere. In that stereotype, only a few well-prepared students ever find this teacher, and even then, only after an arduous search. And so this card suggests the saying, "When the student is ready, the teacher will appear."

One way to understand this is to consider that we hear only what we are ready to hear. If we are not yet receptive to something, we ignore it, discount it, or forget it. So the teacher (or the lesson) may have been there all along, but until we're ready, we won't notice him, or we won't take him seriously. Consequently, advice from this card is to be open and receptive to spiritual learning so that you will find the teacher you need (or so that the teacher will find you).

... the teacher will appear

Just as the Hermit in many Tarot decks holds a lantern aloft in the dark of night, a guru is generally thought of as someone who dispels our earthly ignorance (darkness) with spiritual illumination (light). But a spiritual guide does not give us all the answers; he lights the way so we can find them. And sometimes it may just be the sacred contagion of his life[9] that sparks a deep, forgotten awareness within us and leads us to enlightenment. Truly, the answers we seek lie dormant within us awaiting the proper conditions to manifest, just as a flower sleeps within a bud until the warmth of the sun touches it, and it blossoms.

Being the teacher

We have seen how "When the student is ready, the teacher will appear," but there is another side to this student/teacher equation. Merely having wisdom is not enough to be a guru; one must also have students to teach. In that case there is a less well-known saying that is fitting: "When the teacher is ready, the students will appear." To see how this might happen, consider the following quote from William Butler Yeats:

We can make our minds so like clear water that beings gather around us that they might see their own images, and so live for a moment with a clearer, perhaps even fiercer life because of our quiet.

---

[9] *This phrase is borrowed from the following quote from Walter Rauschenbusch: "We remember with gratitude to thee the godly teachers of our own youth who won our hearts to higher purposes by the sacred contagion of their life."*

This quote makes the point that we may teach by our "being" as much as by what we say, and it's not just a matter of providing a good example. There truly is something magical about the energy or aura of an enlightened person.

What, however, does this have to do with the rest of us common mortals? The idea of "When the teacher is ready, the students will appear" is relevant to all of us, even those of us who are not yet spiritual sages (which of course means most of us), because we learn a lot in the process of teaching others, no matter what level of teaching that may be. It is also important because helping others find their way is part of our own spiritual practice. As Ram Dass says:

We are all on the journey towards enlightenment and at each stage must share what has been discovered with those who will listen. The sharing is part of the work. The listening is part of the work. We are all on the path.

The Hermit Fallacy

"The real transformation of human nature comes not through an austere, ascetic life or a complete withdrawal from the world, but through a gradual and total illumination of life." — Sri Chinmoy

There is a common misconception about spirituality that I call the *Hermit Fallacy*. It says that enlightenment will lead us to abandon involvement with life, to shun the world and go off to live in seclusion in a cave somewhere. (An alternate version of this myth is that a retreat into seclusion is a requirement for enlightenment.)

With this fallacy in mind, many people reject a spiritual path, and some even denigrate it. Perhaps this is because they mistakenly fear that they will have to go off somewhere to live in lonely austerity, wearing only a simple loincloth. Or maybe their ego has convinced them of this negative image of enlightenment in order to protect itself from the dissolution it knows it will experience once they realize their true, enlightened Self.

However, this myth is not a proper account of enlightenment. While it is true that some of the greatest spiritual leaders spent some time in withdrawal, their time in retreat was part of a process by which they sought enlightenment and not the end result of it. For example, the Buddha sat in quiet meditation under the Bodhi Tree for forty-nine days, and Christ sojourned in the wilderness for forty days, but neither of them remained in seclusion. Their period of solitude was a crucible in which they forged their enlightenment, but then they returned, bringing their light—their teaching—back into the world. They completely engaged in the world again in order to relieve suffering in others and to manifest their own divine nature.

This fact is also reflected in the Tarot. The Hermit card is far from being the last card in the Major Arcana, and so it represents just a step on that path, not its destination. In fact, the final card in the Major Arcana is the World card, which depicts the enlightened soul's total engagement in life as a spirit aware of its divine nature even as it functions within the material world. In other words, it is "in the world, but not of the world"—engaged in life, but not governed by worldly desires and not attached to the results of its actions.

Inner depth reveals the beauty of the outer world

Another important facet of the Hermit's message of withdrawal is that our inward journey of spiritual discovery facilitates our realization of the spiritual beauty in the world and in the people around us. After all, how can we find beauty and meaning in the world if we fail to find those things within ourselves?

To be able to perceive the deepest beauty of the world around us, we must also explore our own inner depth and spiritual beauty. The same holds true for our perception of the divine within others. As an example of this, a modern, Western interpretation of the Hindu salutation *Namaste* is: "The divinity in me greets the divinity in you." This is a lovely concept upon which this card suggests a further commentary. The Hermit tells us that we are able to see the divine nature of others only to the extent that we have come to realize it within ourselves.

One way to explore your own inner depths is to spend time alone in peaceful contemplation. This includes meditation, of course, but it is not only that. It can mean being in contemplative awareness of nature, which may involve anything from sitting quietly in your garden to hiking along a remote mountain trail. It also may mean thoughtfully exploring your feelings about your relationships with other people, although it's important to remember to do so with an open heart that is not burdened with judgments or preconceptions. And an inward exploration can also mean contemplation of your own personal connection to the Divine.

Again, the Hermit card is not about permanently disengaging from society. Withdrawal may be something we experience for fifteen minutes each day or for one week in a year, and temporary retreat like that revitalizes us, much like sleep is a respite that refreshes us. This analogy is especially apt when we consider that sleep's withdrawal from consciousness keeps us from experiencing crazy hallucinations about the world. Similarly, a hermit-like retreat helps us develop a saner view of the world as we reconnect with it.

Ultimately, then, the Hermit is not about escaping from the world. It is about withdrawing for a while in preparation for fully engaging in life and experiencing it at a deeper, more spiritual level than before.

10. Wheel of Fortune

"This, too, shall pass away."[10] — *Traditional saying*

This card represents the perpetually changing aspect of life. As Heraclitus famously said, "change is the only constant in life." So it indicates the up and down cycles of life, including those of our successes and failures. Similarly, it is sometimes called the Fate card. It also counsels us to learn from adversity and to learn equanimity in the face of any change.

The "Maybe" parable

The Wheel of Fortune card says that no matter how good or bad a situation is, it will change, and there is a well-known Taoist parable called "Maybe" that illustrates this point. Here it is:

There once was an old farmer who had tended his crops for many years. One day his horse ran away. Upon hearing the sad news, his neighbors said to him in sympathy, "Such bad luck."

"Maybe," the farmer replied.

The next morning the horse returned, bringing with it three wild horses. "How wonderful," the neighbors exclaimed.

"Maybe," replied the old man.

The following day, his son tried to ride one of the untamed horses and was

---

[10] *In a speech in 1859, Abraham Lincoln said of this well-known proverb, "How much it expresses! How chastening in the hour of pride! How consoling in the depths of affliction!"*

thrown, which broke his leg. The neighbors again came to offer their condolences on his misfortune.

"Maybe," answered the farmer.

The next day, military officials came to the village to draft young men into the army. Seeing that the son's leg was broken, they passed him by. The neighbors congratulated the farmer on how well things had turned out.

"Maybe," said the farmer.

Here are a couple of ways to interpret this parable.

ONE: View change with equanimity.

"Pain is inevitable. Suffering is optional." — The 14th Dalai Lama[11]

The Buddha taught that it is our attachment to material, transitory things that causes suffering, not the loss of those things. Of course, it is hard to take this perspective when you suffer a painful loss. Practice will get you there, but that is a long-term strategy. In the short-term, the Wheel of Fortune card suggests the analogy of a spinning wheel. (Think of a record turntable if you are old enough to remember those.) When a wheel spins, anything sitting on the edge will be thrown off, but objects placed on the hub will be safe. This tells us that when life seems to spin out of control, our calm, spiritual center can be a peaceful refuge. Consequently, as we strengthen our inner connection to what is truly eternal instead of that which is transitory we will cultivate a more permanent happiness in our earthly life.

TWO: Everything is a lesson

"There is a lesson—sometimes delightful and sometimes painful—in everything that happens to you." — Rick Fields

It often seems that things (whether good or bad) happen without apparent reason and regardless of what we deserve. That is one way to view life's seemingly capricious nature, but another is to consider life's ups and downs to be life lessons. We often have little or no choice as to what happens to us, but we always have the choice of whether or not we learn from our experiences, and we are free to choose *what* we learn from them. Ultimately, then, it is not what happens to us; it's how we experience it, deal with it, and learn from it that

---

[11] *Another way of putting this is this: "Pain is what the world does to us; suffering is what we do to ourselves."*

counts.

Of course, these two different interpretations ("view change with equanimity" and "learn from change") are not mutually exclusive. After all, it's exceedingly hard to learn lessons from the things that happen to us when we are caught up in their drama, but when we view them with equanimity, our minds remain clear and our hearts remain serene. It is then that we can learn from our experiences rather than merely react to them. And the highest lessons we can learn from our experiences include unconditional love, compassion, generosity, appreciation, forgiveness, and (as we see here) equanimity.

Escape from attachment to results

"You win some; you lose some." — Traditional saying

A great deal of suffering arises from our tendency to attach to the anticipated results of our actions, so cultivating nonattachment to those results is a lesson similar to that of equanimity in the face of changing fortune. And just as with our gains and losses, it is our successes as well as our failures that we need to view with equanimity, for we cannot attach to the one without attaching to the other.

We may enjoy a bit of happiness when we win, but even those happy times may be tainted with fear that we might lose what we have won, or disappointment that the win wasn't big enough, or worry that we were just lucky that time. Inevitably, since we lose sometimes too, we will suffer the unhappiness of failure at other times. As long as we base our happiness on externals like success, we are doomed to suffer from time to time.

We can escape suffering, or at least mitigate it, by cultivating equanimity, which is the wisdom that it's all good since everything is a part of life's lessons, and certainly we can learn as much from our failures as from our successes. So as we develop this composure and release our attachment to anticipated results, we well become better able to enjoy happiness both in good times and in bad times, win-times and lose-times. As the saying goes, "Happiness is an inside job."

The spiritual value of failure

"Failure lies concealed in every success, and success in every failure." — Eckhart Tolle

The Wheel of Fortune says that our lives are part of a vast cosmic dance in which there are eternal cycles within cycles of birth, life, and death. Everything, from a grain of sand to a galaxy, has a beginning and an end, and so it is with us too. Not only are we born, live, and die, but within that overarching cycle, our luck comes and goes as well. Good fortune and bad, gain and loss, success and failure—they all come and go as part of the greater cycle of each individual life.

Although this reality of endless cycles means that change is always inevitable, everything comes in its own time. Sometimes we have some control over that timing; sometimes we do not. In fact, it often seems that during times of trouble, we can only wait it out. Consequently, one lesson indicated by this card is to learn to have patience in difficult times.

Patience requires that we avoid judging a situation, that we suspend our desires and expectations, and that we allow things to unfold as they will. These are all spiritual practices—no judging, releasing our desires, and trusting in the Divine. No wonder it is said that "Patience is a virtue." This is why times of trouble and misfortune are considered to be valuable bumps and potholes along life's journey—they give us opportunities to learn patience, which is made up of several spiritual practices.

Our failures can also return us to our spiritual journey. Eckhart Tolle says, "You must have failed deeply on some level or experienced some deep loss or pain to be drawn to the spiritual dimension." Also, to paraphrase Marianne Williamson, sometimes misfortune brings us to our knees, but that's a good place to be if we are to turn toward the Divine.[12]

So we see that the true gift of failure is that it leads us to give up relying on our own devices and turn instead toward the Divine. In this way, spiritual success patiently waits for us in our every worldly failure.

Permanent joy in the sacred reality

We all want certainties and guarantees in life, but there are none. Life is uncertain. The world is constantly changing, as are we—sometimes for the better, sometimes for the worse. As soon as we find something to support our happiness, it changes, so we engage in an endless struggle to manipulate the world to fit our expectations and to service our desires. But of course we cannot expect to win

---

[12] *The original quote is from Williamson's book,* A Return to Love*: "... many times we are brought to our knees. As always, that's a good place to be."*

every time, so we face the eternal challenge of trying to maintain our balance on the ever-spinning wheel of life.

As discussed previously, equanimity in the face of change helps us avoid suffering, but is the mere avoidance of suffering enough? Even in this ever-changing world, is there not some way to find joy that is profound and lasting? Can we avoid the taint of worldly attachment to make that possible?

Most spiritual teachings talk about the joy that comes from believing in the sacred reality of our spiritual Self. This happiness is both profound and eternal for it is not tied to the ever-changing material world. Consequently, the way to find lasting peace and joy is to detach from the vagaries of life in realization that although all phenomenal reality changes, the divine core of life—the hub of the spinning wheel—is constant. As we move toward that changeless center of our spiritual being and as we root our happiness there, our peace and joy will become unassailable.

The advice of this card, then, is not to let your bliss depend on changing people or conditions that you don't like or on holding on to people or conditions that you do like. Instead, change your perceptions and understanding of the world. Of course, this does not mean that you should just ignore bad conditions and let them continue unchallenged. We should work to right the wrongs of the world because that is the right thing to do. We can make plans and take action, but "the best-laid plans of mice and men often go awry" as the saying goes[13] so we must also learn to trust life and to flow with it. We must learn to take right action but not hitch our wagon of happiness to the results because that brings anxiety.

We must try to see the divinity within us, other people, and the world, and then attach our happiness to that. The most profound spiritual teachers have said that when you do that, something miraculous happens. With our heart in alignment with our soul, we begin to see the world unfolding in accordance with divine Will, and our joy will blossom along with it, now rooted in something permanent.

---

[13] *After a passage in Robert Burns's poem "To a Mouse."*

11. Justice

This card is (obviously) about justice, which can refer to both human and divine justice. In addition, it indicates the cosmic law of "Cause and Effect," which is sometimes called Karma. Note also that the figure of Justice seen on this card holds both the sword of righteousness and the scales of balance, discernment, and wisdom.

Injustice and our humanity

"Injustice anywhere is a threat to justice everywhere." — *Martin Luther King, Jr.*

As its name suggests, this card is often about justice. Whether it is in terms of laws, ethics, or morality, we generally have a pretty good understanding of right and wrong, but we don't always act upon that awareness. Sometimes it seems easier to avoid getting involved if we are not directly impacted by an injustice. We may decide that we can let others take care of it, or we might bury our heads in the sand and ignore the problem since we think it's not ours. But through our shared humanity, it is our problem too. This does not mean that we have to join every crusade that comes our way. However, it does mean that if we see an injustice and we can do something about it—even if it is just one small act—we should, for whenever we tolerate or accept injustice in our midst we lose touch with our humanity, one little bit at a time.

Revenge versus Justice

"A man that studieth revenge keeps his own wounds green." — *Francis Bacon*

There is an important difference between justice and revenge that is often overlooked. While justice is the administration of deserved punishment, typically through an impartial agency, revenge involves the imposition of punishment (often draconian) by someone who is anything but impartial acting in a vindictive spirit.

There are many movies in which a vigilante's revenge is glorified, but there are very few which show its darkness. This tends to buttress the popular sentiment that revenge is good, or at least acceptable. The only recent exception to this cinematic trend that I know of is the 2005 film *The Interpreter* which succinctly describes one of the problems with revenge in this wonderful quote: "Vengeance is a lazy form of grief."

Despite the satisfying picture that Hollywood has painted of it, revenge is bitter, and it often escalates out of control in a vicious cycle. As Confucius said, "Before you embark on a journey of revenge, dig two graves." It also exacerbates and perpetuates the wounding of the spirits of everyone involved. In the pursuit of vengeance, we become mean, violent people. We become that which we think we are chastising, and as a consequence, we corrupt our own lives.

The problems with vengeance do not only apply to dramatic or deadly instances, such as the infamous case of the Hatfield–McCoy feud. Small, everyday acts of revenge corrode our spirit as well. They can be like tiny drops of venom that seem harmless enough by themselves, but their toxic effects build up over time. Beware of them.

Cause and Effect

"Shallow men believe in luck. Strong men believe in cause and effect." — *Ralph Waldo Emerson*

The Justice card advises us to take responsibility for our actions because it is through them that we continually weave the fabric of our lives. Many people mistakenly think this message is about blaming people for their present circumstances, but that misses the point. In stressing the importance of taking responsibility, this card conveys a very positive message of personal empowerment. If the life we are living now reflects our past actions, then surely our present actions are creating our future.

This card also assures us that ultimately no one escapes divine justice, for it sees all. This is why the figure on the Justice card generally is not depicted as being blindfolded like the one we typically see in front of a courthouse.[14] So when we yearn for justice and do not see it coming (at least not quickly enough) we should remember what Martin Luther King, Jr. said: "Let us realize the arc of the moral universe is long but it bends toward justice."

However, although divine justice is inevitable, we must release our expectations about it. Instead we should trust that it will be served in some way

---

[14] *The representation of human justice is blindfolded to symbolize impartiality under the law.*

that we may not perceive, and we should not attach to what form divine justice will take. As a Zen master once advised his students: "Live with cause and leave results to the great law of the universe."[15]   For example, a spiritual life is marked by its generosity and service, but a spiritual person does not practice charity for its reward, which may not be what's either desired or expected. Instead, "we must do this ... as service to God out of love for God."[16]

So first we learn to trust the cosmic law of "cause and effect." Then we learn to release our concern about the effect part so that we may come to do the right thing out of devotion to the Divine rather than with expectations about the results of our actions.

Karma

Karma is generally understood to be the law of cause and effect that governs our lives, whether we see it as operating within this one life or from one lifetime to the next. Consequently, people often talk about "good karma" and "bad karma," considering it to be a cosmic balance sheet. But if the material world is (spiritually speaking) an illusion, what reality is there in material rewards and punishments? And if we are souls having a material experience in order to learn and grow, isn't there a deeper meaning to the concept of karma? Perhaps, then, instead of seeing karma as a system of rewards and punishments, we should see it as being about which lessons we have learned and which we have not. If we can view it this way, we can finally appreciate things that may be considered "bad karma," and we can begin to learn from them in order to relieve our suffering and stop being mired in it.

Choose the right road

"This above all...to thine own self be true." — William Shakespeare

As previously noted, our present life is the result of our past actions, and we are continually creating our future by what we think, say, and do today. Advice about how we can best do this can be inferred from two of the most prominent symbols on this card, the scales and the sword, which stress the importance of

---

[15] Zen Flesh, Zen Bones *by Paul Reps and Nyogen Senzaki*

[16] The Sermon on the Mount According to Vedanta *by Swami Prabhavananda*

"right decision" and "right action." These two are inextricably linked. A right decision without the corresponding right action is tantamount to the proverbial good intentions that pave the road to hell. On the other hand, taking right action without having made the right decision can be like walking correctly along the wrong path, and where does that lead you?

This recipe of right decisions and right actions is vital to our success in every phase of our lives, but one especially important time is early on when we face the classic question, "What do you want to be when you grow up?" If we choose a field that suits our temperament and interests we will be able to swim effectively and serenely with the flow of life, and the channel will be clear for divine will to manifest through us. In this way, we are able to co-create with the Divine.

However, if we do not make a wise decision and instead allow the world around us (our parents, peers, financial conditions, base desires, etcetera) to make that decision for us, then our lives will be marred by a constant struggle between our nature and our chosen path. Living within the turmoil of that struggle, it is very hard to hear, much less act upon divine guidance, and the channel through which divine power can flow into our lives is obstructed by disappointment, confusion, and strife.

This calls to mind Tolstoy's novella, *The Death of Ivan Ilyich*. Ivan Ilyich lived his life in a manner seemingly right and righteous. He did all the right things according to the dictates of society. But on his death bed, he begins to wonder if he lived his life correctly, despite his life's outward appearances of propriety. At the end, he realizes that his work and his relationships have been artificial and meaningless. With that epiphany, however, he also finds serenity and joy. He discovers a depth of genuine feeling for the people close to him that he had never known before. He releases his bitter judgments and dies happy.

So what about those of us who, like Ivan Ilyich, made bad choices in our youth about how to live our lives? The good news is that it's never too late, although hopefully we won't wait until we are on our deathbed to have an epiphany. Some of us can make a midlife career change, but even if we can't, there are other options. We might adjust the details of our job situation, or we can change our attitude about our work to better fit our temperament. We also can take up a fulfilling hobby, or we can do volunteer work that serves our higher calling.

Thus, the Justice card is a reminder to live your truth always. Its encouraging message is that it is never too late to reevaluate what you want to be when you grow up. After all, none of us is ever *completely* grown up, are we?

12. Hanged Man

"When you yield internally, when you surrender, a new dimension of consciousness opens up." — Eckhart Tolle

This card, with its image of a man passively hanging upside-down by one foot, commonly indicates renunciation, sacrifice, and surrender, and it suggests finding a new perspective or looking at things from a totally different point of view. It also suggests the techniques of nonresistance and nonviolence advocated and practiced by Mahatma Gandhi and Martin Luther King, Jr.

Renounce attachment

"A Zen master remarked, 'Renunciation is not giving up the things of this world; it is accepting that they go away.' The result of such acceptance is fulfillment, not deprivation." — Arthur Deikman, MD

One of the spiritual implications of the Hanged Man card is that of the renunciation of materialism, and this scares a lot of people. They think that means that they will have to give away all their goodies. Some versions of this card do show the Hanged Man releasing coins from his hands, but that depiction is metaphorical. Although we should let go of our *attachment* to material things, our actual possession of them is irrelevant in and of itself.

The release of our material attachments is not just to make us less materialistic in order to make room for more spirituality. It is (contrary to what many people believe) to bring us a life of increased joy and fulfillment. We think that having things makes us happy, but this ignores the fact that our attachment to those things has the inevitable consequence of bringing us suffering. This is because all material things are transient, so eventually we will lose them. However, even before that happens, we suffer the fear of losing them, and we expend a great deal of effort trying to maintain our grasp on them. In this way, our possessions own us every bit as much as we own them, so releasing our attachment to them relieves us of a major source of stress.

Ultimately, though, it is irrelevant whether or not we let go of material things because none of those goodies are real anyway since whatever is transient is illusory. In other words, the renunciation of materialism really means giving up the illusion that the material plane is real. This metaphysical concept is extremely hard for us to deal with, though, so for now it's enough to realize that our attachment to material things creates suffering, and suffering is what we are being advised to release.

We are not being called upon to be martyrs or to take a vow of poverty. We are being called upon to awaken to a new reality, to see the eternal value of our spiritual connection versus the fleeting value of our material possessions. And in doing that, we will be helping others to awaken to this higher realization as well.

Sacrifice everything and nothing

"You will come to know that what appears to be a sacrifice will prove instead to be the greatest investment you will ever make." — Gordon B. Hinkley

This card is often associated with the concept of sacrifice (sometimes voluntary, sometimes not) and in that guise, it may seem frightening. Indeed, on a mundane, worldly level, there may be cause for such fear, but that material plane is illusory. On a spiritual level, the Hanged Man's call for giving something up is not a burden; it is a blessing, and it is always voluntary, as is every blessing from the Divine.

Any sacrifice the Divine asks of us is actually a request to give up something of no true worth, to give up an illusion in order that we may gain something of real value: an enlightened vision and experience of life. The requested sacrifice (which is only a sacrifice in our worldly understanding of the word) is onerous merely if we view it through the eyes of materialism. Seen with spiritual vision, it is a blessing.

The power of surrendering

"The curious paradox is that when I accept myself just as I am, then I can change." — Carl Rogers

There is a common misunderstanding about the process of spiritual surrender, which this card advocates. There are some who erroneously criticize it as apathy, giving up, or fatalism, while others fear that it means that spirituality is humiliating, miserable, or even impossible. On the contrary, though, surrender is empowering and liberating.

A great deal of our suffering comes from our resistance to accepting *what is* since our thoughts about a situation, much more than the situation itself, are what torment us. Another way of putting this is beautifully expressed in this Zen proverb: "It is never uncomfortable to be where you are. It is only uncomfortable to want to be somewhere else."

This does not mean we must accept that the way things are is the way they should be or always will be. It also does not mean that *what is* is good, because that is a value judgment, and acceptance transcends judgments. It is observation, awareness, and equanimity.

Similarly, acceptance doesn't mean that we can't work to change ourselves and the world. We just need to accept *what is* right now and not resist it internally. It's a matter of releasing *shoulds* (judgments) and looking for *coulds* (creative possibilities) instead. Thus, as we relax into an internal state of non-resistance, which is centered, balanced, and peaceful, we will gain an expanded consciousness through which we can become an effective force for a positive transformation of the world. This concept of the power of surrender is as old as Lao Tzu and as current as Eckhart Tolle, as the following quotes attest:

"By letting it go, it all gets done.
The world is won by those who let it go.
But when you try and try,
The world is beyond the winning."
— Lao Tzu

"Through surrender, you will be free internally of the situation. You may then find that the situation changes without any effort on your part. In any case, you're free." — Eckhart Tolle

The importance of surrender can also be seen in the old saying "What you resist persists." This adage is true because when we resist something, we give it our attention, energy, and power. Thus, the irony is that resistance is actually an embrace, while surrender is a powerful road to change.

Finally, the deepest importance of surrender is that it brings us closer to a realization of our connection to the Divine. In accepting *what is* we are accepting that whatever happens in the present moment is a necessary step on our path to the Divine. As Ram Dass says, "... whatever is in front of you is a step to God."

Nonresistance

"Nothing on earth can overcome an absolutely nonresistant person." — Zen proverb

The concepts of nonresistance and nonviolent resistance are easily but erroneously confused with cowardice or weakness. On the surface they seem similar, but nonresistance—the kind discussed here—is born not of fear but of courage. It is also a matter of humility, patience, adaptability, and faith. Indeed, the concept of nonresistance indicated by the Hanged Man is a complex and multilayered one. We may come to understand it better, though, by first considering it in light of a fable, and then through the philosophies and careers of Martin Luther King, Jr. and Mahatma Gandhi. Finally, we will view this message in light of the famous saying, "Let go and let God."

In Aesop's fable *The Oak and the Reed*, a lowly reed says to a mighty Oak: "You fight and contend with the wind, and consequently you are destroyed; while I bend before the wind and therefore remain unbroken and escape." Thus we may say that it is the Oak's hubris and rigidity that bring about its undoing, and this advises us to develop humility and flexibility in our lives.

In the works of Martin Luther King, Jr. and Mahatma Gandhi, we see the value and power of the two closely-related concepts of "nonresistance" and "nonviolent resistance."[17] Neither of these men fought in the usual sense of the word, knowing that fighting only creates more violence in the world. On the other hand, they did not submit. They faced the abuse and violence of their persecutors without replying in kind, which took far more courage than to confront it "with sword in hand."

Gandhi wrote that "nonresistance does not mean passive submission to the will of the persecutor." It means refusing to accept injustice while at the same time being willing to accept the consequences of that refusal. Similarly, King said that civil disobedience is not a meek acceptance of evil. It may be passive physically, but spiritually, it is very active. It is standing your ground without putting the other person out of your heart, and it is born of love, not hate. In King's words:

Darkness cannot drive out darkness: only light can do that. Hate cannot drive out hate: only love can do that. The beauty of nonviolence is that in its

---

[17] *In their efforts, "nonviolent resistance" may be the more appropriate term, but often, such as when they and their followers were faced with arrest, non-resistance was literally the case.*

own way and in its own time it seeks to break the chain reaction of evil.

Thus, a powerful message in this card is that we can stand firm against iniquity without resorting to hate, anger, or violence, all of which arise from fear and the illusion of separateness.

"Let go and let God" is a popular saying, and it is a very appropriate meaning for the Hanged Man card. Some people interpret this as "sit back and let God solve all your problems," but it is a much more subtle and profound concept than that. Certainly it is true that in any effort there comes a time when we should stop struggling and allow the Divine to bring us what we need, and when we do that, things turn out better. However, we should do what we can. After all, there is another truism to consider: "Trust in God, but steer away from the rocks."

At a deeper level, "Let go and let God" means that the results the Divine brings us may not turn out to be what we want or expect, but that's okay. The Divine will bring us the results that are right for our spiritual growth. They won't always be what we think are best for our worldly desires, but again, that's okay. So perhaps the most profound interpretation of "Let go and let God" is that we need to stop insisting that our way is the right way; we need to stop resisting the will of the Divine. In other words, this saying may be rewritten as "Let go of your way and let God show you a better one."

13. Death

"What the caterpillar calls the end, the rest of the world calls a butterfly."
— *Lao Tzu*

It is a truism in Tarot circles that the Death card does not usually mean someone is going to die. Rather, this card is generally about profound change, transitions, and transformations. Nevertheless, this card does bring up the topic of the transience of life, which sometimes leads us to profound metaphysical and spiritual insights.

Impermanence

"The Gods envy us. They envy us because we're mortal, because any moment might be our last. Everything is more beautiful because we're doomed." — *Homer*, The Iliad

This quote from the Iliad may not seem very comforting, but its advice is truly powerful. It urges us to appreciate the beauty of everything in our lives because everything is transient, ourselves included. A tender moment with a loved one, a delicate flower in the garden, a crimson sunset—they all change and become something else, which we call "ending." They all are beautifully and exquisitely transient.

Although it may be tempting to see this message as being morose or as a cause for fear, transformation is only loss if we attach to things. If we develop the ability to be thankful for things while they last and then let them go when their time is past, we will be able to appreciate what comes next. Our sense of happiness and wellbeing will be built on the solid foundation of our ability to appreciate rather than on the shifting sand of changing circumstance.

Nowhere is this concept more important than in our relationships. As Thich Nhat Hanh says, "Let impermanence nurture love." Many of us avoid fully committing to a relationship, or we desperately grasp the one we have, because we fear the pain of its ending. Instead, the inevitable mortality of our relationships can make them more precious instead of frightening. In one way or another, every relationship ends, and if we know and accept this, we can cherish every moment we share with the ones we love.

A sentiment similar to Homer's message may be seen in the old saying, "Live each day as if it's your last." So let your realization of impermanence nurture your relationships and enhance your appreciation for the ever-changing beauty that is all around you. But more than that, in realization that the precious gift of life is impermanent, we should always appreciate that gift and everything that comes with it.

Embracing change

"If you are irritated by every rub, how will you be polished?" — Rumi

Everything changes in life, and every change—great and small—presents us with a challenge to learn and adapt. We might say that all change creates friction in our lives, and we often resist it because we don't want that friction to wear us down. But change is a part of life—undeniable and unavoidable—so resisting it is actually a resistance to life. In fact, we experience thousands of little deaths— endings that change our world—in the course of a lifetime. Resisting, denying, and complaining about them only increases our suffering. Celebrating and rejoicing in them brings joy into our lives and into the world, and it allows our soul's beauty to shine. Thus, a profound realization is that it is the friction of life that polishes our spirit, just as the flowing water of a river slowly polishes a rock. In fact, the friction of change can expose the beauty of our soul.

A dress rehearsal for death

Death is said to be the great equalizer since it claims us all. More importantly, though, it is a great instructor. When faced with death, many people finally realize what is important in life. They may see that old grudges are not worth holding on to, or that spending time with loved ones is more important than working nights and weekends in order to have a beautiful home they spend so little time in.

However, it is not necessary to come face-to-face with the Grim Reaper to find such insights. Ask yourself what changes you would make in your life if you found out that you had only a short time to live. What's stopping you from making those changes now? Take this opportunity to learn the lessons that impending death brings before the Grim Reaper actually comes for you.

Looking away from death

In our culture, we avert our eyes from death and refuse to even speak its name. We won't say that someone has died; we say that they passed away, kicked the bucket, or met their maker. Any vicarious brush with death gives us a fleeting glimpse of the doorway to the great unknown and reminds us of our own mortality. And so, in an affirmation of our fear of death, we look away.

Unfortunately, the problem is not just that we have a long list of euphemisms for death; we outsource it too. In some cultures it is not swept under the rug; it is dealt with personally. In ours, however, people often have to die alone. They may be surrounded by other people in a hospital or a retirement home, but they are still alone if there is no one by their side who cares about them. Try to keep that from happening to anyone you love. It may take great courage to offer that sort of support, but the experience can be exquisitely meaningful for you as well as for them if you see it as a passage and allow it to occur with a sense of sacred spaciousness. It helps, of course, to face our fear of the great unknown of death, and the following sections suggest ways to do that.

Conquering the fear of death: Near-Death Experiences

As mentioned in the previous section, much of our fear of death comes from the fact that it is the great unknown. Its mystery scares us. So the more we understand of it, the less frightening it becomes. One way to become more comfortable with the concept of death is through finding out about Near-Death Experiences.

The similarities of the experiences of many people who have undergone a NDE are remarkable. See, for example, the various reports of NDE experiences in the book *Life After Life* by Raymond Moody. Also, an interesting finding about NDE is how it affects those who have experienced it. Again, the similarity of responses is significant. The following is a list of changes common to people who had a near-death experience as described in a Wikipedia article on the topic.[18]

- A greater appreciation of life
- Higher self-esteem
- Greater compassion for others
- A heightened sense of purpose and self-understanding
- A heightened desire to learn
- Elevated spirituality
- Greater ecological sensitivity and planetary concern
- A feeling of being more intuitive

I find it rather reassuring that these are the types of responses that people have after seeing what lies behind that mysterious doorway.

Conquering the fear of death: Dispelling the illusion

"Death is not extinguishing the light; it is putting out the lamp because the dawn has come." — Rabindranath Tagore

Our fears concerning death also arise from the illusion that our bodies and personalities are the ultimate reality instead of our spiritual Self. So we can dissipate our fears about death by challenging that illusion. Interestingly, I have found a wide variety of sources addressing this topic in very similar ways. Here are just a few.

---

[18] *The source material that Wikipedia used is an article in the July 1992 issue of* Psychology Today *by James Mauro titled, "Bright lights, big mystery."*

The *Tao Te Ching* puts it this way:

Each separate being in the universe
returns to the common source.
Returning to the source is serenity.

In his book *Religion in Practice*, Swami Prabhavananda says:

You are not the body, the mind, or the senses. You are the Self, the Spirit [which is] one with God. When you realize this truth in transcendental vision, death won't frighten you. Dying will be like throwing away a worn-out garment, that's all.

In *No Death, No Fear: Comforting Wisdom for Life*, Thich Nhat Hanh presents a useful analogy that compares our life to a drop of water. The essence of this analogy is that a drop of water thrown into the air from an ocean wave may experience the illusion that it has been born and that it will die when it eventually returns to the sea. Part of that painful illusion is the belief that it, the drop of water, is something separate from the ocean, but it is not really, and its return to the ocean is not an ending but a wonderful reunion with its source.

Similarly, Ram Dass discusses the illusion that death is real in an article on his website[19] called "Dying is Absolutely Safe." He says the following:

As long as you identify with that which dies, there is always fear of death. [But] the essence of [our] Being ... is beyond death. ... When the body and the ego are gone, the Soul will live on, because the Soul is eternal.

Also in that article, Ram Dass says that "being with people who were dying [helped] me deal with my own fear of death in this lifetime." Spending as much time with the dying as Ram Dass has is not a viable option for most of us, but at one time or another we all may find an opportunity to spend time with someone who is dying. Many of us want to avoid this, but sharing the experience of death with another living being is an honor and a blessing. Perhaps we would fear death less if we were more willing to do that.[20]

---

[19] *http://www.ramdass.org*

[20] *If you choose to do this, an excellent resource for preparation is* On Death & Dying *by Elisabeth Kübler-Ross. This book is a seminal work in this field.*

Conquering the fear of death: Having a brush with death

Finally, we may gain more understanding of death from our own personal brushes with it, although this does not have to mean a near-death experience. These incidences may create a comforting familiarity with death ... or they may not. The difference comes from the beliefs and attitudes we bring to them. Let me relate one of my own experiences. It is not a near-death experience, but it was one time when I had to face the distinct possibility of my own death.

Many years ago I came down with bacterial pneumonia. There are several types of pneumonia, and this bacterial variety is generally the easiest to treat. If my doctor had diagnosed it properly and then prescribed the most effective antibiotic for it, it should not have lasted very long or been very debilitating. But he did not. So the disease lasted longer than it might have, and it became progressively more incapacitating. In the last few days before I finally got the correct antibiotic that cured the disease, I was convinced that I could possibly die from it.

The interesting thing is that the moments when I thought "I could very well die from this" were the only really peaceful times for me during the illness. Granted, most of the rest of the time I alternated between horrific coughing bouts and bitter complaints about my doctor's ineptitude, so it's not like my life was the height of serenity just then. But I was not panicked by the prospect of death. Instead, in close proximity to it, I felt a serene resignation about death, which was a reaction I found somewhat surprising.

Naturally, my beliefs about death informed my response, but until I was actually faced with the prospect, I did not know for sure how I would react to it. I don't recommend pneumonia as a way to examine your beliefs about life and death, but many of us are confronted with life threatening experiences of some sort on rare occasions, and when they arise, they can be a valuable tool for exploring that part of life which we do not typically see.

Death and rebirth in Spirit

In most spiritual traditions there is a concept that one can be "reborn in Spirit," which, in one way or another, refers to a reunion with the Divine. Many say they want to be reborn in Spirit—in fact, many say they have been—but few are ready to pay the requisite price to get there because the cost of spiritual rebirth is death. No, not physical death, but a dreaded death nevertheless: the release of our attachment to the stuff of our manifest life. This does not just mean our material possessions. It includes our desires, our beliefs, and our judgments of others. And our ego must also die in order that we may be reborn in Spirit.

This does not mean we have to throw out everything we own; it means we have to detach ourselves from all of it. Until we release all those forms of attachment, which is what the previous card (the Hanged Man) represents, we have not yet passed through the required gates of death—we have not experienced the symbolic equivalent of death necessary for rebirth in Spirit.

We must remember, however, that this spiritual rebirth is a process more than an event. We have false starts. We inch toward it and then retreat again. We fall down along the way. But as long as we realize that this is the doorway through which we must pass to reunite with the Divine, and as long as we hold fast to our intention to pass through it, we will succeed eventually, even if it is only at the moment of our last breath.

14. Temperance

"Our real blessings often appear to us in the shapes of pains, losses and disappointments; but let us have patience, and we soon shall see them in their proper figures." — Joseph Addison

The title of this card has several linguistic implications that shed light on its meaning. First, there is the verb "to temper" (as in tempered steel or tempered glass), which can mean making something stronger through a stressing agency. Thus, this card says that our troubles can make us stronger. This verb also means to moderate or mitigate something, often by blending in another agent to bring it into a better balance. For example, we might temper justice with mercy. Then there is the noun, "temper," as in the phrase, "he lost his temper." In this case, temper can indicate a calm state of mind that we can either keep or lose. Finally, the word "temperance" has been used a lot with regards to the consumption of alcohol. However, contrary to popular opinion, temperance means moderation, not total self-denial.

Lessons of our wounds

As noted above, one of the meanings of the verb "to temper" is to make something stronger or more resilient through stress or hardship. Certainly, it is adversity and not comfort that challenges us to grow, although we must make the decision to meet the challenge in order to accomplish that growth. In other words, trials and tribulation are inevitable, but learning and evolution are optional, at least in the short term. So the question is, do we use hardship as an impetus to become more loving and understanding, or do we allow our suffering to make us bitter, angry, and defensive instead?

Nowhere is this question more relevant than in the area of our emotional wounds, which we all have in one form or another. They cause us suffering, and they often control our behavior in nasty ways that we don't realize at the time. But they also can become our greatest teachers if we seek to learn from them with an open heart and mind.

One way to find healing for these wounds is through the water of quiet, meditative exploration of them. This practice brings a soothing understanding of how these wounds affect our spiritual journey. Another way is through the fire of our passion for union with the Divine, which reveals the level of our being that is untouched by our wounds. As the Temperance angel is depicted mixing disparate elements to create something precious and new, the mixture of the water and fire of these two paths will alchemically transmute the lead of our painful experiences into the gold of our spiritual evolution. We are thereby saved from crumbling under the weight of our wounds.

Consequently, as we come to realize the purpose and lessons of a wound, our unfolding wisdom will heal it. However, in addition to our own healing, this process will also facilitate in the healing of the world around us as we become empowered to help others with similar wounds. In this way, we can take on the healing role of the Temperance angel and fulfill our sacred purpose of relieving suffering in the world.

Turn poison into medicine

"Use what seems like poison as medicine. Use your personal suffering as the path to compassion for all beings." — Pema Chödrön

An important aspect of this card's meaning of alchemical transformation may be beautifully summed up in the Nichiren Buddhist term *hendoku-iyaku*—"changing poison into medicine." This is the process by which we transform our problems—anything from our base desires to our troubles and afflictions—into strength, joy, and enlightenment. We can do this by viewing these difficulties with compassion (as suggested by the Strength card), by learning from them (as discussed in the prior section, "Lessons of our wounds"), and by releasing them to a higher power (i.e., by "letting go and letting God," as suggested by the Hanged Man). Specifically, though, let's consider our problems in light of Pema Chödrön's words.

The wounds we carry in our hearts may seem like obstacles in our lives, but through our experience of them, they can make us more sensitive to the problems and shortcomings of others. As we become more sensitized in this way, our compassion increases, which may be the highest lesson we can learn from adversity.

On one level, experiencing a specific problem may show us the way to be more compassionate toward others who are suffering that same problem. For example, recovered alcoholics often help people new to Alcoholics Anonymous. On a higher level, though, we can generalize our lessons and use our problems to develop a universal "compassion for all beings."

To explain this further, let me describe several different types of people. First, there are those remarkable individuals who act with compassion in a given circumstance because they are filled with universal love. Their wounds have already taught them that everyone has their own unique problems and that we should have empathy for them even if we have never experienced their problems. Then there are people who act compassionately in specific circumstances where they have been personally touched by the problem. They have not generalized their empathy, but they have learned enough from their tribulations to have specific compassion. However, if they have not experienced a given problem, they may still lack compassion for those who are suffering it. For example, this includes wealthy people who lack sympathy and charity for the poor. Unfortunately, there are also people who have been touched by a problem but have not yet learned from it. Despite their personal experience, they still fail to act with compassion. In rejecting the learning opportunity, the poison remains poison.

One final comment here is this: Not only should we use the difficulties we experience as grist for the mill in our spiritual journey, but we should also give thanks for them since they actually will improve and enrich us if we allow them to.

Moderation and our spiritual center

"Denying oneself is an indulgence. The indulgence of denying is by far the worst: it leads us to believe that we are doing great things, when in effect we are only fixed within ourselves." — Carlos Castaneda

Some people find moderation to be a hindrance, an inconvenience, or a burden, but the truth is that it is a way to find our spiritual center while traveling in a physical incarnation. Just as we can't create anything of value with too much of one ingredient or too little of another, we need to find a compromise or balance between the two extremes of blithely indulging our passions versus diligently abstaining from them.

The problem with total self-denial is that we cannot learn from our physical incarnation if we avoid engagement in the sensual world. On the other hand, our desires must be appropriately controlled and channeled so that they neither impair our well-being and spirituality nor infringe upon the rights and happiness of others.

Nevertheless, some religious traditions teach that abstinence from pleasures and comfort are the only way to become closer to the Divine. This approach sounds very spiritual, but it can become nothing more than a subtle form of egotism. Indeed, it is an extreme which can easily be a trap if we are not careful since desire and attachment—even desire for enlightenment and attachment to abstinence—hinder our spiritual growth. The risk, then, is that we may become addicted to asceticism and we may develop an attachment to one particular concept or view of enlightenment.

And so one message of the card is that we must find the necessary balance between the two levels of our existence. We must walk this path of a manifest entity, a physical human being, but we must do it in a way that is aware of our spiritual reality.

The Serenity prayer

"God grant me the strength to change the things I can, the serenity to accept the things I can't, and the wisdom to know the difference." — Reinhold Niebuhr

Recently I made a commitment to stop complaining about problems in my life. This doesn't mean not discussing problems when that's useful. If I need to get advice or bounce ideas off someone, then talking about a problem is helpful. However, just complaining about troubles (and about troublesome people) is unproductive. If there is something we can do about a problem, then we should do it. If not, then what's the use of complaining? Why not just adapt?

The interesting thing is that whenever I keep that commitment, an amazing thing happens. I become a happier person, and I find more joy in my life. I also notice how pervasive the habit of complaining is in our culture. When I buy into that habit, it seems so normal that I don't really notice it in other people. But when I don't, it seems strange and puzzling when someone grumbles about a situation or person in their life.

To see the spiritual component of this, consider two hypothetical people who have the same intractable problem. One succumbs to self-pity and complains about it constantly while the other one calmly accepts an adverse situation for what it is. The first has looked inward to the ego and found misery. The other looked inward to the divine Self and found joy and serenity.

Thus, I encourage everyone to make a commitment to avoid complaining. It can help if you have a significant other with whom you can work on this. Make a deal to point out to each other when you start to complain. Just point it out and trust the other person to make a course correction if they can. You won't regret it. Besides gaining the serenity that the famous prayer promises in its title, you'll also find yourself solving more problems as you direct your energy toward solutions instead of complaints.

15. Devil

"The mind is its own place, and in itself can make a Heaven of Hell, a Hell of Heaven." — *John Milton*

Traditional concepts of the Devil and of Hell may inform our understanding of this card, which leads us to interpretations such as temptation, wickedness, addictions, and materialism. Other assessments of this card include dysfunctional relationships, egotism, and distortions of virtues, such as revenge (a distortion of justice) and lust (a distortion of love).

Materialism

An inverted pentacle atop the Devil's head is an element commonly seen on this card. This symbol indicates placing material concerns above spiritual ones and thus indicates the private hell of things like materialism, hedonism, vanity, and jealousy. This is because when we allow material desires to overshadow our spiritual pursuits, we give them undue importance that allows them to ensnare us. Then our attachments to material things become chains, whether we can see them or not. However, if we can see how our desires bind us to our own private hell, and if we make the decision to break out of those chains, we will discover that they are fastened only as tight as we allow them to be.

Addictions to the Material World

"Addictions are not evil or bad, they just cost you too much in lost perceptiveness, wisdom, effectiveness, and happiness." — Ken Keyes, Jr.

When we think of addictions, we typically think of substance abuse, such as alcohol or narcotics, but that's just the tip of the iceberg. More common than substance abuse are our addictions to all the little things in life, such as a favorite TV show, a cup of coffee in the morning, or getting the last word in any argument. Even more insidious are our addictions to our beliefs and our concepts of "should"—what we *should* have, what other people *should* do, what the world *should* be like, and so on. These things may not seem like they are a big deal, but when anything is an addiction instead of a preference—in other words when our need for it rules us instead of the other way around—it is an impediment to our happiness and our ability to live a rich and meaningful life. In fact, even addictions to positive things like exercise or a spiritual practice can be a problem because a failure to satisfy them results in suffering and unhappiness.

Addictions also overshadow our perception and enjoyment of the finer, more ineffable things in life, such as the exquisite mysteries of love, the subtle beauty of every individual, and the divinity shining within everything in the world around us. In focusing our attention on the demands of our desires and cravings, we get lost in the darkness of our addictive behaviors and we miss seeing those shining lights of Spirit that are always around us.

So always remember that your true Self is bigger and better than your cravings, and beware the trap that George Bernard Shaw described when he said, "What is all human conduct but the daily and hourly sale of our souls for trifles?"

The ironic problems of spiritual addiction

"Forgetting God, [man] becomes a slave to the temptation of [the illusion of the material world] and lives in bondage to ignorance and the cravings of his ego." — Swami Prabhavananda

As noted in the previous section, the Devil card may be interpreted as any sort of addiction. It can indicate a specific attachment to something transient, and it may be our more general addiction to the material world overall. The problem is that when our addictions are not satisfied, which is inevitable, we suffer. Then, in addition, we create more suffering around us through our reflexive fear responses such as anger, depression, and jealousy. Consequently this card illustrates our slavery to the temptations of the material world, which is a bondage that will continue until we realize that the material world is an illusion.

Although the temptations of the material world are an obvious source of addiction, attachment can also cause problems on a higher plane. In his book *Be Here Now* Ram Dass says that even the desire to be enlightened is a trap, which seems to be a rather paradoxical concept. It is a trap in so far as it leads us to develop attachments to our concepts and expectations about spirituality, and our desire for enlightenment leads to suffering insofar as we have not yet attained it. So instead of desiring enlightenment, we can instead develop devotion to the Divine and a passion for divine union and let that process unfold as it will. In other words, the advice here is to cultivate a commitment to the process rather than an attachment to and a need for the result.

The value of temptation

"Opportunity may only knock once, but temptation bangs on your front door forever." — Unknown

We typically consider temptation to be a bad thing, but in a way there is a higher purpose to it. It is a crucible wherein we may develop virtue and purity. Certainly the nobility of our lives is not determined by how little temptation we face but by how well we resist it and how well we recover from its clutches if we do fall prey to it. In fact, fearing temptation actually draws it closer to our hearts by the attention our fear gives to it. So a lesson in this card is to embrace temptation as an opportunity rather than fear it as an obstacle, for every time you overcome temptation, you become a better person. See it as a learning experience and a chance to practice your virtue.

Our own private Hell

"Love in your mind produces love in your life. This is the meaning of Heaven. Fear in your mind produces fear in your life. This is the meaning of Hell." — Marianne Williamson

We sometimes feel that we are living in our own private Hell, and at such times there is a great deal of truth to that feeling. However, the Hell we are in is more a matter of our perceptions and attitudes than it is of our external circumstances themselves. It arises from our belief in the final reality of our illusions about life, and the ultimate delusion is that of our separateness from each other and from the Divine. This illusion of being separate from other people allows us to treat them in ways that are "sinful," and the illusion that we are separate from the Divine is the source of suffering that Hell represents: an agonizing separation from divine grace. But when we understand that we are all connected, we see that whatever we do to others, we do to ourselves. And when we recognize our connection with the Divine, we are delivered from suffering.

We see, then, that Hell on Earth can serve a sacred purpose when, in order to escape it, we strive to develop a more spiritual perspective, a vision that sees our difficulties through the eyes of devotion, love, and forgiveness. Indeed, the way out of Hell is the path of love—love of the Divine, of other people, and of ourselves. When we do that, we discover that "the Kingdom of God is within [us],"[21] and Hell was our illusion that it is not.

Resist not evil

"What is evil, after all? It is ignorance, nothing else; a veil of ignorance [that] covers the truth of God." — Swami Prabhavananda

The Devil card is, by virtue of its name, sometimes seen as an indication that something evil is happening. But "evil" is a much trickier concept than we generally assume. For one thing, pretty much everyone who has ever done something that we regard as evil believes (mistakenly, most likely) that they were somehow justified in their actions and that they had good reasons for them. And so we might ask, "Are there evil people, or are there just bad, unenlightened actions?"

---

[21] *Luke 17:21*

As a lead up to addressing that question, allow me to discuss a somewhat puzzling statement about evil that ironically sheds light on our spiritual journey. What I'm referring to is this short quote from the New Testament: "Resist not evil."[22] This seems like a rather bizarre thing for Jesus to have said, but there is a great deal of wisdom to be discovered through a thoughtful examination of it.

First of all, based on its context, it is apparent that this quote is referring to the actions of other people who we label as "evil" and not to temptations that we may face. The following more complete quote makes this clear.

> *Ye have heard that it hath been said, an eye for an eye, and a tooth for a tooth. But I say unto you, that ye resist not evil: but whosoever shall smite thee on thy right cheek, turn to him the other also.[23]*

This, of course, calls to mind the philosophies and strategies of Gandhi and Martin Luther King, Jr. (See the section of the Hanged Man card called "Nonresistance.") Besides being an effective tactic, however, this proverbial turning of the other cheek is an important spiritual lesson for a variety of reasons. For one thing, by responding to evil in kind (i.e., with violence, anger, etcetera) we create more evil in the world. Also, when we resist evil, we focus our attention on it and bring it into our own hearts and lives. We thereby risk becoming as bad as that which we seek to defeat. This is the danger Nietzsche was warning us about when he said: "He who fights with monsters must take care lest he thereby become a monster." On the other hand, when we show compassion and forgiveness to another person, we can disarm them of their perceived evil. This was the brilliance of Gandhi and King.

There is a caveat that is important to make here. Relieving suffering in the world is essential too, so there is merit in being able to properly evaluate an action and then rectify it if it is harmful. But it is important to remember not to judge or hate the other person, and it is important to respond to injustice in a way that comes from the heart and not from anger and fear. As Lao Tzu said several hundred years before Jesus, "Repay injury with kindness."[24]

Now let us return to that original question: "Are there evil people, or are there just bad, unenlightened actions?" First of all, what seems to be evil may be just

---

[22] *Matthew 5:39*

[23] *Matthew 5:38, 39*

[24] *Tao Te Ching, 63*

an illusion born of our imperfect perception of something that a person has said or done. Perhaps they actually had a good reason for their actions, but we are unaware of it, or maybe they were acting out of their own pain or injury-impaired view of a situation. Sometimes we project our own shadow issues onto the actions of other people, as will be discussed in the next section, "Demons in the shadows." In any case, when we set aside our sanctimonious desire to "resist evil," we become more objective about the situation and thoughtfully creative about how to resolve it.

A more important point, however, is this: We are typically seeing the Devil in a person who we feel has done something evil to us instead of compassionately seeing their wounded soul, which is invariably a more accurate assessment. (Remember the adage: "Hurt people hurt people.") And when we label that person "evil," we stop trying to understand why they act as they do, we justify putting them out of our hearts, and we allow ourselves to treat them as less than human. So what does that make us? Evil arises from blindness to our divine connection, and we have lost sight of our innate divinity when we treat someone that way. Remember also that everyone (ourselves included) has their own secret demons. We can always find evidence of those demons in others if we look hard enough, but is that what we really want to be looking for? After all, we find and even create more of whatever we focus our attention on.

Demons in the shadows

"Many of the faults you see in others are your own nature reflected in them."
— *Rumi*

An important meaning of this card is "confronting your demons." This means demons like repressed anger, impulses, vices, addictions, obsessions, and prejudices. These demons also may be called our "shadow issues" for we have thrust them deep into the shadows of our psyche where we can avoid looking at them and pretend they don't exist. But being out of sight does not mean they are gone. They are still able to cause problems, whether we shine a light on them or not. All too often they exert sinister effects on our lives that are inexplicable since we pretend they don't exist.

Actually, we do see these demons sometimes, but we see them in other people instead of in ourselves. Perhaps our heightened sensitivity to these issues makes us keenly aware of them in others. Often, however, we are merely projecting our dark motives onto things that other people say or do, and this is how we see our shadow issues reflected in them. In either case, we are quick and eager to condemn those people, but what we are really doing is trying to deny our own demons by being loudly repelled by them in someone else. For example, it has become almost a truism that the most vociferously homophobic politicians are the ones who end up being discovered in tawdry, clandestine gay affairs.

This is why we should be thankful for the people who really push our buttons—they provide us with a mirror that reveals our own shadow issues that we need to confront and work on. Why should we do this? First of all, as long as our demons remain unacknowledged in the shadows, they can control us, but when we become conscious of them, we are able to get a handle on them instead. Also, since they represent a great deal of energy that the ego has misdirected, if we become conscious of them, we can redirect that energy and reclaim the power we need to move forward with our lives. Finally, we want to confront and banish our demons because the fewer of them we have inside, the more room there will be for the Divine.

16. Tower

The Tower card is typically seen as a harbinger of a sudden or catastrophic change. However, the crisis heralded may be one that gets us out of a situation with bad foundations, one that we needed to escape anyway. With its obvious allusion to the proverbial Tower of Babel, this card also indicates hubris and pride struck down. Less common meanings attributed to this card include anger and a flash of inspiration.

Blowing your top

"... when deep inside you there is a loaded gun, how can you have God [there too]?" — Kabir (as interpreted by Robert Bly)[25]

One way to consider the Tower card is to see it as literally "blowing your top." This reminds me of how often I see people who are mad at the world and are acting out that anger—people yelling at their children, complaining about their boss, or shaking their fist at someone who cut them off in traffic. More and more, though, I am seeing their displays of anger for what they really are: futile bursts of

---

[25] *The Kabir Book: Forty-Four of the Ecstatic Poems of Kabir*

energy that lack a productive focus. When someone has an outburst of anger, the real, underlying cause is rarely the object of their fury; that is just what pulled the trigger. The true cause lies in their own internal powder keg. Benjamin Franklin touched on this centuries ago when he said, "Anger is never without reason, but seldom with a good one."

We get mad at other people because we have unresolved anger lurking inside of us, a vast reservoir of pent-up energy grown from our unhealed wounds. This root cause can be resolved by bringing those wounds to light and then healing them with compassion and forgiveness. This is typically a long-term solution, but there are several things we can do in the short term. For one thing, we can realize that anger is a sadly destructive waste of energy that could be put to much better use if properly channeled. As Marcus Aurelius said almost two thousand years ago, "How much more grievous are the consequences of anger than the causes of it."

We may also find a path to healing by considering this insight from Gary Zukav: "The core cause of anger is a lack of self-worth. Rage is an excruciating experience of powerlessness." When we feel anger, it may be beneficial to try to see where we lack self-worth in the situation or to try to see how we can regain our sense of self-control within it.

Finally, we need to realize that whenever we get angry at someone, two people are negatively affected by our anger—ourselves as well as the other person. Besides the waste of our energy just mentioned, another negative effect to ourselves is that every time we act out of anger we turn a little bit more into a mean person. Perhaps if we keep that in mind we will be able to practice reacting with a practical and measured response instead of with a destructive, angry one. And through such practice, we can change our habit of anger and become more enlightened.

Accepting Change

The Tower card, with its seeming depiction of crisis, upheaval, and disaster is not one that most people like to see in a Tarot reading. Sometimes it seems like the only thing we fear more than change is unexpected and uncontrollable change. But when faced with a Tower event—which can be anything from a life threatening illness to something as trivial as accidentally taking the wrong freeway exit—we have a choice of how we view and deal with the catastrophe at hand. And that decision determines the essence of the outcome more than the event itself.

The approach that many of us often take is to resist the reality of the event. We may deny it, reject it, or resist it. Sometimes we cling to what was, complaining about the changes at hand, and thereby waste a lot of energy.

A better alternative is to accept the reality of what happened. This doesn't mean that we accept that this was what should have happened; just that it is what it is. Then we can see the opportunities hidden within the changes that have come, opportunities to move on to new things that just might be improvements in our life. In other words, we can give our full attention to *what is* and *what may be* instead of *what was* or *what "should be."*

Hubris and the Tower of Babel

"Pride goes before destruction, and a haughty spirit before a fall." — *Proverbs 16:18*

An obvious connotation of the Tower card, with its symbolism of a prideful tower struck down, is the praise of humility and condemnation of arrogance. Even if it went no further than that, it would present valuable advice, but of course there's more, especially when we examine the concept of hubris further.

One interpretation of hubris comes from the ancient Greek use of the term as shaming the victim to gain a sense of self-gratification. And so we can see in the Tower card an admonition against tearing someone else down in order to gain the illusory feeling of pulling yourself up. Ironically, the problem with anyone who does that is a lack of pride, using the word's meaning of dignity and self-respect (versus an inflated sense of self-importance). With a true sense of self-worth, we don't have to shame other people in order to feel better about ourselves. In fact, the more we realize our true, divine Self, the more we want to pull others up along with us, not cast them down.

Hubris also has the connotation of a prideful affront to the gods. Although the ancient Greeks generally used the word in terms of violations against other people, perhaps the most famous illustration of hubris involves the biblical story of the Tower of Babel, which was about an affront against God.[26] In that story, men tried to build a tower to reach heaven. Some say their intent was to enter the kingdom of God and others say it was to storm the gates of heaven. In either

---

[26] *See Genesis 11:4-9*

case, God was not pleased. The popular version of this tale is that God destroyed the tower and disbursed the people building it by confounding their language. (Interestingly, though, the biblical version of the story does not actually mention the destruction of the tower.) Conventional dualistic religion has interpreted this tale as a sign of the inherent separation of man and God. However, another understanding of it (with a non-dualistic view) is that striving to reach the Divine through purely materialistic pursuits (tithing, building temples, etcetera) leads to confusion and failure because reuniting with the Divine is an internal matter accomplished through the heart and soul.

Another message in the tale of the Tower of Babel can be inferred from the account of it by Flavius Josephus in his First Century CE work, *Antiquities of the Jews*. Josephus claims that the tyrant who commissioned the construction of the tower tried to turn his people away from God by telling them that it was not through God that they would find happiness, but rather through their own strength and courage. From this account, we may infer that the Tower is a metaphor for our joy and fulfillment, and the message is that the effort to build that by ourselves (i.e., apart from divine help) is doomed. Also, such an effort results in a loss of our sense of unity with our fellow man, as symbolized by the confusion of languages and disbursement of the people building the tower.

Trapped in the comfort zone

"Life begins at the end of your comfort zone." — Neale Donald Walsch

A tower can protect us or imprison us, but the difference is often subtle and hard to discern. We shelter ourselves in sterilized circumstances—for example, a secure but unfulfilling job or a safe but loveless relationship—that we hope will protect us, but which instead trap us. We don't see it that way, of course, because we have settled into the comfort of the familiar. Our self-made cages may not be gilded, but they are, at least, sufficiently padded. And so we languish in them. We don't understand why we feel so unsatisfied in our comfort zone, but we are afraid to leave it and try something new. So sometimes what we need is a cosmic kick in the pants to get us out of it, which is what the shattering event indicated by this card can be. The crisis usually seems drastic and cruel at the time, but it may be the best (or only) way to get us to take the next step in life and begin the next leg of our spiritual journey.

Whenever we experience a sudden upheaval in our lives, it is beneficial to consider how, perhaps, we are being led to another level of awakening.

Sometimes it may be that we were in an oppressive or restrictive situation that we needed to escape in order to again breathe freely the breath of life. The crisis may be the humbling impetus we need in order to break down the barriers that separate us from other people. Perhaps the reason is that the time had come to stretch and grow in new ways. Or maybe we had refused to let go of an old phase of life and move on to a higher calling.

Of course, in the midst of the crisis we may not be able to make such a dispassionate assessment, but it may be somewhat comforting at least to consider the possibility that there is a higher reason for it. And perhaps afterward, we can seek to find the next step on our spiritual path. It will be there waiting for us just outside our comfort zone.

17. Star

"If you follow your star, you cannot fail of glorious heaven." — *Dante*

This card gains meaning from the traditional associations that we have for the stars in the heavens and the silent serenity that may come to us in the dark of the night. Thus, the Star card can indicate things like divine guidance, hope, and serenity,

Meditation

"... the more you enter a meditative space, the clearer you'll hear your dharma, your flow, your way home, your route back to the source." — *Ram Dass*

Through meditation, we can experience divine communion, inner peace, and renewal of the soul. It takes time and practice, but there is a way to facilitate your progress if this sense of serenity has been elusive so far. It's quite simple, really: just step outside some night and quietly look up at the stars.

Magically appearing every night when darkness falls, the stars embodied divinity to the people of ancient cultures. We too can feel a bit of that sacred connection and experience both awe and serenity when we stand in the silence of the night and stare up at a star-filled sky.[27] It may feel as if your heart so yearns

---

[27] *If you live in a big city where the grandeur of a starry night is washed away by light pollution, take a trip into the countryside some moonless night to see what I mean.*

for that vastness of the heavens that it mirrors it with a vastness of its own.

In doing this, you can get a taste of the peace and oneness that meditation brings, and with that awareness, you will more easily recreate and recognize the feeling when you do meditate. But even more directly, when your eyes gaze silently into the starry heavens, your heart will also catch sight of "your way home, your route back to the source."

Silence

"Come into the silence of solitude, and the vibration there will talk to you through the voice of God." — Paramahansa Yogananda

As noted in the previous section, we may find a profound and healing serenity in contemplation of a star-filled sky. Similarly, the Star card represents the exquisitely beautiful power of silence. We all understand that silence is an integral part of the practice of meditation, but it also may be used in a less rigorous manner in quiet contemplation of something, such as a flower, a scenic view, or a work of art. The stillness in our hearts that results from such contemplation is invaluable for it is then that we feel the touch of the Divine.

In addition, silence can be a precious gift we share with another person. Sometimes the best thing we can do for someone who is suffering is just to be there with them, to sit quietly with them without trying to fix anything. Giving someone space to be who they are and being present with them as they experience their sorrow can be very comforting and healing. Just sharing with them our presence and peace of mind can be the greatest gift of all.

Unfortunately, we usually are reluctant or even afraid to sit quietly with someone else. We often feel a need to fill the silence with words, perhaps because that is what our ego-mind does to the silence within us—it fills it with incessant thoughts. So practice sharing silence by sitting quietly with a loved one. Find someone with whom you can sit for awhile, sharing each other's presence without speaking. If there is no one like that for you, try it with a pet instead. (They love it.)

There are several ways you can do this. You might focus on listening to each other's breath. You may try to feel the energy field of the other person if that works for you. You can contemplate the other person, either with your eyes closed, feeling their presence, or looking into their eyes. (The second way may be more rewarding, but it's more challenging, so feel free to work your way up to it by starting with the eyes-closed method.) You might want to have some physical contact, or you may not. For example, if it seems right, lightly touch the other person's hand. However you decide to do this, do it silently, both externally and internally. Try to quiet your mind as well as your voice, and don't judge what is happening. Let go of your thoughts, and just observe what you feel. In doing this you may discover that in the absence of words, you will hear the beautiful song of each other's soul.

Hope

"In the face of uncertainty, there's nothing wrong with hope." — Dr. Bernie Siegel

The stars in the heavens symbolize our hopes and dreams, and so this card calls to mind phrases like "a guiding star" and "wish upon a star." Indeed, in my childhood whenever I saw the first star in the evening sky I would recite this poem:

Star light, star bright!
First star I see tonight!
I wish I may, I wish I might
Have this wish I wish tonight.

Then I would silently make a wish. Although it was rare that these wishes came true, I continued to make them, for this simple ritual was an expression of my faith that there is always hope for a better and brighter future. Sometimes just having that innocent hope was enough to sustain me, while at other times my wishes sparked my imagination, which then lifted me into a happier world. And so this card urges us to keep hope alive. After all, hope sustains us in times of trouble. It lets us dare to make wishes, and wishes help us create the future that we envision through them. And hope counteracts fear, which is what keeps us in a state of separation, be it from other people, our authentic Self, or the Divine.

We are all stars

A star is a metaphor for the divine light that shines within each and every one of us. We are all stars, points of light shining in the darkness like beacons calling to one another. But just as the glare of city lights can drown out the subtle light of the stars in the heavens, our worldly concerns can obscure the shining star within each of us. And just as clouds will mask the stars, our worldly cares will block our vision of the inner stars of other people. Luckily, however, although our worldly eyes are this easily fooled or blinded, the eyes of the soul are not. When we look at someone with the eyes of our soul, we can see the transcendent beauty of their essential being. But how can we do this?

We may find valuable advice in something Martin Luther King, Jr. said: "Only when it is dark enough can you see the stars." There are a couple ways to interpret this. First, this may refer to those dark times when you are in trouble. At such times, if someone helps you, you may see the light of their inner star. In other words, the darkness of your plight allows you to see the star of their divine spirit. Perhaps this is why the Star card immediately follows the Tower with its implications of crisis and catastrophe.

A second way to interprets King's statement is through an analogy of the chatter of our ego-minds being like the brightness of day. That mental chatter is typically so loud that it drowns out our perception of the subtle glimmer of the stars in other people. In fact, it also blinds us to the star within our own heart. Through meditative silence, however, we begin to quiet that chatter. This is like the setting of the sun, which brings the silent darkness against which the stars shine like diamonds in the night.

The value of both of these interpretations depends on our willingness to see that there is a divine star shining within everyone no matter how much the dross of their worldly concerns obscures it.

Faith

"Faith is the bird that feels the light when the dawn is still dark." — Rabindranath Tagore

I have written the content of this section in a way different from the others; I wrote it as a poem in free verse. I did this because the Star evokes deep, ineffable feelings and thus has a poetic quality. Also, I was inspired to do this because I was reading a wonderful book of poetry (*Ten Poems to Change Your Life* by Roger Housden) when I began composing this material.

Faith

True, abiding faith lies beyond
any knowledge or belief.
It is wisdom of the heart
that transcends
any knowing of the mind.

It holds dearly to a shining hope
that our heart affirms
but that our mind cannot explain.
Meager words pale before it.
If words could *explain it,*
it would merely be belief.

It lifts us and carries us
along our journey
when belief stumbles.
It comforts us
when knowledge fails us.

Whereas knowledge and belief
are ever changing,
it is eternal,
supple and humble.

Faith is the guiding star
that leads us to salvation.
It is a gift of divine grace,
our soul's response
to the divine call
to return home.

18. The Moon

"Everyone is a moon and has a dark side which he never shows anybody." —
Mark Twain

The Moon is the mistress of the night and has two faces, the one she allows us to see and the one she never shows anyone. The darkness of the night can confuse and delude us if we are not careful, but the night also brings dreams, and in this realm of intuition we may find spiritual insights.

Considering the Moon's dualistic nature, this card represents dreams and nightmares, fears and romance, delusion and imagination, madness and enchantment, mystery and magic, the supernatural and the occult.

Monsters under the bed

"One does not become enlightened by naively 'imagining' images of light, but by making the mind's darkness conscious." — *Carl Jung*

The Moon card says that there really are monsters under your bed at night, just as many children suspect. Not literally, of course, but figuratively speaking, there are monsters lurking in our unconscious minds. They are the unreasoning fears, instinctive impulses, and taboo desires we have banished to the deep, dark recesses of our minds. This concept was used in a 1956 science fiction movie called *Forbidden Planet* which featured a "monster from the id" that ran amok carrying out the secret desires that one of the characters, Dr. Morbius, possessed but refused to acknowledge.

Our monsters haunt us and cause us to act irrationally and hurtfully at times, and the only way to conquer them is to have the courage to turn on the light and look for them. You cannot banish the darkness by ignoring it; you must light a torch and explore it. This is a frightening prospect, however. It means that not only do we have to seek and confront these monsters, but we also must admit that they are a part of ourselves. However, it is only when we find the courage to face them that we can banish them, because no matter how terrible they may seem, they cannot long survive the light.

Horrible things

As we may surmise from the previous section about monsters lurking in our unconscious minds, we have all done terrible things—things we are ashamed of, things we want to hide in the darkness. Also, there may be awful things that have been done to us for which we have mistakenly taken on the shame. In either case, the fact is that we all have secrets hidden in shadowy places, and the only way to escape the darkness of our shame is to shine a light on them. That might be through confession and penance, or maybe we just have to stare a secret in the eye so that, unblinking, we can show it that we have moved beyond it.

No matter what it is that we have to do in order to deal with a horrible secret, the important thing is the light. We have to shine a light on it because the one thing we should *not* do is leave it in darkness, for that is where secrets fester and turn into monsters. In the light, though, they can be understood, forgiven, released, and transcended. And in that light, we can atone for what we have done, and we can be redeemed.

Terrible beauty

The Moon represents the terrible beauty of the dark mysteries of life and death—questions like, "Why is there suffering in the world?" and "What lies beyond the veil of death?" These ineffable mysteries are frightening and challenging, but without them, life would be dull and insipid—perhaps even meaningless. Their infinite expanse lies forever beyond the periphery of the finite circle of our rational knowledge. And the more we know, the larger that circle becomes, which means that the periphery of the unknown expands as well. Thus, we will see more, not fewer, of these exquisite mysteries around us, and we will come to cherish them more too, for it is in pondering them that we may catch fleeting glimpses of the Divine and of our Soul.

Intuition and imagination

"Forget safety. Live where you fear to live. Destroy your reputation. Be notorious. I have tried prudent planning long enough. From now on, I'll be mad." — Rumi

The Moon card encourages us to pay attention to the gentle, intuitive voice within our hearts, crazy though it may seem sometimes. Our modern age exalts reason and logic, but imagination and intuition are also important guides through life. So this card urges us to allow our imagination to wander through the untamed worlds of myth and dream, finding enchantment in the unknown. In this way we can rediscover the mystical realm of Spirit. Because it is mysterious, it can be frightening at times, but the path to enlightenment necessarily leads us through the dark forest of the unknown, so we have to embrace that dark part of the journey too.

A portion of our spiritual path, then, involves finding our way through the darkness of life's troubles and dealing with the uncertainty of the eternal unknown. Life is always a bit wild no matter how hard we try to tame it and no matter how hard we try to convince ourselves that it can be tamed. But if we follow our imagination and intuition, and if we overcome our fear of the unknown, the beauty of life's mystery and wildness is exquisite.

The Promised Land and the Wilderness

"The Promised Land always lies on the other side of the Wilderness." —
Havelock Ellis

The pale light of the Moon casts an eerie glow on nocturnal landscapes making the world seem both frightening and mystical. Similarly, our spiritual path sometimes takes us into the darkness where the silvery light of our intuition illuminates the landscape of our minds so that we may confront and overcome our fears and thus find our magic and our authentic selves.

When drawn toward the dark, enchanted forest, we may fear that we are being called to relinquish the comforts of the familiar material world, so we hesitate to enter it. We may also wonder why we have to leave the apparent safety of the rational light of consciousness and travel into the dangerous darkness of a world we can only dimly perceive. The reason is that the conscious mind is as selective and deceptive as moonlight; it's just more certain about its delusions.

Once we venture into that wilderness, we may enter a proverbial dark night of the soul for a while. This is a time when we are turning away from the material world, suspicious that its meaning is shallow, but we are not yet able to see the spiritual world clearly and faithfully. Thus, this time can be a test of faith, a time when we may feel that we have lost our way. For an interim period, then, our transformation is incomplete, and until we rise to a higher level of consciousness, we may feel a desperate absence of light and meaning.

Ultimately, though, we will discover a surprising truth about the supposed darkness of the spiritual world. It is only when we look with our physical eyes that it seems dim like a moonlit landscape while the material world seems bright. When we learn to see with the eyes of our soul, the sacred world of the Divine becomes bright and is revealed to be the real sunlit world, the one we find in the next card in the Tarot's Major Arcana, the Sun card.

19. The Sun

"Exuberance is Beauty." — William Blake

Like its namesake, the Sun card symbolizes the dawning of a new day and is associated with life, optimism, enlightenment, and regeneration. It captures the essence of our life force and the capacity for growth within each of us, and it says that joy and fulfillment are our birthright. Traditionally, it also represents the integration of our conscious and unconscious minds.

Awaken to divinity

"Holding [people] in the glow of our energy may be the best way to awaken theirs." — Eckhart Tolle

The Sun is the source of light and life in our world, so it is natural that it is also a common symbol of our spiritual core. It symbolizes the vitalizing divine light that shines within us and the beacon of our soul that illuminates our spiritual path. This suggests a couple of important spiritual messages for this card. One is the advice to awaken to our own divinity, which will reveal to us our soulful purpose. Another message from this card is that our inner light can awaken the people around us who seem to be unconscious of their divine nature. In other words, once we are conscious of it, the radiance of our divine light can bring about a dawning of their spiritual journey. This is a key point because we often feel that we have to convince people of our spiritual message, but arguments by themselves are often not a very effective means of awakening people. Instead, it may be that the divine light within us is what will awaken them, and we need to trust that. Of course, we also have to realize that everyone awakens in their own way and at their own pace.

The question, then, is how can we shine this light on others? One answer is to be conscious of it and allow it to shine. We can find another answer to this question in an esoteric association for this card. In the Kabbalah, the central sephirah (node) of the Tree of Life is traditionally associated with the Sun as well as with divine love and the heart chakra. The implication is that through our exercise of unconditional love, which is our most direct manifestation of our divine nature, our divine light shines brightest.

Joy in the eternal world of Spirit

In the song *Only the Good Die Young* Billy Joel says that he would rather laugh with the sinners than cry with the saints, which reflects the common misconception that spirituality is dull and dour. People get this impression from a variety of sources, such as Buddhism's admonition to release attachment to material things and the Spartan character of monastic life in most religious traditions. However, giving up our attachment to worldliness doesn't mean we have to live in poverty because whether we have material things or not is beside the point. It is the attachment and not the possession that's the problem.

A spiritual life involves finding joy in the permanent things of spirit (such as compassion, generosity, and unity) instead of basing our happiness on transient, worldly things, which inevitably causes us sorrow and suffering when they pass away, as they must. And rather than resulting in privation, releasing our desire for and attachment to things of the world is profoundly liberating. To see an illustration of the value of renunciation, ask a former alcoholic when were they happier: while in thrall to alcohol or now that they have given it up.

In a metaphorical sense, then, the Sun (which represents our joyful connection to the Divine) shines every day of our lives even though we don't see it when there are clouds in the skies—clouds like unfulfilled expectations, relationship problems, and worries about financial success. But along our spiritual path, material things and worldly desires lose their power to cloud over our skies and blot out our view of the sun.

Every day is a gift

"Waking up this morning, I smile:
Twenty-four brand-new hours are before me."
— *Thich Nhat Hanh*

This card symbolizes the dawning of a new day and suggests the spiritual message that every new day brings the gift of life, the most precious gift we are given. This may seem to contradict statements elsewhere in this book that our material life is an illusion, but these two statements can be reconciled through the analogy of considering life to be like a dream. Is a dream real or an illusion? While we are dreaming, it certainly is real enough, but when we awaken from it, we see that it was an illusion. It is a valuable gift, however, because it is a chance to learn something and a chance to resolve disturbing issues. Similarly, although our mundane life may be an illusion from the perspective of our eternal soul, while we are here, it is real and valuable.

So an important message of this card is to try to see each new day as a new opportunity to learn more fully how to live with joy and optimism, compassion and forgiveness, gratitude and generosity. Remember always that every new day is a renewal of the gift of life.

A new light

The Sun card suggests seeing the same old things in a new light. There are a couple of reasons for this association. First, there is the obvious solar implication of light and a new day. Second, there is a numerological reason. This card is numbered 19 which reduces to 1 (1+9 = 10; 1+0 = 1), and this indicates a new beginning and also refers back to the Magician card. Thus, seeing things in a new light brings a magical new beginning into our lives.

A specific application of this insight is the advice to allow our relationships to start fresh with a clean slate every day. The effects of this can be miraculous because when we let go of the emotional baggage of yesterday through forgiveness, we allow today to shine with renewal and new opportunities. In this revitalizing light, our relationships will blossom like trees in the warmth of springtime.

Finding good everywhere

"The measure of mental health is the disposition to find good everywhere."
— *Ralph Waldo Emerson*

Although Emerson's message may seem to be about optimism and seeing the glass as half full versus half empty, it goes deeper than that. It is about rising above the dark clouds of negativity in order to see the Light, and it is about realizing that those clouds arise out of our ego's illusions about the world.

It is also about seeing the vital divine nature in another person instead of their ego, which obscures it. As an illuminating analogy, consider that the Sun is always shining, even though we don't see it on an overcast day. In this analogy, the Sun represents the divine light that shines within each and every one of us, and the clouds are the thoughts and actions that arise from the ego with its illusions of fear, separation, and desire. Thus, it is important to remember that within each of us, the sun is always shining even when we cannot see it.

So look for the divine light in everyone you meet, and even when you don't see that light shining in someone, know that it is still there behind the clouds.

20. Judgment

"The practice of forgiveness is our most important contribution to the healing of the world." — Marianne Williamson

This card can signify hearing a call, awakening to a higher truth or reality, or a metaphorical resurrection. It also is concerned with the issue of forgiveness. This may seem ironic given its title, but everything is about its opposite, so the issues of judging and forgiving are inextricably linked.

The call to awaken

The Judgment card, with its depiction of a glorious awakening, refers to the spiritual rebirth that occurs when we heed the call to awaken to our own innate divinity. To see the importance of this, consider as an analogy how hard it can be to wake up in the morning. Although it can take some effort, waking up in the morning leads us out of a state of limited consciousness (sleep) to an expanded one (wakefulness). Similarly, awakening to our spiritual life involves realizing that we are spiritual beings having a "dream" of our material life. This can be a frightening prospect because we fear leaving our little boxes of familiar "reality." However, we don't lose our material life as a result of a spiritual awakening; we just discover the deeper fullness and brilliance of our existence, and we lose our fear of it too. In this way we transcend our material life. In other words, we are all living within drab little boxes called "the material world," and we are being called to awaken to the realization that there is a vast, brilliant world beyond those boxes.

The Universal Mind

We may see this card as an indication of our ability to access the wisdom of what Itzhak Bentov termed "the Universal Mind."[28] In his book *A Brief Tour of Higher Consciousness*, Bentov asserts that there is a cosmic consciousness from which a human mind can derive any knowledge needed as long as it is sufficiently prepared to receive it. Of course, the part about being sufficiently prepared is the catch. Metaphorically speaking, we may say that this universal consciousness is a divine Internet and we need to configure our mental computer to access it.

The best way to prepare is through the practice of meditation, which quiets the chatter of our "monkey mind" so that we can hear the wisdom of Deity instead. However, we can also catch a glimpse of this process whenever an answer comes to us after we have left a problem alone and diverted our conscious attention by doing something simple like making a cup of tea or going for a walk. Sleep may be the ultimate diversionary activity since it allows the unconscious mind to explore answers for our problems and communicate them to us in our dreams.

So we see that although our rational thought process has a valuable place in shaping our lives, it can be limited and limiting. When we take our mind off of the issue at hand, however, our unconscious mind is freed to bring us answers from a higher source without the hindrance of the criticism and skepticism of our conscious mind.

Waking up from self-judgment

"Sickness is not a sign of God's judgment on us, but of our judgment on ourselves." — Marianne Williamson

Many spiritual traditions maintain that our physical issues, such as illness, weight problems, and addictions, are ultimately constructs of the mind. They are symptoms of our belief in our separation from the Divine, and that belief is the root problem. So does it mean we shouldn't take medicine or stick to a healthful diet? No, of course not. Should we be blamed for our own health issues? Again, no, for this is not about blame. What this means is that a change in perception—waking up to a higher reality—will change our lives for the better.

Also, the deeper essence of our physical problems lies not in the clinical symptoms per se—things like a fever, extra pounds, or uncontrolled cravings—

---

[28] *Similar concepts include the Akashic Records, the Buddhist doctrine of "mindstream," Vladimir Vernadsky's "noosphere," and, of course, the mind of God.*

but in the suffering that results from them. We sadly tell ourselves that we are not good enough, or smart enough, or rich enough. We think we are fat, weak, or unlovable. This is how we torture ourselves with our self-judgments. This is not to say that there is nothing important about being at a healthy weight, for example. Rather, it means that there is a great deal of importance in releasing our judgment about our weight, for that judgment is what causes our suffering.

There are those who criticize this advice by saying that people must be aware of their problems so that they can deal with them effectively. But this confuses the terms *evaluation* and *judgment* (as I'm using it here).[29] We can calmly evaluate a situation without self-reproach and without the suffering that comes with judging. Also, when we judge ourselves and our problems, we focus our attention on a level of lack, sickness, and adversity, which brings more of that level of reality into our existence. But raising our attention from a consciousness of scarcity and blame to one of prosperity and empowerment brings good fortune on this impermanent physical plane. And even more importantly, raising it from material consciousness to spiritual consciousness leads us to the enduring fortune of Spirit.

The miracle of healing that we experience as we remember our oneness with the Divine may be on a symptomatic level—we may lose that extra weight or recover from that illness—but a truer and more permanent healing comes from being released from our suffering. This is the result of a shift in our perceptions rather than a change in our circumstances.

"Show me the way"

It is said that if we open ourselves to be called to fulfill our soul's purpose, then we will be called to it. So why do most of us not hear this call? The problem lies in the caveat that we have to be open to it, which is not nearly as simple as we might think. This openness includes accepting the possibility that our calling may take us places that are difficult, unfamiliar, and even frightening.

We have to be able to say, with complete sincerity and trust, "Thy will be done," no matter what. This simple statement is not merely a symbolic shrug of our shoulders, however. It is not that we are saying, "Oh, well. You're just going to do what you're going to do anyway, so I might as well resign myself to it."

---

[29] *See the section "Misunderstanding Judgment" on page 97*

Rather, it is a way of acknowledging that the Divine knows best and saying that we trust it and will follow its guidance in order to act according to divine will.

But the ego always fears this loss of control, and we buy into that fear because our faith is not yet deep enough. It is that fear which stops us from opening ourselves to be called. However, if we can see at least a glimmer of what our calling is, it may stop being such a frightening prospect. Thus, we can begin the process of opening up to our calling with a simple prayer: "Please show me the way." And if we can view the response with an open mind and an open heart, our journey of awakening can begin.

<u>You inner light calls others from the dark</u>

When we interact with people from the place of our own inner divinity (i.e., when we let our inner light shine forth) we resurrect other people. By this I mean that they are drawn from the darkness and toward the light within us, and as they are, their own inner light shines brighter in response.

Here's an example of this idea that we have all seen. Consider the response that most of us generally have to dogs. We want to walk up to them, smile at them, pet them, and maybe (if you're like me) give them a big hug. Why? For one thing, dogs have an unflagging look of joy. They seem eternally happy and in love with life. So just seeing a dog can make us love life too, at least for a moment. Dogs also display a simple, unconditional love to which we instinctively respond. It's no wonder that therapy dogs are so effective. In fact, studies show that they are at least as effective as conventional medications for relieving stress.[30]

It's much less common to find this radiant quality in people, but I have seen it. The most intense example was an old man I briefly met once many years ago. He was a Kabbalah teacher, and I believe that his spiritual practice had made the window to his soul crystal clear, for he radiated a warmth and joy to which I instinctively responded. It is impossible to explain adequately in words, but if you think of the dog example I just gave, that might give you an idea. Few of us attain this level of clarity through which our divine light can shine into the world, but we all can become a clearer window than we are now. And as we do that, the people around us will start to respond in kind.

---

[30] *I don't mean to exclude cats or other types of pets here. It's just that dogs are such a perfect example to use.*

So an important message for this card is to remember your innate divinity and realize that you have that radiant light within you. In fact, you *are* that light. In remembering this, your soul will shine through and draw others to you, calling them from the darkness into the light.

Judge not...

"The more one judges, the less one loves." — Honoré de Balzac

There are many reasons why we should avoid judging other people. For one thing, we probably don't know what burdens they carry or what wounds they bear. (Consider the saying, "Hurt people hurt people.") For another, judging others reinforces our illusion of separation, and buying into this illusion keeps us from Atonement. Furthermore, contrary to the popular notion, judging impedes our healing because it keeps us attached to the wound about which we hold a grudge. Finally, there is another cost that we don't usually consider: judging other people burdens us with the awful sense that we are being judged by everyone else. This is due to the fact that we project onto others the faults that we have but do not want to acknowledge. In this case, if we are judgmental, we assume everyone else is too.

Considering the high cost of judging, then, why don't we forgive? One obvious reason is ignorance; we may not realize the price is so high. There are other reasons too, however. One is that holding on to judgment arises from the ego's delusional desire to retain a sense of superiority over other people. We also like to think that we are the arbiters of right and wrong, and we want to believe that we are above the mistakes that other people make. Finally there is the common belief that if we forgive someone an injury, we are condoning their bad behavior. This is not true, however, as explained in the next section.

Misunderstanding *judgment*

As noted in a previous section ("Waking up from self-judgment") there is some confusion about the word *judgment* in spiritual discussions due to the multiple definitions of the word. On the one hand, it refers to an objective evaluation of a situation and the formulation of an educated opinion about it. As such, it is an appropriate exercise of our intellect. However, this word may also refer to a moralistic condemnation of other people and an unfortunate tendency to presume to determine their worthiness. This is an inappropriate mental exercise and, worse yet, an abandonment of our purpose in life to love and forgive. The difference between these two meanings is that the first involves evaluating an action or situation, and the second is about judging people in a way that is moralistic and censorious. We think we are good at the former (although we aren't as good at discernment as we think we are), and we typically don't think we do the latter (although we are practically addicted to it).

Perhaps this explains the vehemence with which some people defend their "right" to condemn another person and to put that person out of their heart. Their defense inevitably hinges on a perceived need to stop or to punish the other person's actions, and this is why they believe that their condemnation of the other person is justified. The truth, however, is that what is justified is only an evaluation of, and opposition to specific actions of the person.

People also commonly confuse justice and judgment. They think that we cannot have justice if we forgive. What they fail to realize, however, is that justice is what we do on the outside, while forgiveness is what we do on the inside. Another way to explain this is to say that while it is right to resist erroneous action, it is not right to hold a grudge and put someone out of your heart. In fact, there is an old saying that holding a grudge is like drinking poison and expecting the other person to die, and indeed, bitterness and animosity toward others will slowly but surely corrode your spirit. Understandably, it can be very hard not to put difficult people out of your heart, but a large part of our spiritual progress involves learning to love and forgive even the seemingly unlovable and unforgiveable people among us.

Release judgment and be reborn into Spirit

"The ego cannot survive without judgment..." — A Course in Miracles

This quote from *A Course in Miracles* provides some insight into why the Judgment card is the penultimate card in the Major Arcana. After learning the lessons of the prior cards, we arrive at the most important lesson: letting go of judgment. Once we stop judging others and forgive them instead, we can be released from the bondage of the ego and reborn into Spirit. It is then that we will discover the Oneness that we see in the final Major Arcana card, the World. It is then that we will find the Kingdom of Heaven which is here on Earth.

21. World

"The kingdom of the Father is spread out upon the Earth, and men do not see it." — The Gospel of Thomas, *Saying 113*

The World card symbolizes our soul operating within the limitations of our physical being, which calls to mind the saying that we are spiritual beings having a worldly experience. And so it suggests the phrase "to be in the world, but not of the world." This card also recommends finding our place in the world and discovering our oneness with everyone and everything in it.

Freedom born of limitations

The typical World card image is based largely on medieval *Christ in Majesty* icons, which were images of Christ, typically in the centre of a mandorla, with the symbols of the Four Evangelists (angel, eagle, bull, and lion), in the four corners. In the Tarot imagery, the angel, eagle, bull, and lion are interpreted (via astrological associations) as being symbolic of the four classical elements, which suggests the structure and physical limitations of our lives while the dancing woman in the center represents our eternal soul. The obvious implication is that of a soul residing within a body (our physical limitation). We may also infer from this a bit of advice about enhancing our spiritual realization.

To arrive at this guidance, begin by considering an aspect of your life where you feel limited or constricted. This can be in any aspect of your life, such as your finances, your health, or your love life. This constraint, which you probably see as an obstacle, can instead become a path to discovering your essential divinity when you release your resistance to it and accept that it is what it is. As you relax into that acceptance, your divine essence will begin to shine through into your life and (ironically) you will feel a surprising sense of freedom emerge.

Incidentally, it is not surprising that this message manifests with the final card of the Major Arcana since it builds upon the lessons of prior cards, such as non-judgment of what is (which we learned from the Judgment card) and the power of surrender (which we learned from the Hanged Man).

Universal Love

There are three cards in the Major Arcana that are associated with the number three: the Empress (numbered 3), the Hanged Man (numbered 12, and 1 + 2 = 3), and the World card (numbered 21, and 2 + 1 = 3). These three cards may be seen as expanding circles of love, beginning with the Empress. That card represents interpersonal love such as the nurturing love of a mother or spouse. The Hanged Man, through its meaning of sacrifice, indicates transpersonal love. Examples of this include sacrificing our time, resources, or energy to help others in our community or risking life and limb to save a group or individual who we don't know. Finally, the World card is about universal love—the love of all humankind and even of all living beings.

Universal love encompasses a sense of our oneness with everything in the world, and getting there is like a dance. When we take a step toward understanding our oneness with everything, we gain a closer experience of universal love, which in turn strengthens our belief in our oneness a bit more. It's an upward spiral toward universal oneness and universal love as long as we keep reaching for it. And the result of our personal, individual awakening is a gradual awakening of the consciousness of humankind, since we are all One. As each individual approaches this awakening, so does humanity as a whole.

The concept of universal love and oneness is itself universal. Although some may discount this as a trendy New Age idea, it crosses cultural boundaries and extends far back in time. There is a Buddhist "Universal Love Prayer" in the Metta Sutta, and in Christian theology, the concept of charity encompasses an unlimited loving-kindness toward all others. Finally, I once found a wonderful essay on universal oneness by Swami Sivananda (a twentieth century Hindu spiritual teacher). Here is a brief excerpt:

> *Feel that the whole world is your body, your own home. Melt or destroy all barriers that separate man from man. ... Feel that one power or God works through all hands, sees through all eyes, hears through all ears.*

As above, so below

"The same stream of life that runs through the world runs through my veins."
— *Rabindranath Tagore*

There is a famous Hermetic saying: "As above, so below," which may also be phrased as "The macrocosm is reflected in the microcosm." Similarly, Christianity says that "God created man in his own image."[31] I don't believe that

---

[31] *Genesis 1:27*

this means that God looks like a large version of a man, however. It means that just as the universe is the body (so to speak) of the Divine, and that body is suffused with divine Spirit, so it is with us as well—our physical body is suffused with our spirit. In this way, we are created in the image of the Divine: a soul operating within matter.

We can use this analogy to explore the concept of the divine nature of the universe. Think about the body you inhabit and consider it for a moment as a self-contained entity. Can you point to where your soul is located? Of course not. It's everywhere, isn't it? It is in your nerves, your skin, and your heart. Every bit of you is alive, but no one part of you contains your soul. Also, what happens to your physical body when you die? At the moment of death, the material makeup of your body doesn't change. Yes, the activity and energy flow of your body changes (specifically, it stops), but from a purely materialistic point of view, the matter in your body does not change at the instant of death. Your body is composed of the same molecules the moment before you die as it is the moment after.

The point here is that the quintessential *you*, which is your soul, may inhabit a body, but it is not the body, and so it is with the Divine as well. The "Anima Mundi"—the soul of the world—inhabits a rock, a cloud, a tree, a squirrel, and a person, but is not any of those things. The Divine is in everything but is not anything, just as we are in a body but are not the body. The difference between us and the Divine is a matter of scope. "The macrocosm is reflected in the microcosm."

In the world, not of it

There is a popular saying that we should be in the world, but not of the world. Of course, if you are reading this, you are living in the world. Aren't we all? The question is, how do we avoid being "of the world?"

As we saw in the section titled "The Hermit Fallacy" (for the Hermit card), we can be fully engaged in life but not governed by worldly desires and not attached to the results of our actions. Similarly, the Fool (in the section titled "Beginner's luck") advised us to be actively involved in the world while also remembering that the deepest truth is that we are of Spirit, not flesh. This consciousness helps keep us from being attached to the results of our efforts. So the way for us to be in the world but not attached to it is to attach our hearts and minds to the Divine instead. But how do we do that?

Although we are functioning within the confines of the world, we can dedicate our actions to the Divine. However, although we can control our intention (i.e., how we dedicate our efforts), we cannot control the results once our actions are done. It is the devotion that matters, though, and when we realize this, every effort can be the source of sacred joy regardless of whether it fails or succeeds.

Although our eyes see the material world, we can turn our attention toward the Divine whenever possible. One way to do this is to find a mantra that works for you, and repeat it with sincerity and dedication whenever your attention is not required elsewhere. Here is an example you might consider: *God is with me always and in all ways.*

Although we live in the world, we can turn our hearts toward the Divine. Indeed, we can fall in love with the Divine. There are various ways that people have done this through the ages. For example, many people sing devotional hymns while others read the ecstatic poems of mystic poets like Mirabai and Kabir, Rumi and Hafez, St. Francis of Assisi and St. Teresa of Avila. Also, the biblical *Song of Solomon* may be seen as a parable of the passionate, loving relationship that is possible between a person and God.

These are various ways that we can attach our hearts and minds to the Divine while being in the world as well.

No man is an island

"No man is an island, entire of itself; every man is a piece of the continent, a part of the main." — John Donne

We may view this card as an illustration of how the countless manifest bodies of the world (symbolized by the beings in the four corners of the card) are all interconnected through our common spiritual core (the dancing woman in the center). Once we realize this, we operate differently in the world.

As an analogy, we all know that our stomach is not something separate from the rest of us, so if we have a stomach ache, we do not hold a grudge against our abdomen. We also would not consider cutting it out of our life. It is a part of us, so we try to heal it. The same is true for the people around us—we are connected in that we are all part of a greater whole. When other people are troublesome, we should not hold a grudge against them; we should try to understand them and help heal them. And this holds true for more than just our fellow human beings. As

Albert Schweitzer said, "Until he extends his circle of compassion to include all living things, man will not himself find peace."

The indwelling Divine Spirit

The World card illustrates our true reality, which is that of a divine spirit existing within the confines of a physical body, but the problem for most of us is that we are asleep to this vital truth. This truth, however, can change our lives subtly but profoundly for "when you succeed in enshrining God in your heart, you will see God everywhere."[32]

When we realize our inner divinity, not only do we begin to "see God everywhere" in a profound shift of our perception, but we also begin to co-create a more divine material world. However, we don't have to become totally enlightened in order to begin to manifest such changes in the world. As we come to realize that our essential being is Spirit and that our outer being—our body and personality—is but a cloak we wear, we shed, bit by bit, our unfortunate facility for doing harm in the world, and we gain, bit by bit, an increased capacity for doing good instead. Also, the more we realize and exhibit our essential spiritual self, the more the people around us will change as a result. They probably won't know why they are changing, and they may not even realize that they are, but they will respond to the divine spark within us that shines ever brighter as we come to realize it.

Why are we here in the world?

"The purpose of life is to increase the warm heart. Think of other people. Serve other people sincerely." — The 14th Dalai Lama

Throughout the centuries, there have been mystics and sages from every religion who have taught that the material world is a dream of the soul. Of course, from the perspective of our material body (which is ephemeral) the material world is quite real, but from the perspective of our soul (which is eternal) it is but a brief illusion. Considering that, why are we here in this unreal world? Is it all just a cosmic joke, or is there a grand reason or purpose to it all? This is certainly the proverbial $64,000 question, and philosophers have argued this point for thousands of years.

---

[32] *This quote has been attributed to Swami Sivananda.*

First, let us consider the following excerpt from a poem by Kabir called "The Time Before Death."

Jump into experience while you are alive! ...
What you call "Salvation" belongs to the time before death.

...

If you make love with the Divine now, in the next
  life you will have the face of satisfied desire.

Kabir seems to say that our salvation arises out of a deep, passionate involvement in life. He also makes the point that this passion should come from a complete willingness to act from the heart in the here and now, and it should be about our love of the Divine. In other words, it is essential that we cultivate a passion for the Divine in this worldly life. But since we are in the material world, where do we find the Divine? The answer is that we find the Divine in everyone and everything around us. Kabir is also saying that rather than worrying about what happens to our spirit in the afterlife, we should concentrate on passionately living a spiritual life here in the mundane world. This is our purpose; this is why we are here.

Kabir's message corresponds well to the traditional image on the World card, which seems to say to us, "May your soul dance with joy in your every circumstance, in whatever tasks you undertake, and in your every personal relationship." And since these are all things that we experience here in the physical plane, it is here that we can learn from them.

To find support of this idea that learning is one aspect of our purpose, let's consider something that the Buddha said about two and a half millennia ago: "Your work is to discover your world and then with all your heart give yourself to it." Similarly, a few decades ago, Rick Fields wrote in the book *Chop Wood, Carry Water*, "The entire world is your curriculum." So perhaps we are here on a journey of discovery. Again, however, it is vitally important that we engage our divine spirit in that process for that is how our journey acquires true meaning. We may also infer from these quotes that the world is like a giant class room where our souls have experiences from which we can learn and grow. As Elisabeth Kübler-Ross said, "There are no mistakes, no coincidences, all events are blessings given to us to learn from." In other words, more than just exploration, perhaps we are each put here to learn specific things.

Finally, in his poem "Zero Circle" the 13th century Persian mystic Rumi tells us that we cannot—should not, even—be sure of the answer to this existential question. He says:

> *Be helpless, dumbfounded,*
> *Unable to say yes or no.*
> *Then a stretcher will come from grace*
> *to gather us up.*

Perhaps it is presumptuous to say we know why we are here, but saying we do not know can shut off our spiritual inquiry. If, however, we are "unable to say yes or no"—if we say we aren't sure—that leaves open an infinite number of possibilities. Then the wondrous curiosity and humility of wanting to find the answers but not presuming to know them invites divine guidance, which will lead us to explore those possibilities.

These are but a few examples of what sages past and present have thought about the question of why we are here in this unreal world. Other philosophers, prophets, and mystics have addressed this eternal question in similar ways. Simply put, though, a common thought that runs through their answers may be expressed like this: *We are souls living a mortal life in search of enlightening experience.* However, as Rumi indicates, we should not presume to think that this is a definitive answer. At best, it may be but a small part of a much larger truth toward which we are endlessly striving, and perhaps it is in this very process of searching for meaning that we manifest our purpose in life.

But if we believe in no other purpose, and even if we can never really know for sure why we are here, I have heard no greater answer to this eternal question than the one given by the Dalai Lama: *The purpose of life is to increase the warm heart.* In fact, if this is the only message you get from this book, it is enough.

Postscript: The poems by Rumi and Kabir that are noted in this section can both be found in Roger Housden's book, *Ten Poems to Change Your Life*.

Cষ ৪০

Part 2: Minor Arcana

*"The great lesson from the true mystics ... [is] that the sacred
is in the ordinary, that it is to be found in one's daily life, in one's
neighbors, friends, and family, in one's backyard."*
— Abraham H. Maslow

*"[Our] challenge ... is to live in such a way that there is no
duality, no separation between the spiritual path and its
manifestation in everyday life." — Rick Fields*

I once read a review of a book that gave some spiritual meanings for each of the Tarot cards. The reviewer's complaint about the book was that "some cards really aren't about spirituality." This is, unfortunately, a common misconception. At first we think that spiritual work is something we do at special times and in special places, but eventually we learn that our spiritual work arises in everything we do. As Dan Millman said in his book *The Peaceful Warrior*, "Not a moment passes that isn't spiritual practice." So I decided to preface this part of this book with a few words about that idea. After all, this book explores spiritual meanings for all seventy-eight cards. This includes, of course, those of the Minor Arcana, which are commonly considered to be depictions of events and people in our daily lives.

Despite their seeming focus on our everyday lives, the cards of the Minor Arcana are, in their own way, concerned with our spiritual journey. For one thing, a spiritual practice is hollow and lacking in transformative power if it is not integrated into our daily activities. That doesn't mean we must change *what* we do; it means that we must change *how* we do everything. Truly, we can incorporate our spirituality into everything we do—work, play, romance—and this book explores that idea for the Minor Arcana cards.

We must also realize that the outward aspects of our activities do not determine how spiritual we are. Tithing, abstinence, wearing modest attire, etcetera—things that many religions claim are important religious practices—do not in and of themselves bring us closer to the Divine. It is the clarity and purity of our hearts as we perform each and every task in our daily lives that does that, and then as we grow in love, compassion, and wisdom, the things we do change wherever necessary. Consequently, just as everything in our lives has an underlying spiritual element, so too does every Tarot card.

There are various ways to approach this understanding of the spirituality of those cards. For example, we can loosely associate each suit with a general theme. For example, the following is something that I adapted from a quote from the *Tao Te Ching*. In that ancient book of wisdom, Lao Tzu says, "I have three treasures: simplicity, patience, and compassion." To that list, I would humbly add a fourth treasure: awareness. These four treasures, then, may be associated with the four suits as follows:

Simplicity: Pentacles
Awareness: Swords
Compassion: Cups
Patience: Wands

Similarly, I was inspired by material I read in *The Path to Love* by Deepak Chopra to categorize the suits as follows: We may say that although we seem to be material beings (suit of Pentacles), in truth we are pure creativity (Wands), pure love (Cups), and pure awareness (Swords). In addition, each suit has an underlying theme due to its traditional elemental association: Wands and fire, Cups and water, Swords and air, Pentacles and earth.

Loosely based on these connections, the following are suit associations that can help us explore the spirituality of the Minor Arcana.

- <u>Wands</u>: Power issues, passion and desire, and action. Consequently, this suit can be about a passion for divine union. It can be about Karma yoga, which is the ancient path of action, meaning selfless work wherein everything we do is offered to God as a sacrament.
- <u>Cups</u>: Love and Compassion, the yoga of relationships, devotion to the divine. Thus, this suit may be associated with Bhakti yoga, which is the path of devotion wherein one cultivates an intense love for the Divine, facilitated by cultivating a personal relationship with the Divine. Often this is accomplished by using a chosen idealization of the Divine.
- <u>Swords</u>: Thought, reason, communication, and attention. The suit of Swords suggests Jnana yoga, which is the path of knowledge characterized by learning how to discriminate between the eternal and the non-eternal. All transitory phenomena are analyzed and then rejected until Brahman alone remains in the spiritual aspirant's awareness.
- <u>Pentacles</u>: Non-attachment, gratitude and appreciation, and simplicity. This suit is also about our perception of the material world. Since Karma yoga,

the path of selfless action, includes charity, the suit of Pentacles may also be associated with that path.

I often discover Tarot meanings and insights in unexpected places, and another way to consider the four suits came to me recently while reading *The 7 Habits of Highly Effective People* by Stephen Covey. I came across a passage in that book which listed the following four most basic needs that people have:

- To live
- To love and be loved
- To learn
- To leave a legacy

(The alliterative nature of this list is Covey's mnemonic device.)

Whenever I see a list of four archetypal or primal traits, qualities, concepts, etcetera, I think of the four Tarot suits and try to find ways to associate them. It's not always a perfect fit, of course, but sometimes, as in this case, the association seems made to order.

"To live" calls to mind the fiery suit of Wands with its indication of our energy, our passion for life, and our libido (the drive to create more life). "To love" and "To learn" are obviously associated with the suits of Cups (love and relationships) and Swords (thought, ideas, and communication), which leaves the fourth need, "a legacy," for the suit of Pentacles, the suit of physical manifestation. An obvious connection comes from seeing this phrase, "to leave a legacy," as meaning a need to create something of lasting value. However, it also refers to our need to find meaning in the things we do and to create meaning in our physical, material lives.

We can also use numerology to help us explore spiritual meanings for the cards. What follows are numerological associations for the numbered cards in the Minor Arcana.[33]

1. ONE indicates the true reality of Unity. We are one with each other and with the Divine. (It is significant that there is a hand of God offering the suit icon on the Aces in many Tarot decks.)
2. TWO is about Duality. It can indicate our illusion of separateness—from each other as well as from the Divine.

---

[33] *Of course, this list provides only a cursory overview of numerology, and there are a variety of numerological interpretations. Use what works best for you.*

3.   THREE calls to mind "Trinity," which is a common conceptualization of the divine. ("Father, Son, and Holy Spirit," "Brahma, Vishnu, Shiva," "Maiden, Mother, Crone," etcetera) THREE is also a first glimpse that things aren't black and white—everything is a shade of gray—which is a first tentative step away from the duality of TWO. This number also symbolizes creativity since something new is created when two elements come together.

4.   FOUR, being the number of structure (four seasons, four directions, etcetera), symbolizes the material world. We typically think this material world is the ultimate reality, but its separate reality is an illusion.

5.   FIVE indicates our humanity (people have five senses, five fingers, etcetera), and the FIVE cards all have an element of the suffering that is common to us all and that results from our illusion of separateness. These cards thus show us our lessons in life. However, this number also calls to mind the "Fifth Element" of Spirit (which is reflected in its assignment to the Hierophant).

6.   SIX represents reciprocity. These cards depict acts of compassion and charity as we overcome the suffering of the FIVE cards and begin to learn their lessons.

7.   In the SEVEN cards, we find tests of our learning so far. In addition, seven is the number of chakras and the classical planets. Thus, it is the number of transcendence, representing our path up from the mundane, manifest world to the transcendental realm of the Divine.

8.   EIGHT is movement and power, so here we see that in working to overcome the duality illusion we can move forward toward the reality of divine unity. Our success here is dependent upon having passed the tests of the SEVEN cards.

9.   NINE is the manifest result of the work of the previous cards. This may be gratifying, wounding, or distressing, depending on the outcome.

10. TEN can be both a return to divine union and a return to our community with the intent to help others along this path. However, it also can indicate that our failure to realize divine union sends us back to start the process over.

Keep in mind that while we can use these elemental and numerological associations to help us expand our awareness of the cards, we should not let them become a straightjacket to constrain and limit our understanding. Each card can encompass a wide range of meaning.

WANDS

This suit indicates (among other things) passion and desire, which can either tether us to the material world or lead us back to the Divine. It all depends on *what* we desire. In its aspect of power, the suit of Wands also indicates our ego, which we must overcome along our path of spirituality.

Ace of Wands

This ace is about inspiration, desire, passion, ego, confidence, and enthusiasm. A common image on the Ace of Wands is that of a divine hand offering a wand, which says that passion is one of the essential aspects of a spiritual path. Like all the aces, though, what it represents is a seed that needs care and nurturing in order to grow.

Unity of Life

"Treat everyone you meet like God in drag." — *Ram Dass*

Seeing the unity of life is perhaps the most fundamental spiritual realization of all. Many religious traditions teach that all life is interconnected, and many spiritual teachers go even further, asserting that all life is One and the entire manifest universe is the body of the Divine suffused with the divine Soul.

This is the secret of life. It sounds simple—and it is—but although we may be able to acknowledge this spiritual truth, it's so much harder to experience it and live it. One way to incorporate it into our lives is by being compassionate toward others, bringing peace into the world, and relieving suffering in others. Through these actions, we affirm this truth and incorporate it into our very being.

The more we treat everyone "like God in drag," the more we experience them that way. We begin to see the Divine in everyone, and as our perception changes, our world changes. To quote Ram Dass again: "When we see the Beloved in each person, it's like walking through a garden, watching flowers bloom all around us."

Inspiration

When we allow the inspiration of the Universe to flow through us and into our efforts, we become co-creators of our lives and of our world. However, it is important to remember that a true spark of inspiration—one that serves the purpose of our soul's journey—comes from the part of us that is connected to the Divine. This is different from egoistic inspiration, which is typically born of fear or selfish desire. We can differentiate between the two based on our consideration of the anticipated effects of the inspired action. For example, we might wonder if our inspiration will uplift us or serve to relieve suffering in others. In that case, it is probably of a divine origin. On the other hand, if it is focused merely on personal aggrandizement or the accumulation of wealth, it is of the ego.

A higher purpose

Many people erroneously think that being on a spiritual path means retreating from our responsibilities in life, but that is far from the truth. Our Higher Self—our connection to the divine Oneness of the universe—urges us to strive to be the best person we can be in the here-and-now and to do what's right with confidence, determination, and vitality. All of this is a reminder that our actions, which are, of course, performed here on this earthly plane, can have a higher purpose when we allow divine inspiration into our lives.

Libido

Our urge to unite with another person is a reflection on this earthly plane of our spiritual yearning for union with the Divine. Indeed, mystics in every religious tradition have expressed their transcendent experiences in terms suggestive of sexual ecstasy. However, sexual activity can become a diversion from a spiritual practice, which is one reason why most religions burden it with so many guidelines, restrictions, and prohibitions. (Unfortunately, the sexual taboos of major religions also reflect the prejudices of the cultural milieu in which they developed, thus either obscuring or tarnishing essential truths about sexuality and spirituality.)

It is not sex per se that is the problem; it is enslavement to lust that blocks our spiritual progress. When seen as a loving, sacred union, sexual activity can be an intensely transcendent experience. In addition, if sexual energy is not dissipated heedlessly, it may be transmuted into passion for divine union. So this card asks this very essential question: "Have you mastered your libido or has it mastered you?"

<u>Refined desire</u>

"Yearn for Him with a longing heart." — Sri Ramakrishna's advice about how to find God

There is a saying that the way to get rid of the darkness is to light a candle. This metaphor illustrates the importance and power of realizing our connection to the Divine and of moving in that direction. But how can we do that? How do we light that metaphorical candle?

In his book *Religion in Practice*, Swami Prabhavananda says that any one of us can experience our connection with the Divine "if the following three conditions are fulfilled: human birth, longing for God, and the society of the holy. When the first two conditions are met, the third fulfills itself." Obviously we have all met the first condition (human birth), so the factor we need to work on is our desire to experience the presence of the Divine in our lives. We can cultivate that desire by turning our passion and attention ever toward the Divine and by surrendering the results of our actions to the Divine. When this purified desire is sustained, it readies us so that the Divine will appear in our lives. And as with everything, when we desire and are ready for things that are in accord with what our soul wants for us, the Universe conspires to bring them to us.

Then, when the Divine brings a candle into the darkness of our lives, it ignites our own spiritual candle as well, which empowers us to co-create light in a world that was dark, for even a single candle can dispel the darkness around it. And with that candle, we can illuminate the way for ourselves and for others, and we can light the candles that other people carry. As the Buddha said, "Thousands of candles can be lit from a single candle, and its life will not be shortened."

Two of Wands

This card can represent domination over others, conflicts about personal power, and decisions about where we direct our passion.

Choice of passion

We may consider this card's spiritual message in light of its numerological and elemental associations. The number Two can indicate choices and decisions, and the suit of Wands, being associated with fire, is about passion. Thus we see that the Two of Wands can indicate the need to make a choice about where to direct our passion.

There is a saying that a man cannot ride two horses at the same time. Similarly, we cannot dedicate our lives to both a passion for material success and a passion for divine union. This does not mean, however, that we have to take a vow of poverty or even that we cannot be successful in the world. It just means that we have to decide which one is of primary importance in our lives. And it means choosing a course of action based on that primary decision of where our passion really lies.

Dominion

The keyword for the Two of Wands in the Thoth Tarot deck is "Dominion," which is a concept that bears investigation. The scope of dominion can be as vast as a conquering army or as small as a schoolyard bully, but in any case, it is delusional for many reasons. First, it is a trap. Consider, for example, that although prison inmates are confined by bars, society is also imprisoned insofar as it is required to maintain the prison and guard the prisoners. The delusion of dominion is also explained by Eckhart Tolle in *The Power of Now* as follows: "Power over others is weakness disguised as strength." The need to dominate others reflects a weakness, such as an insecure ego or a lack of trust in our own ability to secure the resources we need.

Another insidious problem with our power addictions is described by Ken Keyes, Jr. in this quote from *Handbook to Higher Consciousness*:

Our power addiction keeps us from loving people because we perceive them as objects that may threaten our power, prestige, or pecking order.

Similarly, every attempt at dominion over someone else is based on the duality illusion, i.e., the delusion that we are separate from each other.

Finally, we need to understand that cooperation is preferable to conflict for it brings synergy instead of damage and love instead of animosity. And at a deeply spiritual level, cooperation brings us back to oneness instead of moving us away from that realization. Perhaps, then, when a conflict looms with another person, we would do well to seek oneness with them through cooperation instead of separateness through dominion.

Power conflicts

When we release our ego's need to be right and to prove itself better than others, we can escape the power that interpersonal conflicts have over us. Although there is nothing wrong with stating our position assertively, it is important that we do so without being either aggressive or defensive, which are two sides of the same flawed coin.

When we find ourselves acting in either of those ways, it is a warning sign that our ego is controlling our actions in an effort to defend itself while deluding us into thinking that we are virtuously defending the truth. It is also a sign that we are attached to the results of a discussion, which inevitably turns it into an argument instead of a cooperative search for truth. By learning to see when this happens, we can instead observe the situation with equanimity and bring the light of our higher consciousness to it. Then the darkness of our ego will dissipate, power games will recede, and our relationships will heal as a result.

Three of Wands

This card can represent having foresight and patience, exploring new ventures and new possibilities, and expanding our horizons and envisioning our future. As a card with the number Three, it is about creativity and synthesis, while as a card in the suit of Wands, it is about energy, activity, and passion.

Release the results

In many modern Tarot decks, this card is seen as a depiction of a merchant watching his ships sailing out to sea (or returning from a sea voyage) on a commercial venture. While the ships are at sea, he has no control over what happens next, and he has to wait patiently, trusting in providence that their voyage will be successful. Consequently, we may see in this card the spiritual practice of releasing the results and consequences of our actions and enterprises to the Divine. Of course it is important that we take action (i.e., that we do what is right) but at some point we must let go and say to the Divine, "Thy will be done."

This is more than just a matter of trust and faith, though. Releasing our need to control the results of our actions—and even, more generally, the course of our lives—is an act of non-attachment to the material world, which is a vital step toward realization of our oneness with the Divine.

<u>Resolve interpersonal conflicts</u>

A common aspect of the Three cards in the Minor Arcana is their depiction of group interactions. This is obvious in the Three of Cups (friendship) and the Three of Pentacles (working together), but it's also implicit in the Three of Swords (painful or broken relationships) and, as I shall explain here, the Three of Wands.

The fact that the Three of Wands directly follows the struggle for dominion in the Two of Wands leads to some advice about resolving our interpersonal conflicts. When we have a fight with someone, a healthy and creative resolution depends upon rising above a "me versus you" (i.e., dualistic) attitude. When we do that, we begin to see the big picture, which is that we are all interconnected. In other words, we discover that we can't fight someone else without hurting ourselves too. We also need to take a long-term approach to problematic relationships instead of looking for instant gratification, which is an approach that is all too prevalent in our culture.

So a bit of practical advice in this card is that one way to heal a conflicted relationship with someone is to do something for them that is compassionate and generous. It is important, however, to do this without resentment or any expectation of reciprocation or even appreciation. In fact, it's best to do an act of kindness without any regard for whether or not the other person knows that it was you who did it. If you cannot do it anonymously, though, at least don't make a point of mentioning it.

This recommendation of anonymity emphasizes the fact that such acts are not intended to curry favor with the other person. Instead, the point is to change the basic energy of your relationship in order to transform it from a source of conflict into a wellspring of blessings.

<u>Be a visionary</u>

"There are those that look at things the way they are, and ask "Why?" I dream of things that never were, and ask why not?" — Robert F. Kennedy (paraphrasing George Bernard Shaw)

This card urges us to look beyond our current situation in order to find creative solutions for ourselves and the world. When we feel disenchanted or trapped within our circumstances, we would do well to take time to pause, reflect, and see beyond them. Sometimes we need to remember that when we envision a better life and a better world, we are taking the first step toward manifesting that vision.

<u>Accentuate the positive</u>

There is always both positive and negative energy all around us, but often it seems as though negativity is ubiquitous and relentless while positivity is rare, subtle, and hard to find. At such times, we need to rise above the fray of our day-to-day existence and look for the positive things in life with vision, patience, and determination. As we do that, we can also make a commitment to surround ourselves with positivity until we are strong enough to be able to generate positive energy on our own. Here is a way to do that.

We create our lives in large part by the type of people with whom we choose to associate and the types of activities on which we focus our attention and efforts. For example, have you ever known a person who seems to suck the life out of a room with their continual criticisms and complaints? If you spend much time with them, sooner or later they will turn you into a negative person too unless you are very strong. On the other hand, do you know someone who brightens up a room when they walk in or who makes you feel happy just by being with them? That sort of energy is contagious too, and being around it can make you a more positive person.

This is not to say that we have to associate only with bright, cheerful people, but it does mean that we should be aware of the fact that the person we are becoming is affected by the kinds of people with whom we spend time. Of course, we don't always have a choice, such as at our jobs, but often we do have a choice of what we do and with whom we do it.

By choosing the right associations, we can fill our lives with positive energy. And as our lives become filled with such energy, we will begin to see opportunities where others may see obstacles, to see the good in other people instead of the bad, and to count our blessings instead of our problems. Then we will be able to go out into the world and be the kind of person who can help others become more positive.

One thing you can do to start along this path is to make a list of the people you spend time with, the activities you engage in, and the news you prefer to watch or read. Consider them carefully to see which choices are helping you create a more positive life, and then evaluate who and what you choose to surround yourself with.

<u>The observer Self</u>

Like the man standing on a hilltop in the RWS Three of Wands, our eternal, Higher Self is the observer of our lives. Although it does stay involved in life, this eternal part of us also remains detached, much like you or I when we watch a movie.

I have found that when a scene in a movie becomes too intense or stressful, I can regain my equilibrium and equanimity by glancing down, diverting my attention to the reality of the theater to remind myself that the movie isn't real. Our lives may be like that too. When life's burdens become too stressful, we can draw our awareness in to our divine Self—the inner observer. Then we will rediscover the bliss and serenity that is our birthright.

Four of Wands

Bearing the number Four, this card is about stability and security, which sets up a dynamic tension with the energy, activity, and passion associated with the suit of Wands.

This card is also traditionally associated with celebrations and rites of passage. It urges us to create sacred space in our lives for joyful celebrations of our past achievements, new adventures we are undertaking, and our plans and goals for a fuller life.

Honor the path taken

The Four of Wands can indicate a rite of passage (such as a graduation, wedding, etcetera) in which we celebrate entering a new phase of life, but such rites should also involve honoring the phase of life we are leaving. This does not mean dwelling on the past, but rather it's about honoring the path we have taken so far. This is important for a couple of reasons.

First, a sense of gratitude and appreciation for what has gone before has a vital role in creating lasting success in our lives. It is also important that we appreciate the entirety of our lives, and that includes the "good" along with the "bad." (I put those words in quotes because they are subjective. Events are only good or bad when we label them as such.)

Another reason to acknowledge the journey we have completed so far is that it affirms our sense of unity with those who are now setting foot on the path we have just completed. Our acknowledgment says that even though we are on the next leg of life's journey, we do not feel superior to those who are traveling along the path we just completed, but rather, we have a sense of unity and community with them.

All too often people act condescendingly toward those who are still in the phrase of life that they themselves have recently completed. This is not just in terms of our mundane journey through life either. Many who are on a spiritual path take this attitude toward those who seem not to have begun that journey. We can rejoice and celebrate the milestones along our sacred path, but that never means we should feel superior to those we see as not having set out on one. Instead, we should keep in mind our essential unity, because ultimately, we are all on the same journey.

Celebrations: honor who we are

As previously noted, the Four of Wands can indicate a celebration, such as a reunion, a graduation, or a wedding. And we do love to celebrate, don't we! Why is that? One reason, of course, is that it's fun to party, but there is more to it. While a celebration can honor an achievement or an important passage in life, there is another very important reason of which we may be unaware. We celebrate as a way of honoring who we are—either as an individual or as a group. A celebration can be about expressing a sense of joy in our being, making an affirmation of life, or showing appreciation for the people in our life. All of that is tremendously important, so it is always appropriate to celebrate who you are, no matter how small the festivity. You don't have to wait for a major milestone because every moment in your life is a milestone worth celebrating.

So this card urges us to celebrate everything. Celebrate the new day. Celebrate your love for someone else. Celebrate life. That's the secret to joyful living, and it's also one of the secrets to living a spiritual life.

<u>Put away childish things</u>

Just as a rite of passage may be something like a marriage or a graduation, it also may be an initiation into a religious tradition or a private matter wherein one makes a personal commitment to follow a spiritual path. In some rites of passage, the person completing one phase of life and preparing to enter a new one does so by relinquishing things associated with that prior phase and accepting things associated with the next. Therein lies a problem that many of us have with moving from a life based on a materialistic view to one of spirituality.

We fear that we will have to give up all our "things," like an initiate joining a convent or a monastery. That's not really the case, though. We do need to give up our *attachment* to material possessions, but that is not the same thing. We also need to understand that we are not being asked to give up anything of value; we are volunteering to trade in the things of a child for those of an adult (metaphorically speaking). It's like the famous biblical passage about "childish things":

"When I was a child, I spake as a child, I understood as a child, I thought as a child; but when I became a man, I put away childish things."
— 1 Corinthians 13:11

As an example, consider how most children would hate to give away any of their toys, but at the approach of their next phase of life, they release them freely. Those old toys are excess baggage and are no longer wanted or needed because the former child now discovers new fulfillments. Such is the transition to a spiritual life. Material possessions lose their attraction and we lose our attachment to them.

Also, giving up our material attachments is not about imposing restrictions on our lives, for it is our attachments that truly constrain us. Rather, it is about finding new freedom in liberating ourselves from the thrall of materialism.

Five of Wands

This card indicates the struggle and strife that is inherent in our lives. But despite (or, perhaps, because of) such difficulties, we may learn to create greatness in our lives. This is especially true when we are able to find common ground in contentious situations and when we can organize conflicting energies into a creative endeavor.

Life is struggle

This card tells us that life is struggle—a struggle to survive, to thrive, and to excel. That is what life is about, but we often complain about it, resist it, and run away from it. However, we have the choice to embrace it and learn from it. Indeed, to love life is to love it even in times of struggle and strife, to see the lessons and value in everything. And so the trick is to fully engage in the struggles of life while also seeing beyond them into our spiritual reality so that we don't suffer in those conflicts and obstacles. This is how we can transcend the struggles of life.

Avoid bickering

An important message from the Five of Wands is its recommendation to avoid bickering. This advice is about more than merely getting drawn into petty arguments, however. It's also easy to be fascinated as a bystander by the quarrels and fights of others. This may seem harmless enough, but it too can be problematic.

For example, have you ever read the comments section on an online news article and found yourself being fascinated by the arguing going on there? You don't have to participate in those arguments to be adversely affected by them. Just being a mesmerized onlooker allows a noticeable amount of negative energy to seep into your psyche by the anger, confusion, or criticism it stirs up.

In his book, *The Power of Now*, Eckhart Tolle says, "Any negative inner state is contagious. Unhappiness spreads more easily than a physical disease." Tolle's disease analogy is a very useful one. If you're not careful to avoid contagion, a disease will infect you, and through you, it will increasingly spread into the world. A negative inner state is like that too in that we can easily become both victim and propagator of the problem. This is why it is said that the world can only experience peace to the extent that the people of the world experience inner peace.

The disease analogy has one flaw, however. While close physical proximity is required for physical disease, it is not a necessary factor for negativity. Although snide, spiteful, demeaning, or callous remarks occur in face-to-face interactions, we are often exposed to negativity remotely, such as through an internet discourse as noted in the preceding example. Regardless of the forum, however, such comments come from the negativity within people, and unless we have a good way to shield ourselves effectively from such negative energy, it is best to avoid it whenever we can.

Cage your monkey mind

An internal manifestation of bickering is sometimes called "monkey mind," a term that illustrates the way our minds jump from thought to thought like a monkey jumping from tree to tree. We may consider the Five of Wands to be an illustration of this.

To understand this phenomenon, sit quietly for a little while and you'll soon become aware of your own monkey mind. It is the constant chatter in your head, thoughts like "But what about ...?" and "I can't believe what she did!" and "This is too hard," and "I'm hungry; I wonder what's for dinner."

Our monkey mind is easily distracted. It obsesses about the past, and it worries about the future, all the while avoiding a meaningful engagement of the present. It keeps us in chaos and confusion, it keeps us from finding peace, it keeps us from living in the present moment, and it keeps us from hearing the soft voice of our intuition. However, there are times when we are able to quiet this monkey, such as when we are deeply involved in a game, watching a movie, or practicing meditation.

During meditation, it helps to just become aware of your thoughts rather than thinking them. Observe them without becoming absorbed in them and distracted by them. Whenever a thought arises, just notice it ("Oh, that's another thought. Okay.") and then gently return your attention to whatever your meditation focus may be: your breath, a candle's flame, a mantra, etcetera. This will help you get to the point where you can choose what thoughts you want to give space in your life.

Meditation will help you calm your monkey mind, but another useful exercise is to carry around this card—the Five of Wands—to remind yourself that whenever your monkey mind starts to chatter, that's all that's happening. Then quietly return your attention to what is going on around you in the present moment.

Coping with argument monsters

"A power struggle collapses when you withdraw your energy from it. Power struggles become uninteresting to you when you change your intention from winning to learning about yourself." — Gary Zukav

Have you ever been in an argument or a contentious situation where it seemed like the chaos of the dispute took on a life of its own, growing like a monster? Such chaos arises when everyone involved wants to win, when their interactions are of the ego rather than the Soul. At such times, the energy of antagonism and separateness that arises from the egos involved creates a self-perpetuating "argument monster."

Quarrels and fights are, at their essence, chaotic energy, and chaos feeds on chaos. In other words, when we get into a chaotic situation, our minds become more hectic and confused, and that always exacerbates the situation. Then, barring any steadying force, the situation can easily spin out of control. But that part about a steadying force is the key to solving the problem. You can allow your Spirit to become a stabilizing force. As Gary Zukav says, if you change your intention from winning (ego) to learning (Spirit), the energy of the situation will shift from chaos to peace.

Revenge and violence

"Hate multiplies hate, violence multiplies violence, and toughness multiplies toughness in a descending spiral of destruction." — Martin Luther King Jr.

On May 2, 2011 Osama bin Laden was killed in a covert U.S. military operation, an event that initiated a variety of reactions in America, from wild celebrations to spirited conversations. Some of the ensuing discussions were about revenge, including the psychological effects of celebrating it, and the social turbulence it creates. When I considered these events and the breadth of our society's reactions to them, I thought about the Five of Wands, which can illustrate the chaos of revenge and violence.

In our external reality, the most obvious problem with revenge is that it often creates a vicious cycle of violence. (Consider, for example, the infamous feud between the Hatfields and the McCoys, which lasted over a quarter of a century.) Internally, the problem with our cultural fascination with and adulation of revenge is that it acts like a drug. In fact, in one conversation on this topic that I had with an acquaintance, it felt like I was talking to an addict, so desperate was his vehement refrain of "Some things must be revenged!" I soon realized that a rational conversation with this person was impossible at that time.

Like taking a drug, reveling in revenge feels good for a while, temporarily masking our pain but not curing its cause. After the high wears off, we are left with the same underlying problems as before since the wrong done to us did not cause them; it merely brought them to light. Our inner state of anxiety and our inability to forgive were there before we were wronged, and they will still be there after the euphoria of revenge wears off. What we truly need is to find in the depths of our soul a capacity for love and serenity, and revenge does not give us that. Ultimately, though, the problem with revenge is its denial of the healing power of forgiveness and its indulgence in a separation mindset as opposed to a realization of our spiritual oneness with everyone else.

Six of Wands

Many modern versions of the Six of Wands depict a triumphal procession in which a victor rides a horse while surrounded by those who have supported his efforts or perhaps by those who are celebrating his success, depending on your perspective. This indicates encouragement and support of a victory, but it also suggests the trap of pride that may come with success. Alternatively, this card may denote a reciprocal exchange of energy.

<u>Appreciation for encouragement and inspiration</u>

The Tarot's Six cards all express messages of reciprocity—giving and receiving—and consequently they also may be seen as expressing messages about appreciation and gratitude. The Six of Wands advocates gratitude for the encouragement that other people give us, and on a higher level, it can be about having appreciation for the inspiration that the Divine shines upon us. In fact, it urges gratitude for the encouragement and inspiration that the Divine shines upon *all of us*, which implicitly acknowledges that we are all one.

Be happy for the success of others

With its image of a triumphant parade, the Six of Wands urges us to be happy for other people when they succeed in life and to support them along their journey of Self-realization. Indeed, nothing says "We are One" like celebrating someone else's success as much as you would your own.

All too often we give only tepid or grudging praise and congratulations to a friend or coworker when they are successful, usually due to feelings of envy or jealousy. But those dark emotions poison our lives and actually stifle our own chances for success. On the other hand, expressing sincere, joyful support for the accomplishments of other people demonstrates and strengthens our loving, caring spirit. It also affirms our belief that there is enough for everyone; that someone else does not have to fail in order for us to succeed. And when we send that message out into the Universe, we co-create an abundant and joyful world.

Another way to achieve this enlightened perspective of the success of others is to realize a deeper meaning in our own successes. The true worth of our victories lies not in our material achievements themselves, but in our connectedness with others which we discover as we all strive together to fulfill our destinies.

The trap of pride

The Six of Wands, with its depiction of a victory parade, warns of a pitfall that we may encounter along a spiritual path, which is a desire for recognition of our spiritual progress. This desire is one of pride, arrogance, and self-importance, and none of these traits are in harmony with a spiritual quest. It's tempting to boast that we are no longer in thrall to materialism, or we may want to make a point of mentioning our charitable works. When such temptations arise, however, we need to recall our humility and modesty. Some spiritual teachers advise their followers to avoid discussing their spiritual work with others, and this is, in part, why.

<u>Recognize the Supernal Light within</u>

"The Supernal Light in you recognizes the Supernal Light in others and in the world around you." — Tau Malachi

We can see that this quote is applicable to the Six of Wands when we combine the numerological meaning of reciprocity associated with the Sixes and the suit of Wands' elemental association with our inner light. The significance of this is that when we recognize the divine spark within others, we are actually remembering that it is within ourselves as well, which helps manifest that "Supernal Light" within all of us. Every time we do that—even if only for just a moment—we are taking a step toward reunification with the Divine.

To enlighten both our own lives and the world we live in, we can repeatedly remind ourselves that we and everyone else are spiritual beings and that the Divine dwells in us all. Recognition of our divine nature reinforces our recognition of that of others, and vice versa. And so we see that we are all in this together, working to recognize the Supernal Light in each other as well as within ourselves. In this way, we help reveal and manifest the divinity within us and within the world around us.

Seven of Wands

This card is about resolve and perseverance and how we respond to the tests of life. It also indicates competition and the trials and challenges that come from being successful. And it suggests the ego's perception of threats to its existence, and its reaction to them.

<u>Commitment and resolve</u>

The Seven of Wands, with its implications of tenacity and determination, says that to do anything important, we must first make a commitment to it. As we work toward a goal, our dedication will be tested repeatedly in every misfortune, temptation, and setback, and success will come only if we renew and hold firm to our commitment.

The most important commitment we can make is to reconnect with our inner divinity, to realize our oneness with the Divine. This includes becoming the best person we can be with regard to things like honesty, integrity, courage, generosity, and compassion. Obstacles to this goal will, of course, continually arise, so we must renew our commitment daily and reinvigorate our journey along the path our soul wants us to take toward manifesting our highest potential, our Divine Self.

Knowing when and where to take a stand

"Do not compromise on ideals and principles. But when it comes to opinions, appreciate views differing from yours, and accept them when they merit it." — Swami Prabhavananda

A significant theme running through the Seven cards in the Minor Arcana is that of tests and trials, and a message we may see in the Seven of Wands is that every time we feel criticized, insulted, or abused we are facing a test of how to respond.

Situations often arise where we feel personally attacked and generally our first instinct is to fight back, but do we really need to fight? Perhaps we are mistaking our opinions for principles, or maybe we are overreacting and need to set aside our ego so we can take a measured response. To correctly evaluate circumstances where such conflicts arise, it helps to keep in mind a few questions:

Is this a real problem?
Is it important?
Is it something worth fighting about, or am I just defending my pride?

On the other hand, it is important that we recognize when a lack of resistance does not come from transcending a conflict but from fearing it. In addition, this card is not only about knowing *when* to take a stand, but also *where* to take a stand. "Staying the course" is only admirable when we are staying the right course. Otherwise, we are just being foolish or stubborn.

At an even higher level, we should realize that when we take umbrage, it is our ego that is feeling offended. "Don't take anything personally" is the second of the four agreements described by Don Miguel Ruiz in this book, *The Four Agreements*, and it can help us avoid a lot of strife and save us a lot of suffering. The ego typically reacts with either anger or fear to perceived insults, but our divine Self sees no offense, no attack. It does not suffer the dualistic illusion of "us versus them," and so it responds with understanding, equanimity, and compassion. When our higher Self resists something, it does so because it is the right thing to do, not because it feels offended. It is in this way that we may tell on what level we are acting.

Constructive Criticism versus Personal Attack

As noted previously, a negative aspect of the Seven of Wands is a tendency to take a defensive posture against imagined insults. There are two sides to this story, however, which I realized recently when I gave someone what I thought was a bit of constructive criticism that they perceived as an attack. I was dismayed by this reception, certain that I had not meant my comment as an affront. But then I decided to consider the issue from both perspectives, theirs and mine.

From the point of view of the speaker, there are a few things to consider in giving constructive criticism. First, it is important to be sure that your heart is pure. Does the comment come from a place of love and compassion, or is there even a hint of blame or reprimand? Even when good intentions comprise 90% of our motivation, the listener will pick up on the 10% that is reproachful. Understandably, this is a hard call for us to make since a little bit of negativity, which is all too easy for the listener to spot, can be hard for us to notice.

It is also important to consider if it's the right time and place for the criticism. For example, even the most well-intentioned constructive criticism can seem like an attack if given in front of other people. Also, people are not always willing to hear helpful truths or able to make beneficial changes. It takes a clear heart to realize when it might be inappropriate or even callous to force someone to confront something they are not yet ready to face.

Finally, I have found that it is essential to consider if my constructive criticism is accurate. What may be valid for me may not be valid for the other person, or a message that seems vital to me may not be very important to the other person, at least not at this time. So perhaps we need to consider if the issue at hand seems important to us simply because it is one that we need to deal with. We all tend to project a lot, so this is a common mistake when giving constructive criticism.

From the perspective of the listener, a vital piece of advice is to assume innocence. It's all too easy to mistake constructive criticism for an attack when we are dead set on defending our ego (as we usually are). But even if a comment does bear a reasonable appearance of an attack, there is usually at least a kernel of truth in it, and we can benefit from finding whatever advice there may be in it.

Playing a zero-sum game

In many decks, the image on the Seven of Wands is reminiscent of a children's game called "King of the Hill." That's the game where you struggle to get to the top of a hill and then have to defend your position from everyone else who is now fighting to displace you. In the "real world" this reflects our society's paradigm of winners and losers, which typically results in defensiveness, anxiety, and insecurity.

Consequently, this card can indicate a zero-sum game in which a person can win only at the expense of other people who lose. This idea that winning can only be achieved through the defeat of someone else is pervasive throughout our cultural mindset of materialism and scarcity-consciousness. We tend to think of it as inevitable and inescapable, but a more highly evolved view is that life can be a non-zero-sum game, and an attitude of looking for win-win solutions can lead us all to abundance.

Of course, this shift in our cultural consciousness will be difficult and slow, and in working to bring it about, we may feel like the figure on this card who displays the courage to fight for what's right and to stand up for his convictions against all odds. It is important to remember, though, that changing the world starts with each of us, as individuals, changing the conduct of our lives. If we can see the world as a cooperative win-win game instead of as a cut-throat zero-sum game, we will all benefit from the resulting collaboration since ultimately we must all win together.

On a metaphysical level, the realization of our essential oneness with everyone else makes a zero-sum game mentality unthinkable. After all, how can we justify making someone else lose so that we can win when, on a deep, spiritual level, we are all One?

Bless also the bumps on the road

"Bless not only the road, but the bumps on the road. They are all part of the higher journey." — Julia Cameron

In the Summer 2012 issue of *Parabola Magazine*[34], architect Barry Svigals says, "We rarely talk about how difficult it is for a person in a family ... to live a spiritual life while the kids are crying, diapers need to be changed, a job has to be

---

[34] *http://www.parabola.org/*

done, all those things." Indeed, it is a universal truth that life is a struggle, and that includes all the little challenges of our everyday life. Look around and you will see it everywhere, from a chick straining to crack open its eggshell to a gazelle desperately running from the claws of a pursuing lion. We all struggle, but not all of us suffer as a consequence. The important question is this: Do we get beaten down by the effort and become cynical, pessimistic, or dejected, or do we see tribulations as an integral part of life, and thus celebrate them and use them as "grist for the mill?" The choice is ours, and the decision we make and the attitude we assume profoundly define our lives. As Joseph Campbell said, "Opportunities to find deeper powers within ourselves come when life seems most challenging."

Eight of Wands

The fiery energy of the suit of Wands is combined with the strength of the number eight in this card of passion and power.

<u>Carpe diem</u>

The Eight of Wands illustrates a rush of energy, which implies moving forward with renewed optimism and vigor, perhaps in consequence of some inspiration or in pursuit of a dream. This does not mean we should chase base desires or pursue just any chimera with unbridled passion. However, when considering a new endeavor, fear of failure or non-conformity may cause us to react with misgivings, apprehension, or anxiety. But if a deep, heartfelt examination reveals our dream to be in alignment with our spiritual purpose, we should pursue it fervently.

Similarly, this card suggests the ability to live in the moment with enthusiasm and vitality. We are not meant to trudge through life; we are here to live it fully, in joy and wonder, to engage in life with a sense of *joie de vivre*. In the 1989 film *Dead Poets Society* the lead character tells his students, "Carpe diem! Seize the day, boys. Make your lives extraordinary." This advice is relevant to all of us, no matter our age or circumstance.

So an exquisite piece of advice in this card is to think about something you can do to make your life extraordinary—wonderfully and beautifully your own—

even if in only some small way, and then go for it. Carpe diem!

<u>Importance of sacred passion</u>

"Love's journey would be terrifying if we didn't have passion to give us courage." — Deepak Chopra

When we fall in love, our passion gives us the courage to overcome our fears of, and defenses against letting someone else into our lives. We are emboldened to make a mad dash into the unknown. This opens up the wondrous experience of love, which is a preview of what our pursuit of a relationship with the Divine can be.

Following a spiritual path—pursuing an intimate, loving relationship with the Divine—can have the zealous character of falling in love when we do it on the level of passion and not just on the level of intellect (such as studying about spirituality), which is as far as some of us take it. Indeed, spirituality merely through study is like trying to fall in love by reading romance novels. Others travel a sacred path on the material level through, for example, charity or tithing to a church. This practice is valuable too, but you don't fall in love just by giving someone a dozen roses; you give them a dozen roses because you fell in love. Or we may equate spirituality with professing our love for the Divine, which also is an incomplete path. Study, charity, and devotion are, of course, essential parts of a spiritual journey, but passion is the spark that enlivens those other aspects.

Does all this mean we should not bother with reading spiritually inspired books, we shouldn't be generous and charitable, or we shouldn't profess or express our love of the Divine until we feel the passion? No, of course not. Any (and all) of those things can lead us toward sacred passion. What it does mean is that we should pray for that passion and then expect to feel it, for it is the flame that will propel our flight toward union with the Divine. So if you pray for nothing else in your life, at least pray for that. Say, for example, "I pray that a passion for union with the Divine, and for realization of my divine Self, be kindled within my heart." Try it! You may be surprised—and very pleasantly so—by the results.

<u>Finding Sacred Passion</u>

What else can we do if we still do not feel a passion for our spiritual progress, for union with the Divine? Doing charitable work, studying spiritual texts (which can be anything from the *Bhagavad Gita* to *A Course in Miracles*), or expressing devotion to the Divine through sacred chants—these are not substitutes for sacred passion, but they are useful vehicles to take us there. They can carry us toward a state of sacred passion if we realize that they are a means toward that end and not the passion itself. In other words, it is important not to mistake the vehicle for the destination.

Consider the truism that you don't act bravely because you are courageous; you are courageous because you act bravely. Things are never quite that simple, of course, but finding our passion for the Divine can be like that. It's a cyclical progression, a positive feedback loop. When we act as if we have sacred passion, we begin to manifest it, and as we discover more of it within our hearts, our actions will reflect our passion with increasing regularity and ease. The one feeds and supports the other.

It is also valuable to consider how the mundane, earthly passions that we have may be affecting our spiritual journey. We may want to ask ourselves questions like: What do I have a passion for? Does it control me? Where is it taking me? How well is moving in that direction serving me? The less we squander our energies on trivial, materialistic pursuits, the more power we will discover in our passion for spiritual ones.

However, we may discover that almost any passion can be transformed into a passion for the Divine. The key is to use it in a spiritual way and to turn over the results of our efforts to the Divine. If you have a passion for art, for example, use your art as your devotion to the Divine and as a way of expressing your divine Self.

At first it may be hard to understand how to do this, but reflect upon it and in time it will come to make sense, and it will begin to happen naturally. And if you do this with an honest and pure intent, the Universe will conspire to direct you and help you along this path.

Nine of Wands

This card is often about boundaries and defenses, and it says that the strength of our spirit is often achieved through the lessons of our wounds.

Everyone has their own wounds

"Be kind, for everyone you meet is fighting a hard battle." — Plato

It's easy to forget that we are not the only ones with battles to fight and wounds to heal; other people have problems too. They need our compassion when their heart and spirit are damaged, and they need our understanding when they act badly because of their problems. Plato's words were spoken over two thousand years ago, but they are just as true today as they were then. In specific situations, merely remembering that they, too, are "fighting a hard battle" can help us be patient and kind to someone else. In general, though, we can become more understanding and compassionate by learning from our own wounds.

The value of a wound

As noted in the section titled "Turn poison into medicine" (see the Temperance card), there is a Buddhist term, *hendoku-iyaku*, which means "to change poison into medicine." We usually see a wound as a problem, handicap, or a source of shame. However, at its core, a wound is frighteningly beautiful, and it has great value when faced courageously. It not only reveals our vulnerability but leads us to our strength as well. It connects us to other people with a bond that unites us, for we all are wounded in some way. The details may differ from person to person, but the essential truth crosses all boundaries. And so a wound is a badge honoring the exquisite uniqueness of our journey while also highlighting the universal nature of our soul.

Consider also this quote from Friedrich Nietzsche: "What does not kill us makes us stronger." This is only true, however, when we learn from our adversity. The value of a wound lies in what we learn from it. Some of us do become stronger and wiser as a result of our wounds, but others let their troubles make them cynical, distrustful, and quick to lash back at any perceived offense. The choice as to which course we follow is, of course, ours to make, and our decision is of vital importance for our spiritual journey.

Barriers against relationships

Relationship disasters—rejections, painful breakups, betrayals, etcetera—wound us and can result in us withdrawing behind a barrier that we hope will protect us from such pain in the future. These barricades don't indicate that we do not want a relationship. We do, or at least we tell ourselves that we do. Unfortunately, retreat isolates us, and in hiding behind a wall, we avoid intimacy, trust, and commitment, which are all prerequisites to a healthy relationship.

Although there are some rational cautions that we should take when entering into a relationship, many of our doubts, worries, and reservations come from a place of hurt-based fear and not from reasonable considerations. And yes, it is true that when we let down our defenses we can get hurt, but those defenses imprison us much more than they defend us. Even more than that, they keep us from growing, from learning important lessons about trust and commitment, forgiveness and love.

The true defense against being emotionally hurt is not to withdraw from love, but to fully engage in it while also loving yourself enough so that you are not dependent upon someone else's love and approval. Specific relationships may come and go, but your relationship with your true, essential Self—once you cultivate that—is eternal and beyond harm's reach.

So if someone breaks your heart, forgive them and move on with your life. Go and love again with an open heart. Discover loving relationships in your life and travel your path to the Divine through your discovery, experience, and creation of love.

Never give up

"There is no failure in the spiritual life, as long as we do not give up the struggle." — Swami Prabhavananda

There is a story that Thomas Edison failed more than 1,000 times (or 5,000 or 10,000 times depending on the version of the tale) when trying to find a suitable filament to make a commercially viable light bulb. When asked about his repeated failures, he allegedly said something to the effect of, "I have not failed 1,000 times. I have successfully discovered 1,000 ways to not make a light bulb. When I have eliminated the ways that will not work, I will find the one that will." Although this quote may be apocryphal, the lesson behind it is valid. Even if you try and fail, it does not mean that you won't learn something. It is only when you don't try at all that you don't learn anything.

Applying this to our spiritual quest, we must realize that when we make a mistake, when we let our hearts wander from our goal of divine union, we should not be discouraged. Instead, we should be like a baby that falls down when it is learning to walk. Always get back up and try again.

Ten of Wands

This card typically depicts a person trudging along, struggling under the weight of a heavy load. Hence it suggests our burdens in life.

Everyone carries their own burdens

Just as the Nine of Wands says that everyone is fighting a hard battle, the Ten of Wands says that it's important to realize that everyone is carrying their own burdens. When you get mad at someone because they aren't doing what you think they should or because they seem not to be doing things correctly, try to understand that they have their own problems and, as a result, their own reasons for doing what they do. This does not mean that you have to give everyone a free pass. It means that when you understand the load that someone else is carrying, you will come to a place of compassion for them, which will lighten your own load of anger and judgment.

So if, for example, someone cuts you off in traffic, consider that maybe they're harried because they're running late or perhaps they're distracted by their worries. Then shrug it off and let it go because you have enough of your own burdens, and adding anger to the list certainly won't lighten your load.

The burden of success

This card sometimes indicates the "burdens of success," which is a phrase that people often find puzzling. "Success isn't a burden," they think, "It's a blessing." But it can be a burden for a variety of reasons including heightened expectations about future performance, the increased scrutiny of the limelight, and diminished freedom of expression when you are expected to create something that is like your last effort.

From a spiritual perspective, a great burden of material success is that it reinforces our erroneous belief that our accomplishments in the physical realm are important and truly valuable. Success can also burden us with a fear of losing whatever it was that we may have gained. We then hold on tight to that boon, and that becomes an effort that saps our energy, binds us to the material world, and blinds us to new possibilities and new adventures. It's like the fable about a monkey who stuck his hand into a jar of figs. He grasped all he could, but then was unable to extract his hand from the jar through its narrow neck. He refused to let go of his prize, but at the same time was distraught about the fact that his hand was now stuck in the jar. And so it is with us. When we grasp as much material success as we can, it traps us.

This is not to say that success in the material world is bad. However, it is much easier for those who have nothing to lose to begin a spiritual journey than for those who have attained worldly success. (Remember the biblical admonition: "It is easier for a camel to go through the eye of a needle than for a rich man to enter the kingdom of God.") Also, the greater our achievements, the harder it is to see beyond them, for they can take on a life and importance of their own. They grow large in our eyes and block our view of what is truly important.

The ego's sense of burden

One way to view the sequence of the numbered cards in the Minor Arcana is to see the Aces as beginnings and the tens as the results of those beginnings. We can use this concept to find a spiritual message for the Ten of Wands.

A dark side of the Ace of Wands is egotism and megalomania. It can indicate those times when we think we are the center of the Universe instead of realizing that we are a vital part of its oneness. An unfortunate result of this is that we come to believe that we, as individuals living in material form, have the power or the responsibility to create the circumstances of our lives, as well as those of other people around us. Beginning from this egotistical perspective, we end up with an oppressive sense of burden, which the ego loves in that it can now say, "Poor me. See how burdened I am."

The irony here is that as spiritual beings connected to the oneness of the Divine, which is a positive interpretation of the Ace in this suit, we *do* have the power to create our lives. In fact, we are doing this constantly whether we know it or not. So we can carry the load as seen in the Ten of Wands when we realize that we are not carrying it alone; we are supported by the Universe.

Ultimately, the difference lies in our perspective. If we see ourselves as alone and separate (i.e., if we take the ego's perspective), then creating our lives can be an onerous burden. But if we see ourselves as being a part of the Divine, then we, as conduits of the power of the Universe, can carry a great load and do great things in joy instead of in sorrow. In other words, the difference lies in the power of our separate physical being versus that of our shared, immortal Self.

A blessing or a burden?

Do you view your journey along your spiritual path as a blessing or as a burden? We may start out thinking of it as a burden, a heavy task to undertake grudgingly, but with time, practice, and experience we will discover the wisdom that it is a blessing. However, from time to time it may still seem to be a heavy load. At such times, don't beat yourself up about not being spiritual enough, not loving enough, or not being generous or forgiving enough. If you see your spiritual journey as an onerous task, you'll soon want to set down the load. Instead, do what you can and you will find joy in it. That's really what it is about.

Being "should upon"

When life seems too arduous and our load too heavy to bear, it helps to consider that perhaps we have taken on too many obligations. Maybe we have allowed ourselves to be burdened by things that other people feel we should do. When we realize that we have let ourselves be "should upon," it is time to reexamine what we want to do in life. Perhaps the countless mundane things we think we "should" do are weighing us down and blinding us to the only thing we truly should do, which is to remember the reality of our divine Self.

A feeling of being weighed down and trudging through life may be our deep, unconscious realization that we are not doing the important work of seeing the Divine in everything around us and in everything we do. If we can see that, we will release our sense of being burdened so that we may travel our path in ease.

I must point out that this does not mean that we should neglect or walk away from our true responsibilities to other people. Instead, this message includes a call to reevaluate what is important and to reassess what we can do to shoulder our responsibilities. For example, if you have children, can you walk away from the responsibility of taking care of them? No, of course not. However, that certainly does not mean that you have to work long hours to give them a wealth of material gifts. Giving them your presence and being involved in their lives can be a spiritual practice in itself, one that can renew your soul as much as it enriches their lives.

Page of Wands

The Page of Wands represents youthful energy, such as playfulness, eagerness, and enthusiasm. It also implies the trust of a child and the loyalty of a pet. Indeed, this card says that there is much we can learn about authentic living from our children and our pets.

Play and have fun

"You don't stop playing because you get old; you get old because you stop playing." — Unknown

Recently while on a walk, I passed a park where a group of children were playing with an abundance of enthusiasm and joyfulness. Kids do that so well, but we adults seem to have lost that capacity, which is sad. If only we could keep living like that, i.e., with joy and enthusiasm. As Balzac said, "We are here to live out loud," but we usually don't. How can we recapture that youthful joy?

The sense of playfulness in the Page of Wands can indicate the thrill and excitement of learning and playing a game. I have found that when I play a game, I can get quite absorbed in it and lose myself in it. When I do that with a sense of excitement and enjoyment, but without a feeling of attachment to the results, I am happy when I win, and when I lose, that's okay too; it doesn't make me sad or dejected.

This is a wonderful model for relating to life in an egoless way. It suggests that we try to treat our life experiences with a sense of play and delight. It also says that we should engage in that play completely and with a sense of joy, but not with a sense of attachment to the outcome. That's how we can learn to be "in the world, but not of the world."

It is also significant that every enlightened person I have ever seen has exhibited that playful air of a child. Such people are not as bland, serious, or dour as we think they would be. They have the playful air of a child. This is not to say that we become enlightened merely by playing (although it can help), but that playfulness is a part of enlightenment, a symptom or result of it.

So this card urges you to go out into the world and be playful. Give yourself permission to be a kid again once in a while. The next time you are involved in something—anything, really—recall how you feel when you are playing a game that you enjoy and try to get into that same sort of "space."

Reconnect with enthusiasm

"The worst bankrupt in the world is the person who has lost his enthusiasm."
— *H. W. Arnold*

The following traits, which are characteristic of the Youth of Wands, are important features of a spiritual journey, especially when one is just beginning.

Enthusiasm: A sense of wonder is like a spark that ignites a candle to light the way.

Trust: Especially in the beginning, we need to trust that this is the right path. Then as we gain experience, our trust will be validated and turn into belief.

Loyalty: This is where many of us fail; we stop practicing. In the beginning, it helps to make a commitment to continue our spiritual journey faithfully for a given amount of time, even in those times when our enthusiasm wanes and our trust is challenged.

These traits are usually easy to manifest at the start of the journey when everything is new and exciting, but later on we may lose them. When that happens, it's important to reconnect with our inner Page of Wands and rediscover these characteristics in our spiritual pursuits.

One way to do this is to remember what it was about this path that attracted us in the first place. Another is to hook up with other people who are traveling along a spiritual path. Or you can mix up your practice a bit and do something new and different. This will put you back into "beginner's mind." For example, if you have been meditating using attention to your breath, you may want to try a meditation technique that uses a mantra instead or try a "walking meditation."[35] However you do it, you will find your journey along a spiritual path to be facilitated by reconnecting with your enthusiasm, recommitting to your trust, and remaining faithful to your practice.

Knight of Wands

This knight rides his passions. He can be dynamic but restive, he can be enthusiastic but reckless, and he can be like a wildfire that burns brightly but that

---

[35] *For more about walking meditation, see* Peace Is Every Step *By Thich Nhat Hanh*

also burns out quickly.

Riding your passion

"We're so engaged in doing things to achieve purposes of outer value that we forget that the inner value—the rapture that is associated with being alive—is what it is all about." — *Joseph Campbell*

When we are adolescents and young adults, our passion for life is directed toward the future and we are in a rush to become something other than what we are right now. We can't wait to finish school. We can't wait to get a good job. We can't wait to fall in love. And so on, and so on, as we ride our passions forever looking forward. But when we finish school, we may miss our classmates, and when we get a good job, it may consume so much of our time and energy that we are never able to relax. When we fall in love, we might get hurt, or we may take our relationship for granted and let it grow stale. In short, to quote Neil Gaiman, "The price of getting what you want is getting what you once wanted." As a result, we may turn our passion toward the future again.

As we get older, however, our energy and optimism wane, our plans may fade and crumble. All too soon, the time left to us seems limited, fleeting, and diminished in its possibilities. So we begin to look back at our lost youth with the longing with which we used to look toward the future. But this desire will never be fulfilled—we can't go back—and that brings sadness and regret.

We may wonder what happened. Were we wrong to ride our passions? No, not at all. The problem was not that we acted with passion, it was that we didn't realize that it was the ride itself that was important, not the destination. We must learn to ride a passion for what is, not what might be or what once was.

Fortunately, it is not too late to enjoy the ride we are on right now. This applies to our life in its every detail. For example, whenever we say, "I can't wait until ..." we are deferring our happiness instead of experiencing the joy of our life right now. To quote Eckhart Tolle: "It is not uncommon for people to spend their whole life waiting to start living." So ride passionately toward the future, but always enjoy the ride as it exists in this perfect moment of *now*.

Smell the flowers along the way

"You're only here for a short visit. Don't hurry, don't worry. And be sure to smell the flowers along the way." — Walter Hagen

Doesn't it seem like we're always in a hurry? We live our lives in fits and starts, rushing to complete something, hurrying to get somewhere. Then when we get there (wherever "there" may be) we may stop, relax, and enjoy the moment briefly, but then we dash off again to somewhere else.

So when are we actually enjoying life? It's hard enough to live in the moment, but our hectic, fast-paced modern world makes it even harder. Much of the time we are focused on getting to our next experience, and we are only living authentically (i.e., living with conscious attention on our lives) on rare and brief occasions.

It is not as if some moments are valuable and others are just preparation time whose only value is being a bridge to somewhere else. Every moment of life is a precious one, even the ones we hate, such as time spent stuck in traffic running late for an appointment. But it is impossible to stop and smell the flowers when we don't even see them, especially when we are zooming past them at 60 miles per hour. But we can learn to pay attention to where we are and what is going on around us—flowers or no flowers—even when we are rushing along from here to there.

The next time you're running late (which is one of the hardest times to live in the moment) take a few deep breaths to relax yourself. Then, without any judgment, focus your attention on where you are and what is happening. Pay attention to your breath and if any worrying thoughts intrude, just notice them, dismiss them, and return to your breath. Worrying about getting there on time will not get you there any faster, and getting stressed will not make your life any better.

Doing is believing

There is a saying that "seeing is believing," but the Knight of Wands says that "doing is believing." This means that it is in acting upon your beliefs that you "prove" them to yourself and (more importantly) that you make those beliefs real and concrete in your life. In short, it is when you invest active energy in your beliefs that they become manifest.

Queen of Wands

The Queen of Wands has a happy, sunny disposition. She is characterized by her strength, enthusiasm, cheerfulness, and optimism, as well as by her self-confidence and self-control.

The sacred practice of service

"The best way to cheer yourself up is to try to cheer somebody else up." — *Mark Twain*

The Queen of Wands offers advice and encouragement regarding the sacred practice of service, which is an important part of our spiritual path. Service does not merely involve material aspects such as charity. It can also indicate the other elemental aspects of mind, heart, and energy—the latter aspect being most relevant to this queen's expertise.

The Tarot's queens personify the feminine aspects of wisdom, which includes understanding other people and being supportive of them. When we couple that with the energy and creativity that is characteristic of the suit of Wands, we see the advice to recognize, inspire, and support the creative spark in other people's lives. This card urges us to find opportunities to encourage and motivate other people to do the best they can in any situation. This can be anything from helping your child do well on a test to motivating a coworker to do a great presentation at work to supporting a friend's effort to start a new hobby. In short, the Queen of Wands urges us to realize that we are a conduit for the energy of life (rather than the source of it), and our strength, enthusiasm, and optimism are enhanced, not diminished, when shared with others.

Be a kinder person; make a kinder world

The Queen of Wands indicates the attributes of being open and warm, giving and supportive, cheerful and gregarious. But more than just advocating that we cultivate these traits for our own sake, this card says that we can create a better world by manifesting them and thereby being an inspiration to others. It is through example rather than either advice or rebuke that we transform the world. As Gandhi said, "Be the change you want to see in the world." And so we can make the world a kinder place by being kinder to other people; we can make it a more cheerful place by smiling at the people we encounter every day.

Criticism and self-improvement

"Each of you is perfect the way you are ... and *you can use a little improvement." — Shunryu Suzuki*

This queen exhibits self-confidence and self-control, which are among the greatest assets we can have, and these qualities may be tested the most when someone criticizes us. Criticism hurts when we lack self-confidence, and we react badly to it if we lack self-control. However, we do have a choice as to how we respond to it.

Most of us let our egos take control at such times, which causes us to become offended, defensive, or aggressive. Such responses are of the ego, not of the soul, and they will further our suffering, not relieve it. On the other hand, we can evaluate the validity of the criticism and choose to learn from it if there is truth to it. Then we can move on. This is the serene reaction to criticism that comes from our Higher Self.

At a deep level, all criticism is the Divine helping us to realize our true, eternal Self. It is a call to return to a state of divine union. Of course, it does not seem like that at the time, but it is through our constant inner work that we can achieve this realization of our true Self. This does not mean that another person's analysis of our shortcomings is always spot on—in fact, it may be totally off the mark—but if we get a visceral reaction to it, something inside needs attention and correction. Perhaps, at the very least, the issue may be that we need to stop basing our sense of self-worth on the opinions of others.

So try to use whatever criticism is leveled against you as a means of self improvement, not as an excuse to get mad or hurt. If someone criticizes you, take a moment to carefully examine what that person said. See if there is some truth to it. (Although it's true that at the level of our soul we are all perfect, at the level of our earthly incarnation we all can use a little improvement.) If there is a bit of truth, commit to doing something to correct the problem. If not, just shrug and let it go. Learn to overcome your sensitivity to the opinions of others.

King of Wands

The King of Wands is a leader who exemplifies the qualities of charisma, courage, and strength of character. Also, he has achieved maturity and mastery with regards to his desires, passions, and ambitions.

<u>Choosing a leader</u>

"The goal of many leaders is to get people to think more highly of the leader. The goal of a great leader is to help people to think more highly of themselves." — J. Carla Nortcutt

There are many self-proclaimed spiritual leaders vying for our attention (and our resources) and seeking to lead us. Many have great charm and strength of character, but does that mean they have spiritual awareness? We should not mistake charisma for spiritual enlightenment or we may end up following a magnetic leader whose spiritual message is not valid. To evaluate a spiritual leader, we must also evaluate his or her message. Is it based on universal love? Does it place the spiritual above the material? Is it of the ego, or is it of the divine Self? And, above all, does it call forth our own divinity?

<u>Captains of our own spiritual journey</u>

This King urges us to realize that we are the masters of our own destiny and the captains of our spiritual journey, and being the masters of our own fate empowers us to create a life of joy and fulfillment. To realize this mastery, however, we must first believe that our lives have purpose and that our work has meaning. So take time to consider what your purpose in life truly is. Then, as you begin to have a clear vision of that purpose and follow it faithfully, you will find that your life does have meaning. This will make a difference in everything you do and everything you experience. And through this, you will make a difference in the world.

<u>Lead the world</u>

"Do not go where the path may lead, go instead where there is no path and leave a trail." — Ralph Waldo Emerson

I associate the King of Wands with leadership, so to understand this card's spiritual message we might first consider what leadership is.

Leadership encompasses the qualities of courage, self-confidence, strength of character, a sense of purpose and destiny, clarity of vision, firmness of conviction, a desire to make a difference in the world, and dedication to a cause. Of course, all of those qualities would be for naught if a leader doesn't also take action based on them. But what does all that have to do with us "ordinary people"?

As noted previously, this card tells us that we are all the captains of our own spiritual journey. In addition, though, we all may be leaders in the world to some degree. As Mahatma Gandhi said, "What good you do may be of little significance, but it is very important that you do it." And as Mother Teresa said, "We ourselves feel that what we are doing is just a drop in the ocean. But the ocean would be less without that drop."

Also, where our leadership is taking us is of paramount importance, so it is essential that we also consider this quote from Martin Luther King, Jr.:

> *Life's most persistent and urgent question is: "What are you doing for others?"*

So consider that question, and then find or develop within yourself the qualities of leadership noted above so that you may take action on your answer, no matter how small that action may seem.

What is the Ego?

Recently a conversation about the question, "What is the ego?" came up on an online discussion group. As a result of thinking about that issue, I arrived at the following analogy to explain the ego, and it reminded me of the King of Wands. In this analogy, the Dark Side of the King of Wands represents our ego, and the Light Side represents the rightful ruler of our lives, i.e., our divine Self. With that in mind, then, I explored the role of the ego and why it can be such a problem.

The ego is a valuable tool when we are children as it functions to ensure our early survival. Unfortunately, that tool—that servant, actually—usurps the throne of our mind. It is like old folk tales about a selfish regent who takes control of a kingdom and refuses to relinquish authority to the young king when he reaches the age of maturity.

A king, in the ideal form of the archetype, rules for the sake of all the people in the realm, and thus symbolizes our Higher Self, which recognizes our oneness with everyone and which embodies our selfless desire to relieve the suffering of others. The selfish regent, on the other hand, symbolizes the ego which has taken ownership of the kingdom (i.e., our lives) for itself, and jealously guards that control. It thinks that it is separate from everyone else, and it acts only for its own benefit. Alas, then, for the unlucky kingdom, which suffers dearly as a consequence. Alas, too, for our lives.

However, when we understand that our ego is not the true ruler, that it has illicitly usurped control, and when we realize that the true monarch of our lives is our divine Self, then we can begin the task of returning the true king to the throne.

Maturity of Conduct

Among its many meanings, the King of Wands can indicate "maturity of conduct" since the Tarot's Kings suggest maturity and the suit of Wands encompasses the concept of action. One place where we sorely need more maturity of conduct in the world is in the arena of our disagreements, which all too often degenerate into angry insults and reckless accusations. As an extreme example, consider Internet discussions such as online chat groups and the comments section of news items. Such Internet discussions may be an extreme example, but a consideration of them can be illuminating.

I have noticed how easily rudeness infects such venues, perhaps because people feel insulated by online anonymity. Does this online discourtesy indicate that the reason we treat people with (relative) respect in face-to-face interactions is because we can't get away with being ruder? Or maybe the problem is that we more easily forget the humanity of the person we are talking to if we cannot see them.

Perhaps a penchant for rude conduct is symptomatic of a deep malaise that we all need to address. The best therapy for this that I've ever heard is the following saying attributed to the Fifteenth Century mystic poet Kabir:

Do what you do with another human being, but never put them out of your heart.

No matter the situation, when we treat anyone with disrespect and a lack of regard for their humanity, we are, by extension, treating everyone (ourselves included) that way too due to our shared humanity. So if we keep in mind Kabir's beautiful piece of advice it can lead us to treat others with kindness, respect, and consideration, even if they disagree with us or oppose us. And when we act with this maturity of conduct, we will lead others to act that way also. Some may follow quickly and some may not, but that is their concern, not ours.

CUPS

This suit is about love and compassion, and also relationships—both personal and sacred. Being the suit of emotion, it can refer to guidance from your heart and it may be associated with the path of spiritual devotion called *Bhakti Yoga*.

Ace of Cups

"While infused with love you see fewer distinctions between you and others. Indeed, your ability to see others—really see them, wholeheartedly—springs open." — Barbara Fredrickson

A common image on the Ace of Cups is that of a divine hand offering a cup, which indicates that love is a precious gift from the Divine as well as an essential part of a spiritual path. This card also indicates self-love, new love, universal love, purity of heart, and loving relationships.

See love first

"I have found that if you love life, life will love you back." — Arthur Rubinstein

An ace is the first card in its suit, and the suit of Cups is about love, so one message of the Ace of Cups is to see love first. Before you see flaws, weaknesses, or vice; before you see differences, disparity, or separation; and before you see invective, abuse, or insults; before any of that, see love first. Love everyone, and whether they are in your presence or merely in your thoughts, see their good first and foremost, for that is what's real. All else is illusion, either their illusion of separation or yours.

Many people resist this message, insisting that we have to face the evil in others. The problem with that argument is that it misunderstands this message. It does not mean that we should ignore the problems in the actions of others. It merely says that we should always see love first and realize that the darkness and negativity in other people is either a matter of our illusions about them or a manifestation of their illusions about themselves and the world. With this perspective, we can act from a place of love instead of from a place of fear. Again, keep in mind the Kabir quote mentioned previously in the King of Wands section titled "Maturity of Conduct": "Do what you do with another human being, but never put them out of your heart."

The healing power of love

We all know that love makes us feel good, but we probably don't realize how much more it does for us. When we experience love, our bodies produce hormones that have healthful benefits. In fact, studies at the *Institute of HeartMath*[36] have shown that merely focusing our attention on a loving memory and its associated positive feelings a few times a day promotes good health. So if you are not currently in a situation that evokes feelings of love, you can at least spend a few moments now and then with memories of loving experiences. You will feel better for it.

Discover love; create love

"The purpose of life is to increase the warm heart." — *The 14th Dalai Lama*

There was a time in my life when I thought that our reason for being here on Earth was to discover how to love, but I have since modified that belief. I now believe that we are also here to *create* love in the manifest world. Of course the two (learning to love and creating love) are not all that different; we do both at the same time. In either case, the Ace of Cups suggests that we ask ourselves each day, "Is there one thing I can do today to create a little more love in the world? Or at least, is there something I can do to help myself discover a bit more about how to love?"

To find, experience, and create love in our lives, it is important to understand what love is and is not. A common mistake is to conflate love and lust, but a strong sexual attraction is not the same thing as love, and neither is a need for someone else. In a broad sense, love is the feeling associated with our realization of our divine connection and oneness with all humankind—with the whole world, in fact. At a more specific level, when we truly love someone, we consider the other person to be an integral part of our life and we see things from their perspective as well as from our own. We place that person's needs on a par with our own and thereby find a healthy balance that nourishes and supports both of us.

---

[36] *www.heartmath.org*

Sometimes it is hard to allow the other person to grow in whatever ways they need to, though, especially when that entails changes we don't understand, but that is an essential part of love, too. It is even more difficult to accept that love sometimes means letting go of a relationship when the other person needs to leave and (harder still) wishing them well. However, if we cannot do that, our love must have been conditional on the other person serving our needs. But love is only authentic to the extent that it is not subordinate to our selfish desires, and selfless compassion is the authentic love we are here to create and experience.

Cultivate universal love

In *The Brothers Karamazov*, Dostoyevsky said, "What is hell? I maintain that it is the suffering of being unable to love." I would add the following: "And what is heaven? It is the bliss of loving everyone."

According to most religious traditions, one of the primary elements of right living is universal love. This is not about the preferential feeling of attachment we have for one specific person. Universal love comes from the realization of our oneness with everything. It is the purity of heart that sees beyond distinctions between people. It is of oneness and unity, not divisions and separation.

It is hard for us to rediscover our sense of union when we are living in a culture that exalts an illusory sense of separation, but there are many ways to cultivate unconditional love and to practice this purity of heart. For example, try the following exercise for one day to see how it feels and how it affects your life.

Every time you encounter someone—whether it's a loved one, a friend, a casual acquaintance, a stranger, or even an enemy—silently say to that person, "I love you." This thought of love will probably be easy if the other person is a member of your family, it may feel a bit awkward when the other person is a stranger, and it can be very hard to do when the other person is an adversary of some sort. However, the amount of benefit this will bring into your life and into the world is highest in that final case. Also do this whenever you even think about someone else. For example, this may be someone you hear about in the news or someone from your past who comes to mind for any reason. Try to make "I love you" your first thought about other people, and as you do this, you will find your life drawn toward the light of unconditional love, which is the essence of your innate, divine nature.

You can only pour water into an empty cup

"Grace fills empty spaces, but it can only enter where there is a void to receive it." — Simone Weil

There is a well-known (although probably apocryphal) story about a scholar who went to see a Zen master. The scholar was very excited to meet this holy man, so when he sat down across from him, he began to speak excitedly, expounding on his ideas about Zen. The master nodded quietly and began to pour his guest a cup of tea. But when the cup was full, he continued to pour, and the tea spilled over onto the table and splashed onto the ground. The scholar cried out in alarm, "Stop! There is no more room in the cup." The Zen master then spoke. "You are like this tea cup," he said. "You are so full that there is no room for anything I can tell you."

This story is commonly thought to mean that if we think we know everything, we are not able to learn more. However, I see other nuances in it as well. It says that if we fill our minds and hearts with too many trivial and mundane concerns, there is no room for the Divine to pour purpose and bliss into our lives. Moreover, this tale is relevant to the way that many of us undertake a quest for love and romance.

Many people try so very hard to find love, not realizing that typically, love finds you instead, often when you are not looking for it. But when the Divine brings love into your life, is your heart ready to receive it? The trick is to keep your heart open like an empty cup. A heart that is full of other emotions such as fear, desperation, or resentment about past relationships, has no room when the Divine tries to pour love into it. But if you work to empty your heart of expectations and negative emotions, it will become an empty vessel that can receive love when it arrives.

How to cleanse a troubled heart

I once read another wonderful cup metaphor in a book called *The Sermon on the Mount According to Vedanta* by Swami Prabhavananda. Briefly, it uses an analogy of a bottle that is stuck to a table and full of filthy water. Since the bottle is stuck to the table, you can't pick it up to clean it out, but you can pour clear water into it so that the dirty water spills out. If you continue pouring in clear water, the bottle will eventually become clean and filled with clear water instead of filth.

This analogy explains how repeating a mantra, such as a name of God, or saying a prayer to God, can work to purify a troubled heart. Similarly, in *A Return to Love*, Marianne Williamson suggests that when we are faced with difficulties in a relationship, we can find a peaceful resolution by repeating a phrase such as, "I surrender this relationship to the Holy Spirit" whenever anxious or angry thoughts about the relationship arise. In this way we can purify our troubled hearts by allowing divine love to pour into them continually.

Two of Cups

"Without love, we are birds with broken wings." — *Morrie Schwartz*[37]

This card deals with romantic attraction and relationships, choices about relationships, and the healing power of love.

Choose love every day

The Tarot's Two cards are about decisions and choices. Since the suit of Cups is about our emotions and relationships, one insight the Two of Cups reveals is that love is a choice. Of course, we don't choose with whom to fall in love, but we do make choices about love—whether romantic, platonic, or universal—every day. As a result, this message is relevant in all our relationships. To love or not is a decision we face continually in all areas of our life, so consider the following questions regarding your interactions with other people:

Am I seeing this person through the eyes of love?
Am I treating this person with love?
Am I acting from a place of love?

With these questions in mind, you can begin to choose love in all aspects of your life.

---

[37] *This quote is from the book* Tuesdays with Morrie *by Mitch Albom*

Love: a verb and a feeling

"They do not love that do not show their love." — *William Shakespeare* (Two Gentlemen of Verona)

There are times in any romantic relationship when we just don't feel the love. At such times, it is important to remember the difference between love, the feeling, and love, the verb. In other words, having loving feelings about someone is not always the same as acting in a loving manner toward that person.

We think that we act lovingly toward someone because we feel love for them, but it is at least as true that the feeling of love results from our acts of love. It's a dance of sorts. Our feelings of love impel us to act lovingly, and our loving actions nurture our feelings of love. The important difference is that we cannot always control how we feel, but we *can* choose how we act toward another person. Consequently, at those times when we are not feeling the love, it is vital to the health of the relationship (and to our own wellbeing) to act lovingly—to practice love (the verb) in order to rediscover and rekindle love (the feeling).

This message also operates at a higher level since our interpersonal relationships serve as a metaphor and a model for our relationship with the Divine. Thus, again, it is precisely when we are not feeling love for all humankind or for the Divine, that acts of loving kindness are of vital importance.

Love is a communicable disease

"Love is essentially self-communicative. Those who do not have it catch it from those who have it." — *Ram Dass*

The Two of Cups offers the whimsical insight that love is contagious. One implication of this is that we should never give up on loving other people even if it sometimes seems like it isn't affecting them. Like a true disease, love's path and rate of contagion are variable, unpredictable, and difficult to chart. Also, some people seem to be more resistant to infection than others. However, no one is totally immune.

We should, however, recognize the difference between authentic love and its faint echoes and parodies, such as desire, jealousy, and lust. Those feelings may masquerade as love, but being counterfeit, they are powerless to infect others with true love. It's important, then, to be able to tell the difference between love and its false imitators. Although authentic love is ineffable, we may point toward it with several descriptions.

In *1 Corinthians 13:4-8*, the Bible says that love is patient and kind, persistent and hopeful, optimistic and enduring. This passage also lists things that love is *not* so that we may recognize its imposters. It is not jealous, proud, rude, demanding, irritable, unforgiving, spiteful, judgmental, or unfair.

In addition, true love is selfless and looks for nothing in return. It cares about the well being of others and is willing to sacrifice for them. It seeks to understand and is always ready to forgive. The saying, "Love is blind," may be a cliché, but it has some truth that is instructive, for authentic love is blind to superficial things such as wealth, appearance, and social status. It does, however, see the profound, essential beauty in the heart and soul of another person. In other words, love is unconditional and nonjudgmental, as illustrated in the following quote.

> *"When you love someone, you love the whole person, just as he or she is, and not as you would like them to be."* — *Leo Tolstoy*

So this card suggests that we should consider our feelings about and actions toward the people we love. Our hearts may not be perfect, but as we evaluate our capacity for love, we will discover ways to guide it toward authenticity. Then, with an improved realization of what true love is, we can go out into the world and spread a purer love. Perhaps we will start an epidemic.

Believe you are lovable and divine

> *"If your compassion does not include yourself, it is incomplete."* — *Buddha*

In his book *The Path to Love*, Deepak Chopra suggests that a way to bring romance into your live is to first learn to see yourself as being loveable. Traveling a spiritual path brings this enlightened self-realization, so if you want to manifest romantic love in your life, work on cultivating a belief in your intrinsic, loving unity with the Divine. However, it is also true that romantic love can aid us on our quest for reunion with the Divine. Taken together, these two statements seem to present a "chicken or the egg" causality dilemma, but experiencing romantic love and seeking divine union facilitate each other, and we don't have to accomplish one before we can work on the other. We can strive for both at the same time, and our progress with one will help us realize the other.

As Deepak Chopra tells us, our spiritual progress aids in our pursuit of romantic love, but how does it work the other way around? To understand this, first consider the following quote:

"Human affection ... becomes spiritualized when it is given unselfishly, without possessiveness or bargaining for return." — *Swami Prabhavananda*

Refining our love for another person so that it becomes increasingly selfless is an important factor in our spiritual transformation. Learning to put another person's needs ahead of our own is a learning experience that can be both preparation and training for the spiritual practice of selfless love of all humanity. Also, in a truly loving relationship we come to see the two (the self and the beloved) as one, and through this we have the best chance of seeing the Divine in the heart of another person.

So if you are in a romantic relationship, consider how it may be a path to realizing divine union. If you are not in a relationship, work directly on your relationship with the Divine for now.

Icons of devotion

"We must begin with a specific relationship with God; later we come to the understanding that He is all in all." — *Swami Prabhavananda*

The Two of Cups typically shows two people who seem to be initiating a close, intimate relationship. This may also be seen as a metaphor for our relationship with the Divine, although there is an obvious essential difference in that the Divine is indefinable and both omnipresent and intangible. So how can we experience a relationship with something that is both everything and nothing? The answer is that we can begin with an approximation, an incomplete and imperfect representation of the formless Divine. While it is true that this is inescapably a limiting concept of what is ineffable, infinite, and all-pervading, it serves a valuable purpose. Our human need to perceive and relate to tangible forms means that it is much easier to focus on and connect with the Divine as represented by a form.

Many religious traditions offer specific images of the Divine, such as a crucifix, a statue of Vishnu, or a painting of Guanyin[38] in order to facilitate worship. Even though any such representation is limiting, religions realize that at the beginning of our journey toward divine union, conceptualizing divinity in concrete, human terms can facilitate our meditation upon, devotion to, and

---

[38] *Guanyin is the Bodhisattva of Compassion and Mercy.*

relationship with the Divine. So we may use such a representation as a point of devotional and meditational focus in order to foster our love of and passion for the Divine. However, we should not forget that any such image, icon, or idol is merely a surrogate, a symbol of that which is beyond any representation.

Healing a relationship through love

The Two of Cups says that we can heal a relationship (whether it be platonic or romantic) through the power of love, and what follows is an exercise that can help you effect such a healing by bringing another person into your heart.

The first step involves sending healing energy to the other person. Everyone has unresolved issues, unacknowledged fears, and unhealed wounds that cause them to act badly at times. If we can heal those wounds, the behavior will improve. We aren't responsible for the healing of another person, of course, but we can send them healing thoughts which may be anything from a prayer to a visualization. Use whatever method works best for you. If you know what the other person's wounds are, be specific as you send out those healing thoughts. Otherwise, you may pray something like this: "I don't know what your wounds are, but I am sending you positive energy so that they may be healed and you may find peace and joy in your life." Similarly, it is also helpful to send healing thoughts to yourself, since your wounds may have contributed to the problems in your relationship too.

The next step is to send the other person your love. Silently repeat "I love you," or words to that effect, even though it may be hard to do that at first if your relationship is badly wounded. You might resist doing this because you think that the other person doesn't deserve your love, but that is an irrelevant consideration and, in fact, a meaningless one. *You* deserve to manifest your true loving Self. In addition, it is therapeutic to realize that everyone deserves love because we are all One and, at our core, a part of the Divine. Indeed, withholding love from others withholds it from yourself. So no matter how hard it may be to do this at first, keep at it. The more you do it, the easier it becomes.

An important result of this exercise is a shift in consciousness. With this shift, you will change and so will your relationship with the other person. Often the way the other person acts toward you will change too, but regardless of how much or how little they change, your suffering within the relationship will dissolve as you transform your thoughts and feelings about it.

<u>Soul mates</u>[39]

"When will I meet my soul mate?" This is a question most Tarot readers have encountered, perhaps rather often. However, what is truly important is our ability to create a soulful connection, for I believe that soul mates are forged in the crucible of our daily lives, not assigned in the heavens. So instead of hoping for Mr. or Ms. Right to come along, we should focus our attention on becoming the best person we can be, i.e., on realizing our divine Self. This is how we can manifest our ability to create, nurture, and sustain a healthy and successful romantic relationship. As Ken Keyes, Jr. says in his book *Handbook to Higher Consciousness*, "It is more important to *be* the right person than to *find* the right person." And as we become "the right person," we also develop the ability to look into the eyes of another person and feel the truth of Rumi's words of almost eight centuries ago: "I always thought that I was me, but no, I was you and never knew it."

Three of Cups

This card is about friendship and all that it entails. It indicates the value of our platonic relationships and how they both support and challenge us.

<u>Friendship advice</u>

As the "friendship card," the Three of Cups calls to mind a wonderful line from the 1946 movie, *It's a Wonderful Life*: "No man is a failure who has friends." (This refers to authentic friendships rather than casual acquaintances, "fair weather" friends, or your 693 Facebook friends.) It also suggests an Erma Bombeck quote, which contains a wonderful bit of advice: "If I had my life to live over I would have invited friends over to dinner even if the carpet was stained and the sofa faded." And it urges us to remember the old maxim, "A friend in need is a friend indeed." The obvious implication of this quote is that we should help a friend who needs assistance, but it goes much deeper than that. It offers the following advice for making deep, meaningful friendships.

Listen with your complete attention when a friend needs to talk.

---

[39] *Recognizing that there is honest disagreement on the topic of soul mates, I offer these thoughts as reflecting my beliefs while also respecting opposing points of view on the subject.*

Give advice when asked, but only then.

Share your friends' sorrows as well as their joys.

Believe in your friends and see the best in them when they have lost faith in themselves.

Accept your friends when it would be easier to judge them; forgive them when it would be easier to hold a grudge.

With practice, we can develop these caring skills and eventually be able to treat everyone this way, for friendships are a wonderful proving ground for our sacred work of developing an open, caring heart. So enjoy your friendships and celebrate them, for they are a bridge to universal love and compassion.

Quality time with friends

"We find rest in those we love, and we provide a resting place for those who love us." — Bernard of Clairvaux

We do things with friends like going to a party or out to dinner, but perhaps the best times spent with friends are quiet moments together, times when our souls are united in joy even if outwardly we are not doing anything special. Those may be the most special times of all, for they demonstrate the beauty of Spirit, which surpasses that of material and sensual pursuits. So this card suggests making plans to spend quality time with a friend. It's good for your soul, and it's good for theirs too.

The influence of friendships

"You are the average of the five people you spend the most time with." — Jim Rohn

Did your mother ever tell you that you couldn't be friends with someone she considered to be a "bad influence"? Or maybe she encouraged you to play with a child who she felt was a "good influence"? Even as adults, our friendships influence us and help shape who we are.

Traveling a spiritual path, we begin to find that some friends are not on the same wavelength as we are. As a consequence, we may find those personal connections diminishing as we come to have less in common with those people. This should not be seen as a judgment of them since everyone travels their own path in their own time and in their own way. The challenge, then, is to reevaluate old friendships and to find new ones that resonate with our path in life for the truth is that we travel our spiritual path (or not) with our friends.

Friends and enemies

Sometimes, in a seeming contradiction, a so-called enemy can be your truest friend, for he or she may tell you things your friends won't tell you. Our friends tend to sympathize with us, which is good up to a point. The problem is that they also tend to agree with us when we are upset, which validates and reinforces our conceits of being in the right and our illusions of victimhood. If, however, you want to see what your problems and issues really are, listen to your enemies, since they are not inhibited about giving you hard truths about yourself. They often have their own agendas too, though, so you have to evaluate their statements carefully. Obviously, not everything they say is true or constructive. But if you have a visceral reaction to something an "enemy" tells you about yourself, there may be a truth or a lesson to be considered there even if it is just to learn not to hitch the wagon of your happiness to the opinions of others.

Four of Cups

"Now and then it's good to pause in our pursuit of happiness and just be happy." — Guillaume Apollinaire

The typical image on this card speaks of boredom and ennui, as well as of not seeing the advice, gifts, and opportunities that the Divine offers us. It also comments on the stability of our emotions and the security of our relationships.

Boredom versus your fuller life

"Our lives are mostly a constant evasion of ourselves." — T. S. Eliot

If the Three of Cups is seen as the "party card," we may consider the Four of Cups to be the "hangover card." It indicates the dissatisfaction we might feel subsequent to indulging too much in the more trivial pursuits of life. As such, it can depict boredom and apathy or perhaps withdrawal into an emotional shell.

On a deeper level, this card can indicate a resistance to finding meaning in life, as illustrated in the following quote from *The Heart of the Soul: Emotional Awareness* by Gary Zukav and Linda Francis: "Boredom is your 'fuller life' calling you, and your fear of hearing that call." Similarly, in *Man's Search for Meaning*, Viktor Frankl defines "existential vacuum" as not having a sense of meaning for your life, and he says, "The existential vacuum manifests itself mainly in a state of boredom." Perhaps this lack of a sense of meaning is why "the mass of men lead lives of quiet desperation," as Thoreau wrote in his classic tome, *Walden.* [40]

On a spiritual level, then, this card reminds us that we should look within our hearts for meaning and renewal rather than search for an artificial means of escape to distract us from our troubles or to fulfill our sense of emptiness and longing. Our moods and emotions are constantly shifting, but we can stabilize them by centering on our spiritual core.

So if your life feels dull and you feel as if you are stuck in a rut, take time to sit quietly and listen for a higher calling. Don't be afraid of the message you may receive; not hearing it is the real danger. After all, there is great truth in the saying, "The only difference between a rut and a grave is the depth." Also, consider (or reconsider) opportunities that you have ignored or brushed off because they have been outside your comfort zone. They may be exactly what you need since the magic in life rarely happens *within* our comfort zone. In short, look to find purpose in life so that you will not go to the grave with your unique song still unsung.

Prayer and guidance

Many people use prayer like it's a letter to Santa Claus, and they try to use God like an ATM. However, this misses the truly great opportunities of prayer. In praying for a boon and then waiting passively for it to come to us, we miss the real gift, which is guidance on how to create miracles for ourselves. So we should listen as well as speak when we pray and then act upon the guidance we receive.

Beyond our desire for gifts and miracles, though, there are better reasons for prayer. We may pray to gain an understanding of a troubling situation or for strength when facing a difficult task. We can also use prayer as a means of giving

---

[40] *An interesting misquotation of Thoreau's classic line is "Most men lead lives of quiet desperation and go to the grave with the song still in them."*

thanks for our blessings or even for the challenges we face, since they are opportunities for growth. In *A Return to Love*, Marianne Williamson suggests that when we are faced with a troublesome relationship with someone it helps to pray, "I surrender this relationship to the Holy Spirit." The famous Serenity Prayer is another excellent example: "God grant me the strength to change the things I can, the serenity to accept the things I can't, and the wisdom to know the difference."   Finally, perhaps the best prayer of all is a request for help and guidance in our quest to discover our divine nature and to realize our union with the Divine.

An anchor for emotional stability

"Stop letting other people control your happiness." — *Traditional saying*

Anchoring our emotional wellbeing on material circumstances, which are (at best) variable, creates emotional distress. Thus, for example, if your happiness depends on what other people do or say, then it is those people, and not you, who control your ability to be happy. Also, since our circumstances are constantly shifting, they will throw us off balance emotionally if we depend on them for our happiness. Finding and focusing on our divine core, however, can help us achieve emotional stability. One way to return to our spiritual center is suggested in the following poem by the Spanish mystic, Saint John of the Cross.

I was sad one day and went for a walk;
I sat in a field.
A rabbit noticed my condition and
came near.
It often does not take more than that to help at times —
just to be close to creatures who
are so full of knowing,
so full of love
that they don't chat,
they just gaze with
their marvelous understanding.

We need not depend upon the fortuitous arrival of a wise rabbit, however, for the Divine often shines through the eyes—the proverbial windows of the soul—of someone near us, whether that be a friend, a loved one, or a pet. We just need to look for and be receptive to their quiet gaze of "marvelous understanding." However, since it is the Divine within them that is the source of this marvelous understanding, we can also find such comfort directly through a meditative practice, since that enhances our own spiritual connection. In any case, it is important to remember that emotional stability comes from anchoring our wellbeing on our spiritual core, which is steady and unchanging.

As a corollary to this message of the Four of Cups, it may be valuable to consider that when someone we care about is sad, perhaps the best remedy we can offer is our own quiet gaze of marvelous understanding.

Non-attachment versus apathy

The Four of Cups is sometimes interpreted as meaning "apathy," and in that guise, it reminds me of a misconception that I sometimes encounter when I talk about cultivating non-attachment. "It sounds like you're advocating apathy," some people say. However, non-attachment to things and to the results of our actions is very different from being apathetic about the events and circumstances around us, and it is important to understand the difference.

For one thing, in apathy, we avoid doing anything to improve the world and our circumstances, but contrary to what some people assume, non-attachment does not mean that. Even when we have reached a state of non-attachment, we can totally engage in life as we work to relieve suffering and make the world a better place, since doing so manifests our divinely compassionate nature. However, we can do this without having our happiness or satisfaction depend upon the results of our actions, i.e., without attaching to those results. Practicing non-attachment means that if we fail, we don't suffer as a consequence. Instead, we pick up the pieces and say, "Okay. That didn't work; let's try something else." With apathy, we just say, "I don't give a darn, and I'm not even going to try."

Another difference arises from the fact that apathy is associated with a retreat from our problems out of a sense of hopelessness or a fear of failure. Non-attachment, however, comes from a sense of trust in the Divine as we release our need to control how things turn out. In addition, non-attachment can help us overcome apathy since our anxiety, indifference, and dissatisfaction will dissolve when we are not attached to the results of our endeavors out of a sense of fear or need.

In short, non-attachment and apathy may seem similar, but they are very different. The former comes from a place of deep, abiding strength; the latter, from weakness.

Listening to your heart

We may say that we want to listen to the wisdom of our hearts, but we often fail to do so. This is often because it is hard to tell the difference between the directives of the heart and those of our base desires, and it is hard to differentiate between our intuition and the hopes and fears that arise from our ego. So if we don't know which is which, how can we know what to trust? Succinctly, the answer is this: When the message is one of love, compassion, and unity, it comes from the heart; when it is of fear and separateness, it comes from the ego. Put another way, when advice from within makes your heart feel expansive, it is of love, and you should follow it. When it makes your heart feel constricted, it is of fear, and it is leading you in the wrong direction.

Five of Cups

This card is generally seen as an indication of loss and of the sorrow we feel as a result. It is about experiencing grief, and it also can be about self-pity and the way that our sorrow about what is lost can blind us to the joy of all that we still have in our lives.

Experiencing grief

We know that when a loved one dies, grieving is a necessary step on the path toward healing. However, this is also true for things other than a physical death—things like the loss of a job or relationship. In fact, it is important that we not gloss over any sorrow, for unacknowledged or unresolved pain may bury itself deep into our hearts and take unsuspected residence there. We may think we are through with it, but if a feeling is not through with us, it will resurface in other circumstances, which can mystify us. "Why did that emotion arise in this situation," we may wonder. In addition, actions that result from the echoes of sadness past will generally seem inappropriate, and they will bewilder or aggravate the people around us. So when inexplicable sadness arises, which is often signaled by strange behavior, consider what past grief or sorrow may be the unseen origin. And when a significant loss occurs, give it an appropriate amount of grieving so that you may let it go and move on.

Releasing grief

The flip side of this card's message about the importance of experiencing our grief is the fact that there is a point at which grieving stops being therapeutic and starts to become dysfunctional and harmful. Consequently, an implicit message in this card is that emptying our hearts of residual grief is part of a purification process that enables the light to come back into our lives.

We all have our own personal histories of pain, and we often keep the resulting sadness locked up in our hearts. It's important to realize, though, that when we hide such sorrows from the light, they aren't locked *out*; they are locked *in*. In fact, one might even say that we are locked in by them. It is only when we are able to expose them and release them that we can finally be free of them. Sometimes it is enough just to have a silent witness to enable us to come to a place of closure, to enable us to let go and move on. For example, the Catholic confessional is intended to do something similar for our guilt, but we also need something like that for our feelings of loss, loneliness, and shame.

So think about whom you can talk to about your sorrow—someone who will listen to you without judging, and who will acknowledge your pain so that it can then dissipate. That may be all you need. But even if there is no person to do that for you, remember that the Divine is always available if we but ask.

Heal and move on

There is a holiday celebrated in many parts of the world called *The Day of the Dead* which typically involves rites such as placing flowers on the graves of dead relatives or anointing tombstones with holy water. The intent of this holiday is to commemorate the lives of the deceased, and its mood is generally brighter than one might think. This difference indicates the contrast between how we tend to react to loss versus the spiritual perspective of loss as the beginning of a new phase of existence to be celebrated. As noted previously, a period of mourning is necessary, but sometimes we get stuck there, and then our losses begin to define us in subtle but harmful ways. We may manifest a belief that we are damaged goods and that we are undeserving of happiness. It is important that we discover and remember that this is just our pain talking. We are not damaged; we are whole. And everyone deserves to have a joyful life.

An important message here is that to heal from our past losses, we must move beyond them. Part of that healing process is saying goodbye to that which we have lost (which may include a good cleansing cry, if need be) so that we can move on. Another part is the realization that our losses do not mean that we are damaged. Thinking that way creates a life in which we manifest a lack of love and joy, and that is not our true essence. That is not what the Divine intends for us. So find comfort in knowing that a bright and beautiful life awaits you when you are finally able to set aside the darkness of past wounds and tragedies.

Leave the pity party

"If you want others to be happy, practice compassion. If you want to be happy, practice compassion." — The 14th Dalai Lama

Sometimes the Five of Cups reminds me of someone indulging in a pity party. When we are on the outside looking in, it is tempting to judge such people harshly, but when we are the woe-begotten one, it is easy to justify a morose celebration of all that has gone wrong. In either case, it's important to remember that we are all doing the best we can with what we have. Then, setting aside both judgments and justifications, it's important to know that there are ways out.

An excellent way out of a pity party is to help others who are worse off than we are. First of all, this puts our own problems into perspective, as indicated by the old saying, "I was sad because I had no shoes until I met a man who had no feet." But secondly, and more importantly, it presents us with the wonderful opportunity of helping ourselves through helping others. After all, we are all One.

Say goodbye

"The bitterest tears shed over graves are for words left unsaid and deeds left undone." — Harriet Beecher Stowe

The Five of Cups advises us to participate fully and unreservedly in our relationships for we never know what tomorrow may bring. This is an extremely important message that we usually ignore when we get caught up in the hectic rush of modern life. Our lives will be more blessed if we can take a moment now and then to think about the kind words and generous deeds we would regret not having shared with a loved one.

The above quote from Harriet Beecher Stowe also acknowledges how hard it can be to find closure after the loss of a loved one. This is a lesson I learned many years ago when my life was shattered by a personal tragedy.

This story began when I was sixteen years old and one of my brothers was in a fatal traffic accident. At that age, I was not old enough to know how to properly process this tragedy, and my parents—the people who otherwise might have been responsible for helping me—were suffering so much themselves that they were not able to provide the assistance I needed. Consequently, I was left with unresolved grief and a damaging lack of closure, which lasted for more than a decade. Finally, a friend gave me the simple but valuable advice to say goodbye to my brother. At first I protested, "How can I say goodbye to him? He's gone." But my friend assured me that all I had to do was imagine that he was there and talk to him.

This process helped me immensely, which is why I tell people that when they lose someone, they need to say goodbye at some point. They may not be ready to do that for a while, but they need to do it eventually in order to find closure and healing. The process I have worked out over the years to help other people is a bit more complex than what I did originally, but the basic process is this:

First, imagine that the loved one is there with you. Tell them whatever you need to, including, but not limited to "goodbye." Then listen for a response, which there will be if you listen close enough, and don't worry about whether or not it's your imagination. As Professor Dumbledore said to Harry Potter, "Just because it's happening in your head doesn't mean it isn't real."

Finally, it's important to know that saying goodbye does not mean you intend to forget the person. It only means that you are willing to give up your attachment to your grief. This letting go allows you to create a safe place where you can visit your memories of him or her when you choose to, rather than being helplessly forced to revisit them in sadness whenever they happen to arise.

Six of Cups

"The more we care for the happiness of others, the greater is our own sense of well being." — The 14th Dalai Lama

The Six of Cups offers a message of unconditional love, urging us to have compassion for everyone around us with the innocent love of a child. It also is about sincere sharing, which both arises from and replenishes the deep well of our heartfelt generosity.

Namaste

"Too often we underestimate the power of a touch, a smile, a kind word, a listening ear, an honest compliment, or the smallest act of caring, all of which have the potential to turn a life around." — Leo Buscaglia

The suit of Cups represents love, and its cards indicate various aspects of that emotion. For example, the Ace embodies the essential power of love and compassion, the Two is about romantic relationships, and the Three signifies the platonic love of friendships. (These are simplifications, of course, but they are a good way to see the difference between these cards.) My personal favorite in this suit, however, is the Six of Cups, which typically shows two children and symbolizes their innocent and unconditional love. Unfortunately, when we grow up, we lose our childlike ability to love so simply and deeply, and regaining that quality is one of our greatest spiritual quests.

Similarly, this card also can be seen as a call for our inner child's unconditional love to connect with that of another person's inner child. This statement reminds me of the Hindu salutation of *Namaste*, which is sometimes interpreted as "The divine within me greets and honors the divine within you." This is a beautiful way to initiate contact with other people and to view our interactions with them. Of course, while there are some people we can greet in this way, there are others who might not react as well to that. But even if we cannot say "Namaste" aloud when we greet someone, we can think it and thereby remind ourselves that our inner child of unconditional love shares a connection with theirs.

Generosity begins in the heart

"Always be a little kinder than necessary." — James M. Barrie

True generosity begins in the heart. Giving something to another person is not really charitable if it is not done in a spirit of love, if it doesn't come from the heart. Worse yet, if done grudgingly, with expectations or strings attached, or for the sake of appearances, an act of generosity actually may be detrimental to your soul's journey since it is a lie. Therefore, cultivate a kind and loving heart—a charitable heart—and keep in mind that it is not just what you give; it's how you give it that counts. Give to others out of compassion, and your spirit will thrive. Indeed, with a heart that is pure, loving, and generous, almost any act can be one of generosity.

An offering of love

"The very nature of kindness is to spread. If you are kind to others today, they will be kind to you, and tomorrow to somebody else." — Sri Chinmoy

One way to deepen our understanding of a Tarot card is to consider it in light of the card that precedes it in its suit. In the case of the Six of Cups, the preceding card, the Five of Cups, is commonly seen as representing loss and grief. One inference we can draw from this sequence is that since everyone has suffered such heartache, they can always use a smile and a kind word to relieve a bit of their pain. As Mother Teresa said, "Every time you smile at someone, it is an act of love, a gift to that person, a beautiful thing." However, although it is easy to smile at a happy person, it may be harder to smile at someone who looks like a poster child for the Five of Cups, even though they need it the most.

Thus, the Six of Cups advises us to transform our emotional connections with everyone around us, even people who are only passing by. This includes little things like giving a warm smile to a beggar on the street. In fact, our compassion for others, in whatever form it takes, may be considered an offering we make to the Divine. As Jesus said, "Even as you have done it to the least of these, you have done it to me."

This practice can lead us to see the divine nature within everyone, but to do it effectively we must avoid worrying about whether or not other people will love us in return or even if they will smile back. An offering of love must be made with no strings attached and no expectation of a reciprocal display of compassion. We can love other people with a smile or a sympathetic touch, and in living a life filled with love, we will create a more loving world for everyone.

Love even the unlovable

"Unconditional love is not the hole in us that receives the dirt, but the sun within that never stops shining." — Mark Nepo

The Six of Cups may be seen as a message to love everyone without judgment. It urges us to approach everyone from a place of love and oneness instead of from a place of fear and separation. It may be easy to do this with those who are closest to us and less easy with strangers, but the hardest people to love unconditionally are the seemingly unlovable people in our lives. However, they are the ones who it is most rewarding to love. After all, if we can love someone who we feel is annoying, abrasive, or disruptive, then we are on our way toward mastering unconditional love. Unfortunately, we tend to justify withholding our compassion from such people. We tell ourselves that they don't deserve our love or that they will take advantage of us if we open our hearts to them. However, as the quote from Mark Nepo points out, loving such a person does not mean being a doormat for them. We can love the unlovable by shining emotional sunlight upon them, and that will brighten the shadows in their lives.

Seven of Cups

"Follow your bliss." — Joseph Campbell

Although this card is sometimes interpreted as an indication of illusions and daydreams, it also includes a spiritual connotation of seeking the true direction of your heart. In the realm of our spiritual path, this can refer to discovering our devotion to the Divine.

Follow your bliss

Sometimes people misinterpret Joseph Campbell's famous saying as advice to be selfish or hedonistic, but that isn't what he meant. Our mundane desires and fleeting earthly pleasures are not true bliss. Bliss arises when we are in harmony with the inner voice of our soul.

So how do we know if we are following our bliss? We can sense the direction of our calling by listening closely to our feelings. When we feel a deep sense of joy, serenity, and fulfillment we are headed in the right direction. It is like being "in the zone" with our life. And the more we follow our bliss, the more we live an authentic life in accord with our spiritual path.

Finally, the universality of this advice may be inferred from the fact that it has been a recurrent spiritual theme throughout the ages as we can see from the following selection of quotes:

"Everyone should carefully observe which way his heart draws him, and then choose that way with all his strength." — Hasidic Proverb

"Let yourself be silently drawn by the strange pull of what you really love. It

will not lead you astray." — *Rumi*

"Go confidently in the direction of your dreams. Live the life you have always imagined." — *Henry David Thoreau*

"The minute you choose to do what you really want to do, it's a different kind of life." — *Buckminster Fuller*

Loving a personal image of the Divine

There is a spiritual practice called *Bhakti Yoga*, which refers to the cultivation, experience, and expression of love and devotion for the Divine. There's just one problem, though. Deity, being infinite and formless, is beyond our ability to grasp with our minds. Luckily, however, there is a workaround, so to speak, which is to use a stand-in, a model.[41]

George E. P. Box said, "Essentially, all models are wrong, but some are useful." An image or conceptualization of the Divine is a model, and so, as Box said, it is wrong (i.e., it is flawed and limited), but it is useful. Despite its flaws, it gives us a focus or object for our devotion that we are able to use. Early in our sacred journey, imagining the Divine in human terms facilitates our spiritual devotion since we are better able to form a deep relationship with a specific, personal construct. Such a conceptualization may be limited, but this is only a problem if we forget that fact and begin to confuse it with the infinite and ineffable Divine.

Thus, the Seven of Cups can signify choosing a personal representation of the Divine, of which there are many. For example, it can be an image of Christ, Vishnu, or Buddha. You may visualize this personal image of the Divine and then, keeping it in your heart, cultivate loving devotion toward it and use it as you "walk with God."

Note that this emotional attraction is typically modeled on a form of human love, such as romantic partners or a parent/child relationship. Use whatever will lead you to a passionate devotion for the Divine. Our facility for human affection serves as a template for our devotion to the Divine, but another goal here is to realize that the Divine is in all people, so we should find love in our hearts for everyone around us too.

---

[41] *For another discussion about this suggestion, see the Two of Cups section titled "Icons of devotion."*

Finally, there is an important warning in this view of the Seven of Cups. We must realize that, consciously or not, we are always choosing something to love and worship. It may be fame, fortune, or sensual pleasures, or it may be the Divine. This card advises us to choose well.

Eight of Cups

"Not all who wander are lost." — J.R.R. Tolkien

This card is often seen as an indication of leaving something behind or finding a new direction in life. Similarly, its common image of someone hiking up a mountain suggests embarking on a spiritual quest and a search for enlightenment.

Leave behind emotional distress

In her book, *Who Would You Be Without Your Story?,* Byron Katie asks someone who is going through a difficult and painful experience this question:

If that were your only way to God, would you take it?

This question reminded me of the Eight of Cups, which symbolizes traveling a path toward enlightenment. It also added an interesting nuance with its advice to reconsider difficult situations in such a way that we let them lead us to the serenity of divine union instead of following them into turmoil.

This card is often seen as an indication of leaving something behind, such as a problematic situation or a troublesome relationship. However, what we need most to leave behind is our emotional distress and anxiety. We don't necessarily have to leave a bad situation itself—indeed, it's not always possible to do that—but we can change our perspective about it.

As Katie points out, one way to consider a difficult situation is to realize that everything can be a path to the Divine, and all problems may be considered "grist for the mill." This is a sentiment we also see in the following quote from Elisabeth Kübler-Ross: "There are no mistakes, no coincidences; all events are blessings given to us to learn from."

Our problems can put us into a state of mind where we have no alternative but to surrender. Thus, they may move us to live in the present moment in a state of acceptance, instead of living in anger about the past or anxiety about the future. But our problems can move us in this way only if we let them, only if we choose to trust the Divine and see the path we are on as our way to God.

<u>Leave behind emotional attachments</u>

"New beginnings are often disguised as painful endings." — Lao Tzu

A figure hiking up a mountain trail, which we typically find on this card, symbolizes a search for enlightenment, and one requirement of such a quest is leaving behind emotional attachments. However, it is important to understand that eliminating emotional attachments does not mean that we should become uncaring or aloof. Rather, it involves the unfolding realization that our joy and serenity are not dependent upon things outside of us.

We also need to realize that this advice refers to the emotional attachments we have to the good things in life as well as to the bad, the successes as well as the failures, the pleasures as well as the aggravations, the happiness as well as the sadness, and the affection as well as the animosity. We become attached to all those things—good and bad—as their familiarity becomes a source of security. And such attachments often lead to irrational behavior—words and deeds that arise from a place that is unworthy of us, instead of from a place that is in accord with our divine Self.

You can discover what some of your dysfunctional attachments are by thinking of something in your life that you do not like and then try to release your attachment to it. If you encounter strong internal resistance, then there you are; you found one. For example, does someone in your life (a friend, neighbor, co-worker, family member, etcetera) aggravate you? The next time you start thinking about what a jerk that person is, try to stop thinking about that and replace that thought with one of compassion and understanding. Can you do it? Probably not easily, and that indicates that you are emotionally attached to that aggravation. Practice replacing negative thoughts with positive ones anyway, even if it feels false at first, and eventually you'll find yourself leaving that attachment behind and moving forward in your quest for spiritual enlightenment.

<u>Many paths up the mountain</u>

"All religions are true inasmuch as they lead to one and the same goal—God-realization." — Swami Prabhavananda

Contrary to what some religious leaders would have us believe, there are many paths up the mountain of enlightenment, and each one reveals sacred truths in its own unique way. A wonderful example of this multicultural view is a book called *The Sermon on the Mount According to Vedanta* by Swami Prabhavananda, a Hindu philosopher and scholar. In this book, he presents interpretations of the Sermon on the Mount, an essential part of Christian teaching, that reveal a practical way to live your daily life in a more spiritual manner.

This idea that there is some amount of spiritual truth in all religious teachings is valuable to understand so that we can release our prejudicial judgments about other religions, and thus, by extension, our judgments of other groups of people. Of course, this unfolding realization is also valuable for humanity as a whole because as individuals set aside their judgmental views, their minds become more peaceful, which manifests as an increasingly peaceful world.

Also, this poly-spiritual view is important for us to embrace so that we may explore the truths revealed in many different spiritual traditions, not just the ones we were taught as children. It is in this way of openness to all paths that we, collectively, discover the spiritual whole through our exploration of the individual perspectives of differing spiritual traditions.

Spirituality and bliss

The Eight of Cups may indicate mundane meanings such as seeking a new relationship or leaving behind an outmoded situation, especially while looking for something more fulfilling. It suggests a realization that our present circumstances are untenable, undesirable, or obsolete. At such times, however, our concerns tend to be more about what we may have to leave behind than about what we might be moving toward.

This is also true about embarking on a spiritual quest because there is a common misconception that doing so involves a painful renunciation of material things and that although it may be a peaceful pursuit, it is one lacking in joy. The truth, however, is very different from that. Although spirituality is about releasing attachments to mundane concerns, this is not a matter of loss but a matter of growth beyond such concerns, and according to all accounts, spiritual enlightenment is blissful and sublime. In fact, there are many examples in the recorded experiences of religious mystics about the ecstasy of their spirituality.

A Judeo-Christian example may be found in *The Song of Solomon* in the Old Testament, which uses passionate and erotic poetry about romantic courtship and consummation as an allegory for a relationship between the human soul and God. In addition, many Christian mystics have shared blissful visions of their soulful union with God. For example, Saint Teresa of Ávila related that she often felt the intimate embrace of God.

Similarly, Sufism, a mystical branch of Islam, often talks about a euphoric state of union with Allah, and the thirteenth-century Islamic mystic Rumi wrote fervent poetry about the ecstasy of divine love.

Some other examples, which come from India, are:

- Kabir, a fifteenth-century mystic poet who had an important influence on Sikhism, wrote spiritual poetry that was intensely rapturous.
- Mirabai, a sixteenth-century Hindu mystic, celebrated her intense devotion to Krishna with over one thousand passionate songs in praise of Him.
- In the twentieth century, Meher Baba wrote that God-intoxicated souls are desperately in love with God, or consumed by their love of God.

So we see that we need not glance back sorrowfully at what is past when we embark on a spiritual path. Rather, we should gaze forward with longing and joyful expectation.

Nine of Cups

The Nine of Cups is sometimes called "the wish card" which, of course, implies the warning to be careful what you wish for since it might come true. It also can indicate enjoyment, satisfaction, appreciation, and satiation.

Be careful what you wish for

"I wish I could join the Solitaries instead of being a Superior and have to write books. But I don't wish to have what I wish, of course." — *Abbot John Chapman*

Getting what you want can be both a blessing and a curse, since wishes are powerful things. A wish sets an intention that, if fueled with passion, enables a person to change his or her life.[42] However, wishing is a dangerously subtle process. For example, a thought like "I wish I could be young again," is not going to turn back the hands of time. It does, however, implicitly project an intention to relinquish the positive gains of age, such as wisdom and patience, which is a self-denigrating and counterproductive desire. Of course, any wish for your life to be different risks being counterproductive, at least to some extent. The danger arises when such desires are tantamount to saying something like, "I am not good enough," which affirms the illusion of our separation from our true, divine Self. Also, wishes for a change in our circumstances may be a longing to shirk the learning experiences that our soul is providing us at this time.

Consider, for example, how often children wish that they were grown up and independent, and how often we adults wistfully look back at our childhood, longing for that simpler time. We want to change our current situation when we would do well to try to understand and appreciate it. We seem to wish away our lives instead of living in the eternal *Now*. So this card advises us to examine the things in life that we wish were different, find the meaning and lessons in them, and seek satisfaction and gratitude in them, instead of regret and discontent.

Live life fully and appreciate everything

We know that gluttony, hedonism, and decadence can impede our spiritual progress. However, tipping the scales to the other extreme and denying our sensual experience of life does not necessarily serve our soulful purpose either. (Unless that is actually what you feel called to do.) We are here to live life fully and to find joy and fulfillment, although with the caution that our sensual experiences should neither control us nor impinge upon the liberty and evolution of others.

The Nine of Cups depicts contentment, pleasure, and satisfaction, but these feelings depend upon appreciation, which is an important aspect of spirituality. Of course, it is easy to appreciate success and fortune when they come to us, but it's the much harder practice of appreciating the value of *everything* in our lives that brings us deep and lasting joy and serenity. This includes the intangibles of life, such as love, hope, and tranquility, and it even includes our problems, which challenge us and help us grow in wisdom and compassion. So we should be grateful for everything in life for it is all a divine gift, and we must remember that

---

[42] *For a detailed account of this process, see* The Law of Attraction *by Esther and Jerry Hicks.*

appreciation is a matter of attitude more than circumstance. Indeed, good fortune is not the same as material success; it is a state of mind. It both reflects and arises from a willingness to look for and recognize the wondrous things in our lives and having an appreciative attitude about them.

Thus, it may seem a bit strange that appreciation arises from good fortune, and good fortune is made possible through appreciation. "Which comes first?" we might wonder. This conundrum can be resolved when we realize that appreciation and good fortune evolve together in an upward spiral that begins with an act as simple as saying "thank you," which is a habit we should cultivate. Say it to yourself, say it to other people, and say it to the Divine. Say it about everything you can, and say it often. And always mean it.

Finally, a valuable piece of advice we may find in this card is to take time now and then to list some of our smaller and less-obvious blessings and then acknowledge and give thanks for them. In cultivating our appreciation for these blessings, we also cultivate our enjoyment of them and of life.

Self-righteousness

As noted in the previous section, the Nine of Cups can indicate having a sense of satisfaction with what we have. However, a dark side of this card is taking satisfaction to a negative extreme, i.e. being self-satisfied or self-righteous. One implication of this is a warning to avoid being smug about our spiritual practice. This does not just mean "Don't brag." It is also a warning against feeling superior to other people who may seem less spiritually "evolved" than we are. Truly, if we think we are superior because of our spiritual work, then, ironically, we are missing the point.

Similarly, this card warns us not to be sanctimonious and scornful of other people who are on a different path, or of those who seem not to be on any spiritual path at all. Humility, non-judgment, and a realization of our unity with all humankind are all important parts of our progress, so the minute we judge or condemn the progress of others, we prove how far *we* still have to go.

This is an easy trap to fall into, so a useful exercise is to think of someone on a very different spiritual path from yours, and consider how their journey has improved their lives. (Even if you think it has had detrimental effects, there are bound to be some positive ones as well.) Also, try to do this without making comparisons between their journey and yours. Finally, look within yourself to find a place of happiness for that person.

Ten of Cups

This card indicates a sense of community, emotional maturity, universal love, and the archetype of a happy home.

Love everyone, near and far

"Your home ... should be the center and not the boundary of your affection."
— *A. Parthasarathy*

The number ten reduces numerologically to the number 1, which indicates "self," so it may be seen as an indication of a higher level of self, such as "community." Since the suit of Cups is associated with love and relationships, the Ten of Cups asks us to consider questions like:

Do I understand my relationship with my community?

Do I realize that at a deep, spiritual level, I am one with my community?

Do I have unconditional love for the people around me—from my family to my local community to the world?

That last question is an especially difficult one. Universal love is not an easy reality for most of us. For example, it can be hard to love an unappreciative boss or a disruptive neighbor. But even though your heart may not be there yet, just being mindful of the ideal of loving everyone in your life and of making that your goal can move you in the right direction. You may also take the love you feel for your family as a guide and apply that love—both the feeling and the way of relating—to everyone in your life.

Finally, for a different perspective on this subject, consider the following quote from Mother Teresa.

It is not always easy to love those close to us. It is easier to give a cup of rice to relieve hunger than to relieve the loneliness and pain of someone unloved in our own home. Bring love into your home for this is where our love for each other must start.

Loving Kindness

In the preceding section, we considered this card's meaning with regards to its numerological association of "community." However, the number ten also denotes the results or consequences of completing a cycle, thus representing an epilogue or foreshadowing the start of a sequel. So the Ten of Cups can imply the attainment of compassion for all through the integration of our emotional experiences. It suggests coming full circle from the unconditional love of a child, which arises from innocence, to an emotional maturity wherein we have discovered the joy of loving unity with everyone. And so this card indicates the blissful serenity that results from being at one with all humankind and with the world.

In Buddhism, there is a meditation for cultivating this type of universal compassion or "Loving Kindness."[43] It may be described succinctly as an intentional wish for all beings to be happy and safe. This practice begins with directing loving-kindness toward oneself, and then, progressively, toward a friend, a "neutral person," a difficult person, all people, and finally, the entire universe. For example, you may recite the following lines, repeating each one three times before progressing to the next one:

May I be free from anger, adversity, and suffering, and may I live happily.
May [a friend] be free from anger, adversity, and suffering, and may she live happily.
May [a neutral person] be free from anger, adversity, and suffering, and may he live happily.
May [a difficult person] be free from anger, adversity, and suffering, and may she live happily.
May all people be free from anger, adversity, and suffering, and may they live happily.
May the entire Universe be free from anger, adversity, and suffering, and may it live happily.

(Insert specific names for "a friend," "a neutral person" and "a difficult person.")

---

[43] *For more about this Buddhist practice, I suggest Sharon Salzberg's book,* Lovingkindness: The Revolutionary Art of Happiness.

<u>Home is where the heart is</u>

Just as this card can represent an idealized version of a family, it also may indicate "home" in a spiritual sense. To explore this metaphor, let us first consider the quote, "Home is where the heart is." This means that our true home is with the person (or people) we love most. It can also mean that finding what we love (which, in addition to a person, may refer to something like a career or hobby) gives us that comfortable feeling of returning home. Thus "home" may be a feeling we yearn for more than a place we long to be.

This metaphor goes even deeper, however, since many religious traditions compare death to "going home." For example, consider the following quotes.

"Life is a dream walking; death is going home." — *Chinese proverb*

"I am not going to die; I'm going home like a shooting star." — *Sojourner Truth*

"Death is nothing else but going home to God." — *Mother Teresa*

Of course, we don't have to die to return home if we realize that we can do so through traveling a spiritual path. And perhaps this shows us how we can stay true to that path. If it feels like going home, then we are probably following the guidance of our spiritual compass. So again, "Home is where the heart is," but in this case, this aphorism means that our soul realizes that divine union is like going home. And perhaps when we feel ill at ease with our lives, such as when we feel stressed, bored, or angry, we are homesick—we have strayed from the path and are yearning to return to that primal, archetypal home: divine reunion.

Page of Cups

"Suffer little children, and forbid them not, to come unto me: for of such is the kingdom of heaven." — *Matthew 19:14*

This card indicates a childlike enchantment with the mysteries of life, new explorations of imagination and intuition, and simplicity and innocence in a relationship. It also denotes emotional inexperience or naiveté.

Embracing mysteries

This card typically expresses a theme of being enchanted by the mysteries of life, and we may see it as urging us to embrace that which is mysterious, unknown, and even unknowable. It can say, "Embrace the mysteries of life for they will enchant you, and your pursuit of them will lead you into wondrous realms you never before dreamed of."

Thus, a bit of advice here is to take time now and then to consider something mysterious in life. It can be anything from the "big" questions like "What is love?" and "What's the meaning of life?" to more personal ones like "How can I truly love myself?" or "What is it about a beautiful sunset that makes me so happy?" However, don't try to definitively answer the question or analyze the mystery. That just crams the ineffable into a neatly labeled box. Instead, just feel the mystery, experience it, and let your heart travel the path that your contemplation reveals.

Eternal mysteries of the heart

"The heart has its reasons which reason does not know." — *Blaise Pascal*

In our youth, the mysteries of the heart seem almost infinite. Although there was a sweet agony in our earliest forays into romance, there was also an ecstasy in them, a profound spiritualism even. They were breathtaking and energizing, and they filled us with wonder. Sadly, though, we generally lose that sense of awe and that easy openness to an intense experience of love as we grow up.

The Page of Cups indicates a new blossoming of the heart, a fresh awareness of love. This is not something that should be limited to our youth. Even in old age, we may discover new things about relationships, and we may fall wondrously in love, perhaps even discovering a feeling of new love for an old lover. However, this happens all too rarely, although that is not because a fresh understanding of love and relationships cannot occur when we are adults. It's that as we grow older we become less emotionally open, inquisitive, and supple, less open to new (or renewed) love. We buy into the delusion that "young love" is only possible when we are young. But that is not really true unless we let it be.

So this card urges us to be young at heart, to regain a youthful sense of joy and wonder about love and relationships, and it tells us to reexamine the mysteries of love. Just because we will never completely unravel those mysteries does not mean we should abandon the quest. Our life and loves can become all the richer for the exploration. And in the process we learn to listen to the wisdom of our hearts, we regain trust in the power of love, and we reopen our hearts to let other people in.

Imagination and intuition

In addition to its message of embracing the mysteries of life and love, the Page of Cups suggests beginning a journey of discovery into the mysteries of our unconscious minds. It can signify our imagination, which is a wonderfully creative tool that is strong in our youth but becomes stifled as we grow older. If we can revive it, though, we can use it to envision a better life and a better world.

This card may also suggest that we explore our intuition further, since it may allude to surprising messages from our unconscious mind, such as those that our dreams reveal. The soft whisperings of our intuition speak to us from deep within our soul, and when we are open to such intuitive messages, instead of being dismissive or fearful of them, we are apt to receive surprising insights that can help us comprehend the mysteries of our soul's journey. Thus another aspect of this card is its advice to become more amenable to an emerging spiritual awareness. In all these things, though, the underlying message is to be like a child—to have an open and eager heart—for that is the key to spiritual wisdom.

Innocent love

When we consider the love of a child, it seems so unconditional and heartfelt that we may bemoan the fact that we adults are not like that. Why is our emotional maturity so sterile compared to a child's emotional innocence? Indeed, one of the saddest parts of growing up is losing that innocent ability to love so purely. But have we really lost it, or is it still there deep inside our hearts, buried beneath layers of pain and worry and fear?

On a recent trip to the grocery store I noticed a child sitting in a shopping cart next to me, staring at me with a big, happy smile, and it gladdened my heart to smile back at her. In fact, I found myself making a funny face in a successful effort to make her laugh. Now, you have to understand, I don't generally go around making funny faces at people to make them laugh, especially not strangers, but I rarely think twice about doing so when the other person is an infant. And why is that? Because I know the child will find an innocent delight in it and will respond in a joyful way while I don't expect adults to react that way.

(Quite the contrary, in fact.) Of course, I'm not unique in this; I often see people openly captivated by the tender gaze of a child they have never seen before and probably will never see again.

There are two complementary messages in all this. The first is the advice to love everyone as unconditionally as a child does. When we learn to explore our relationships—platonic as well as romantic—with the unconditional love of a child, we will find them to be full of wonder and delight. The other message is that as we become emotionally open like a child, we will draw other people to us. Our open and loving hearts will invite a like response from others. They probably won't make funny faces at us in a giddy attempt to make us smile, but they will respond with their hearts more open than usual, and that is delightful enough.

Knight of Cups

We may interpret this card as actions (Knight) of the heart (Cups). This leads us to its meanings of movement (or even recklessness) in our relationships as well as following and acting upon the advice of our heart. The Knight of Cups can also indicate a spiritual quest.

You can't swim wearing armor

Many years ago I took a Tarot workshop with Mary K. Greer in which she had us conduct an internal mental conversation with a card, and the card I pulled was the Knight of Cups.[44] This was a wonderful exercise, and in my conversation with him, this knight was both humorous and profound. One of the things he said, which I'll never forget, was this: "You can't swim wearing armor." The context of this statement was a discussion about personal relationships, and what I understood from it is that you cannot have vital and meaningful relationships with other people if you insist on being guarded. You have to open up. You have to allow yourself to be vulnerable.

Think about how open you are to other people. How guarded are you about yourself? Are you afraid to reveal your own feelings, and are you reticent to ask about or listen to the feelings of other people? Consider questions like these, and

---

[44] *You can read more about this exercise and many other interesting techniques in* Mary K. Greer's 21 Ways to Read a Tarot Card.

as you become more aware of how you relate to others, you will become better able to do so with an open heart.

<u>Purity of Heart</u>

"My strength is as the strength of ten because my heart is pure." — Alfred, Lord Tennyson (from the poem Sir Galahad*)*

None of us has the absolute purity of heart of Sir Galahad, but it is an ideal toward which we may strive. Moreover, it is an ideal toward which our soul will lead us if we pay attention and consent to follow. Our hearts can show us the way to find true happiness and fulfillment, but this is a message easily misinterpreted. It does not mean that our yearning for someone will bring us true happiness. In fact, that usually is not the case, for feelings like lust and craving are desires of the ego, not of the love that comes from the heart. Rather, it is our love and compassion for other people that fulfills us; it is our love and compassion that gives us "the strength of ten."

<u>Let your heart guide you</u>

Sometimes we feel lost and bewildered as if we are wandering through a dark forest without direction or purpose. It's not that we have succumbed to temptation or taken up with bad company. We do want to live a spiritual life, and we want to stay on the path our soul has set for us. However, we cannot figure out how to do that when we are overwhelmed by problems that we don't know how to handle.

Things like depression, financial difficulties, or frustration with a relationship can throw us off course like a ship tossed about in a storm. As the saying goes, it's hard to remember that you're there to drain the swamp when you're up to your neck in alligators. Luckily, however, this is not usually an "either / or" situation; we can work on both draining the swamp and fighting off the alligators. Occasionally taking a little time off to listen to our hearts can improve our ability to fend off those alligators because doing so refreshes us and gives us a much-needed improvement on our perspective of life.

So whenever you feel you have lost your way, take a break and let your heart show you how to regain your bearings and find your way along your spiritual path again.

<u>When you are ready, your soul mate will appear</u>

The Knight of Cups is a card often associated with romance (albeit with perhaps a touch of longing or idealism to it), as in the famous song title from the classic Disney movie *Snow White and the Seven Dwarfs*: "Someday my Prince will come." Consequently it reminds me of one of the more common questions for a Tarot reading: "When will I meet my soul mate?"[45]

Perhaps a better question in such circumstances would be something like this: "What can I do to be ready for a positive, loving relationship?" This line of consideration recently led me to recall another famous saying: "When the student is ready, the teacher will appear," which I have used as a template for the answer to that common soul mate question. In other words, the answer to the question, "When will I meet my soul mate?" is always (at least to some extent) "When you are ready, your soul mate will appear." In fact, a soul mate may have appeared in your life already, but if you are not emotionally and spiritually prepared for it, a loving relationship may not manifest, or if it does, it may not last.

Unfortunately, I have found that some people don't want to hear this sort of advice. They don't want to admit that they may not be ready for a soulful relationship, and they don't want to bear the responsibility of doing the spiritual work of improving themselves. But the hard truth is that this is what is necessary. The wonderful truth, though, is that once you have done that work, the Universe will conspire to bring you the love that you want and deserve.

Queen of Cups

This queen's characteristics of emotional self-sufficiency, compassion for others, and unconditional love inform and shape her message of the divine power of love.

---

[45] *Although some people consider a soul mate to be a unique person with whom they are destined to fall in love, I see this term as referring to any person with whom we have a loving and deeply spiritual relationship. (For more on this topic, see the Two of Cups section titled "Soul Mates.")*

Find the Divine in those we love

I once heard a story about a woman who told her spiritual teacher that she no longer believed in God because she couldn't see God anywhere in her life. The guru asked her if there wasn't someone, just one person, whom she loved. The woman replied, "Well, yes, I do love my little nephew very much." Her teacher smiled and said, "That's where you will find God in your life."

I love that little story. It is a reminder that we both manifest and discover our divinity in those moments when we feel unconditional love for another person. So whenever we are beset with doubts, that is where we can look to rediscover our faith.

Love of others is our spiritual practice

This card tells us that our love of other people helps us fulfill our desire for spiritual perfection when we express our love and when we realize how blessed we are to have others in our life. So this card may urge you to consider someone you love deeply and to ask yourself if you have told them lately how much they mean to you. Indeed, you may even consider whether you have ever told them what a blessing it is to have them in your life.

We often assume that the people we love know that we love them, and they probably do, but hearing it can bring a spark of the Divine into their lives as well as our own. Thus, this card says that expressing our love of other people is a spiritual practice in and of itself.

The free benefits of love

The Queen of Cups advises us to find the loving, caring, and compassionate part of ourselves that she represents, the part of us that is able to see everyone through the eyes of love, as a mother sees her children. But how do we find that feeling of love within our hearts? This card reminds us that we don't act in a loving way because we are full of love; we are full of love because we act in loving ways. In other words, as we practice compassion in our relationships with others, we fill our hearts and lives with love.

This seems ironic when we consider it from our ordinary perspective, which is trained in the materialistic paradigm of limits and scarcity. But the truth of the spiritual world is that we gain love by giving it away. And so our love for others

Tarot and Your Spiritual Path

has a magical way of multiplying and bringing more benefit to our lives and the lives of those around us than it costs us, for indeed giving love costs us nothing at all.

Unconditional love and emotional security

Unconditional love is a hallmark of a spiritually enlightened person, but a persistent question about that ideal is how to attain it. The Queen of Cups suggests that one path toward unconditional love involves working on loving ourselves enough so that we can become emotionally secure. Indeed, most of us could use a bit more of this queen's emotional self-confidence.

When we do not love ourselves sufficiently, we develop a need for someone else to love us instead in order to compensate. This can result in dysfunctional relationships in which we love other people with strings attached. In subtle ways, we say, "I'll only love you if you love me back. And you have to love me enough. And you have to constantly say and do things that assure me of your continued love and affection. And, most important of all, you can't ever leave me, or even let me think that you might leave me."

Learning to love unconditionally begins with learning to love yourself, and to do that, first learn to forgive yourself. Don't judge yourself so much. Of course you should evaluate your beliefs and actions and then correct or adjust them if they are causing problems, but you can correct your mistakes while also forgiving yourself for them. Judging ourselves is different from self-evaluation. It includes things like getting mad at ourselves for the common human errors we make or criticizing things like our physical characteristics. It is the harsh way we sometimes tell ourselves that we are bad or ugly or insufficient in some way. So one way to learn to love yourself is to develop a positive self-image and a positive attitude about yourself. For example, if you have an attribute that you don't like, change it if you can, and learn to accept and love it if you can't.

There is something else you can do to develop unconditional love, and that is to seek to rediscover your true, Divine Self. Those flaws and mistakes you see within yourself are not the real you. The essential, eternal you, which is always there to be seen when you are ready to see it, is your own inner divinity. When you realize that, you will love yourself and other people unconditionally.

Page 186

King of Cups

The King of Cups is the epitome of emotional control, maturity, and serenity. He exhibits tact and diplomacy and works compassionately to bring peace into the world.

Peaceful depths

On the RWS version of this card, we see a king sitting placidly on a throne in the midst of a stormy sea. A message we may infer from this is that our total being is like the ocean even though our consciousness bobs around on the surface. Our lives may be agitated by the vagaries of life, which is like being tossed on the waves, but deep down we have a peaceful core that remains calm like the depths of the ocean, even when its surface is agitated by a passing tempest. External conditions can stir up that which is superficial in our lives, but they cannot disturb the deep, true essence of our soul.

Unfortunately, we think that our real identity is defined by the waves of external problems. We identify with the volatile surface and fail to realize that our essence goes much deeper, all the way down to a calm, silent, impenetrable depth. One way to connect with that depth of being is through meditation, which trains us to maintain serenity in the midst of emotional turmoil. Then, as we come to believe in our true Self, which lies in the steady, peaceful core of our being, we will discover the profound, abiding serenity that provides safe haven in times of trouble and doubt. We can then maintain an emotional calm that allows us to deal with other people with tact and diplomacy, even if they lose themselves in fear and anger. Like the King of Cups, we can live placidly in the midst of any emotional tempest.

Emotional control

The preceding discussion may sound like it is saying that we should control our emotions. Indeed, this card, the King (control) of Cups (emotions) seems to advise that, and both history and literature are full of cautionary tales about people who fail in their struggle to do so. But how right or effective is emotional control? Certainly, suppression of our emotions is counterproductive (unless you want to create an ulcer), but contrary to popular notions, suppression and control are not the same thing. Also, it is clear that we should not allow our emotions to control us. But is controlling them the only alternative?

Depending on how deeply you do it, controlling your emotions can keep you from experiencing them, and they are an integral and vital part of life. We should feel and experience them—even the negative ones like anger and grief—but we should also know when to release them. They ebb and flow on their own if we do not hold on to them, so the trick is to avoid clinging to our emotions and to avoid allowing ourselves to become captivated by them. That's how emotional control becomes vital.

In addition, we can and should control our attention to the thoughts that our emotions thrust upon us as well as the actions that they urge us to take. For example, continually engaging a thought like, "I'm so mad at him! Who does he think he is? How dare he treat me that way!" just encourages an emotion (anger in this case) to take up permanent residence in your heart. So when such thoughts arise, just observe them and say, "I'm done with that now," and change the subject. To do that, you can shift your attention to your breath, plan your activities for the day, or think about a pleasant experience. Better yet, if you can, send loving thoughts instead of angry ones to the person you're mad at. In this way you can guide your emotions rather than suppress them.

Compassion and inner peace

In Buddhism, it is said that Kannon, the Bodhisattva of Compassion and Mercy, hears the cries of suffering in the world and as a result, strives ceaselessly to free all sentient beings from their misery. In seeming contrast to all that "striving," however, Kannon is typically depicted in a meditative or contemplative pose, representing someone who is at peace with the world.

There are a couple of inferences we may draw from this. One message is that the qualities of compassion and inner peace are inherently and inextricably intertwined. Compassion for others comes from having peace within, and peace within comes from being a compassionate person. This sounds like another "chicken or the egg" conundrum, but we do not have to be fully proficient at one to work on the other. We can work on compassion and serenity jointly, and they will progress together, hand in hand.

Another message is that being at peace is the way to lead others to serenity, whereas distress leads to more agitation and suffering. For example, doing something like protesting for world peace is ultimately self-defeating unless that protest is of a peaceful nature itself. This is because you cannot truly create something in the world around you while manifesting its opposite within yourself.

It is an easy and common mistake to act out of anger toward people who are causing suffering in others. At best, though, you might stop that one specific act in the other person, but in the broader scheme of things, you will have created more suffering than you eliminated. As Ram Dass says in his seminal book *Be Here Now*, "You can only protest effectively when you love the person whose ideas you are protesting as much as you love yourself." Thus, it is through the example of our own serenity and equanimity that we contribute to the end of suffering in the world.

SWORDS

"There is no coming to consciousness without pain." — *Carl Jung*

This suit is infamous for its portrayal of trouble and sorrow. But Swords are associated with elemental Air and thus with the mind, so how do the two relate—thought and distress? First of all, there is the truth that much of the suffering we experience arises from our thoughts about things, not from the things themselves. We may also consider that the difficult parts of life are typically the ones from which we learn the most.

Ace of Swords

"You can lead a person to truth, but you can't make him think." — *A paraphrase of a traditional aphorism.*

The Ace of Swords indicates the wondrous power of thought. Indeed, what we communicate to ourselves and to the world brings creative potential (for better or for worse) into our lives. At a deeper level, this card represents the divine consciousness that underlies all reality. The image most commonly seen on it is that of a heavenly hand offering a sword, thus indicating a state of pure consciousness. Also, a state of unadulterated awareness—a state wherein we leave distractions, labels, and judgments behind—is the way to see the world from a divine perspective.

Singularity of consciousness

"Consciousness is a singular for which there is no plural." — *Erwin Schrödinger*[46]

An analogy (admittedly, a very approximate one) that may help us understand Schrödinger*'s* quote is to say that there are many drops of water in the ocean, but there is only one ocean. Thus, while there are an infinite number of manifest minds (such as yours and mine) that may be observing the universe with

---

[46] An alternate version of Schrödinger's quote is this: "Vedanta teaches that consciousness is singular, all happenings are played out in one universal consciousness and there is no multiplicity of selves."

awareness, there is only one transcendental consciousness (i.e., a divine consciousness) of which they are all a part. And so the transcendental question is not, "What do I need to learn from this experience;" it is, "What can We learn from this experience." Each individual experience is a learning opportunity for the transcendent, whole Self—the consciousness for which there is no plural.

Similarly, there is one transcendent truth, which is that we are all One. The challenge of life, however, is not so much to search for this truth, for it is already there before us, but to have eyes that see it in all that is and to have a consciousness that experiences it in all that we do. We can meet this challenge through pure awareness of the proverbial "here and now." As James Thurber said, "Do not look back in Anger, or forward in Fear, but around in Awareness." As we cultivate that sort of awareness, we will begin to see this singularity of being.

Pure awareness

"The aim of life is to live, and to live means to be aware, joyously, drunkenly, serenely, divinely aware." — Henry Miller

From Ram Dass (in his seminal work, *Be Here Now*) to Eckhart Tolle (in his bestseller, *The Power of Now*), the message of modern spiritual leaders is increasingly clear: spiritual enlightenment arises out of a state of awareness that comes from living in the present moment as we focus our attention on the here and now. This is not a new message, of course, but it is entering our collective consciousness now more than ever. A benefit that we will derive from awakening to the present moment is a transcendent bliss and serenity.

In addition, this focused attention on the here and now creates an uplifting quality in our relationships as it facilitates our spiritual connection to others. Richard Moss said, "The greatest gift you can give another is the purity of your attention." Unfortunately, instead of giving the purity of our attention to someone when they talk to us, we are usually thinking about what we are going to say in response. Or we are judging the person and thinking about why what they are saying is wrong. Or we are thinking about other things entirely, such as what we want to eat for dinner. So try giving your pure attention to other people when they talk to you. You will discover an amazing improvement in your interactions with them.

The way of divine recollectedness

"Whenever you think of God, you are in the sanctuary." — Swami Prabhavananda

In *Religion in Practice*, Swami Prabhavananda advises us to think about the presence of God whenever we can. He tells us that if we practice this "constant recollectedness" of the Divine, we will eventually see the presence of the Divine in other people and in the world around us. In his book *The Eternal Companion*, he quotes Swami Brahmananda's succinct explanation of this path to divine union:

> *Repeat the name of the Lord. Whatever you do, let the name of God flow like a current within you.*

But how do we find a way to recall the Divine frequently? Certainly, a constant recollection of the Divine is not easy at first, but many spiritual traditions provide some tangible means of assistance. In some traditions, people chant a name of the Divine. Followers of the Hare Krishna movement, for example, are quite well-known for this. Even a simple affirmation, such as "God is with me always and in all ways" can serve this purpose. In other spiritual traditions, a ubiquitous icon (such as a cross or crucifix in Christianity) is used as a reminder, or a talisman of some sort (such as prayer beads) is kept on one's person so that touching it may recall the mind to the presence of the Divine. In the latter case, even a Tarot card with a divine depiction on it (such as, perhaps, the Ace of Swords) may be used.

See with new eyes

"I found that the chief difficulty for most people was to realize that they had really heard 'new things': that is, things that they had never heard before. They kept translating what they heard into their habitual language." — P. D. Ouspensky

The Ace of Swords symbolizes new ideas, and the quote from Ouspensky is a comment on how people typically avoid, ignore, or discount them. Another way to put this, however, is to say that it is very hard to see new ideas except through the filter of what we already believe. It is easy to see how other people do that when we tell them about new truths we have discovered, but it's not so easy to see how we do it too. But truth, as they say, is a two-edged sword, so let us look at this phenomenon from both sides.

If we listen carefully when people respond negatively to insights that we share with them we can see how this works. They don't hear what we are saying; they hear what they are conditioned to hear and what fits into their existing belief system. Also, it may be that they are not ready to hear what we are saying, but we have to allow and accept that because everyone has to progress in their own time. As Sri Ramakrishna said:

Dislodging a green nut from a shell is almost impossible, but let it dry and the lightest tap will do it.

Once you've heard uncomprehending reactions from other people often enough to recognize it easily, listen for it coming out of your own mouth so that you may come to question your own "habitual language" (to use Ouspensky's term) whenever it keeps you from hearing something new. Doing that is not easy, but it will enable you to begin questioning your preconceived notions and paradigms so that you may hear new truths and see the world through new eyes. At a profound level, that is the shining promise of this card: new eyes to see the world clearly and new ears to hear the message of the Divine.

Thought manifests in reality

The Ace of Swords tells us that we manifest what we focus our attention on (like it or not) because our thoughts are like seeds that sprout and grow into the circumstances of our lives. They are the first phase of our role as co-creators of our lives.

This is something that we may think is a bit of New Age thinking from tomes like *The Secret* and *The Law of Attraction*, but actually, it is a truth that has been revealed in one way or another since antiquity. Consider, for example, the following quotes from the Buddha and Marcus Aurelius, as well as more recent thinkers like William James, Swami Prabhavananda, and Ram Dass.

"All that we are is the result of what we have thought. The mind is everything. What we think we become." — *The Buddha*

"The soul becomes dyed with the color of its thoughts." — *Marcus Aurelius*

"There is a law in psychology that if you form a picture in your mind of what you would like to be, and you keep and hold that picture there long enough, you will soon become exactly as you have been thinking." — *William James*

"Whatever you think, you become; so if you think you are a mortal human

being and a sinner, you will stay that way. But, instead, if you tell yourself, 'I am free, perfect, and divine,' how then, can anything evil come from you?" — Swami Prabhavananda

" [At] every moment you are a full statement of your being. And you're sending out vibrations that are affecting everything around you, which in turn is affecting everything that comes back." — Ram Dass

While recent books about manifesting what you want through attention and visualization tend to focus mainly on romance and finance—circumstances outside ourselves—the sage messages noted above also tell us that our thoughts create who we are, which focuses on that which is essential: our character and our soul. This is a subtle, but important distinction. It is the difference between the fleeting currency of the physical and material world versus the timeless treasure of the soul.

So pay attention to your thoughts. When you find yourself thinking negative thoughts about someone (including yourself), stop and divert your attention toward something else. You might find a basic meditative technique like focusing on your breath to be useful. You might want to use a specific positive thought or memory, such as a particularly enjoyable experience you had on a past vacation. Or you might shift your thoughts to a positive affirmation like, "I am a loving, caring person," or Prabhavananda's "I am free, perfect, and divine." The important point is to get into the habit of replacing negative thoughts with positive ones, for this will transform your world, your character, and your life.

Words matter

In an open field behind my home there is a young Orchid Tree, which I like to call "my" Orchid Tree due to its close proximity to my home. Not long ago it bloomed for the first time in its relatively short life. At the same time, a more mature Orchid Tree growing a few blocks down the street from me was covered in a showy profusion of blossoms. One day as I passed by it, I remarked, "I can't wait for my Orchid Tree to look like that."

After I said that, however, it occurred to me that my statement exhibited impatience, and more than that, it was impatience with Nature, which can't be hurried. This expression of dissatisfaction with Nature's pace, as well as my lack of appreciation for what blossoms there were on the young tree struck me as a bit of negativity that I didn't want to put into my mind, my heart, and my life. So I silently acknowledged that Nature unfolds perfectly in Her own time and that the little Orchid Tree was beautiful in its own unique way. I also made a mental note that statements beginning with "I can't wait until ..." are not ones that I want to make. In small ways like this, I try to pay attention to the words I use and the ideas I implant in my psyche so that I can consciously and deliberately improve them.

We all create who we are—either consciously or not—by the things we say and do, and if we make a conscious effort to pay attention to our words, we can choose (or change) them in order to transform our lives for the better.

Look for truth

"The wise are pleased when they discover truth, fools when they discover falsehoods." — Unknown

Sometimes when I share a wisdom quote with someone, I find that they have a swift negative reaction to it ("Oh, I don't believe that!") instead of considering it to see what insight there may be in it and what they might learn from it. Of course, short quotes are open to interpretation, and no one, regardless of how many wisdom quotes are attributed to them, is perfect. But it always amazes me when someone is so quick to assume and eager to insist that they are wiser than Plato, Mahatma Gandhi, or Albert Einstein.

Of course, we all do something of this sort from time to time. Are we so completely wedded to our worldview that we resist any challenge to our opinions? Or do we, impelled by our egos, try to prove that other opinions are wrong (and thus that we know more than other people do) in an ongoing attempt at self-aggrandizement? Perhaps sometimes we misinterpret things people say because we are hearing them through the distortion of our fears. Indeed, I have often found that when I ask someone why they disagree with a quote, their explanations reveal their own fears and past wounds rather than their understanding of what I have said. Probably, however, it is a mixture of all of these.

And so this card reminds us that a search for truth is of the soul whereas a search to find fault and prove people wrong is of the ego. Thus, it urges us to look first for the value in what we hear and to resist the temptation to attack and prove people wrong out of reflex.

Two of Swords

The Two of Swords is about duality, choices, decisions, and balanced ideas. It also can indicate a need for objectivity, a willingness to compromise in the interest of fairness and harmony, and an awareness that there are two sides to every story.

Polarity

"If you're in polarity, you're creating polar opposites." — Ram Dass

When we see the world defined by an "us vs. them" paradigm (instead of "us *and* them"), we are living in a world of polarity rather than one of unity and wholeness. As a result, we struggle and fight with people and situations instead of looking for our connection and common ground with others. We look for (and find) conflict instead of compromise or cooperation, so we end up creating results that are the polar opposite of what we intended.

Ram Dass also said, "You can only protest effectively when you love the person whose ideas you are protesting against as much as you love yourself." In other words, protests and resistance to injustice must come from a place of peace and harmony or they will ultimately create more conflict and discord. Whenever we push the pendulum in one direction, we are setting it up to swing back in the opposite direction.

But when we understand that there are two sides to every story, when we see that on a deep, spiritual level, the other person is also "me," when we withdraw from the arguments of life, and when we try to find ways for everyone to win— when we can do all that, then we will stop life's pendulums from swinging from extreme to extreme. And as that change gradually happens, we will create peace and happiness in the world as well as within ourselves.

Quiet listening

"The quieter you become, the more you can hear." — Ram Dass

In the RWS version of this card, the ethereal image of a seated woman holding two crossed swords exudes a quiet serenity, albeit perhaps one of indecision or stalemate. Her blindfold can indicate impartiality, or it may be interpreted as having an undistracted mind. These aspects of this card relate well to the above quote, although it is important to realize that the quietness Ram Dass is referring to is not just that of not talking for a while, although that is often good advice. He is referring to the cultivation of a meditative quietness of mind in order to truly listen to the Divine, or, at the very least, to people talking to us.

First let us consider our ability to listen on the level of our interpersonal interactions. I have noticed that human conversations are often more like serial monologues than true dialogs. When not speaking, we sometimes are more interested in preparing for our turn to talk than in listening intently to what the other person is saying. This habit is related to our ego-illusion that we are separate from each other and that we are more important than other people. It would help if we could cultivate the habit of conversing with a balance of speaking (which we love to do) and true, thoughtful listening (which we do not).

Worse yet, we treat our relationship with the Divine the same way, only more so. If we listen at all, we listen through a distorting filter created by our hopes, fears, and prejudices. Usually, our "conversations" with the Divine are merely a litany of our complaints and requests. This is unfortunate because the Universe constantly whispers so much wisdom in its every detail—from the rumble of a storm to the sudden appearance of a butterfly—if we will but watch and listen with a peaceful heart and a quiet mind.

An example of this listening mind is Neale Donald Walsch who, in the mid-1990s, wrote a series of books called *Conversations with God* in which he relates his extensive discussions with the Divine on a variety of topics. Some people have found it highly unlikely that God would pick this particular man to give his wisdom to. However, I doubt that God actually did think that Walsch was more deserving than anyone else. His specialness was simply his willingness to listen, which is something that the rest of us rarely do.

These two aspects of quiet listening (in both spiritual and mundane matters) are not so different from each other. One way to learn to listen to the Divine is to practice listening to the people around you. You may want to try this exercise: For just one day, really listen to what people say when they speak to you. Give them your full attention and think about what they have said before you even begin to consider your response. Not only will you begin to hear things you don't expect, but you will find that people will like talking to you a lot more. Then take that attitude into your discourse with the Divine and silently listen for answers and responses whenever you pray. The quieter your mind, the more surely they will come.

Decisions and choices about existence and reality

"Every decision you make is not a decision about what to do; it's a decision about who you are." — *Neale Donald Walsch*

Every day, circumstances and events in our lives confront us with choices by which we shape the character of our being and create who we are. Thus, for every decision we make, we would do well to keep in mind the profound, underlying question, "Is this who or what I want to be?" In light of this consideration, we can choose our thoughts and actions in ways that affirm our divine nature and our deep connection to everyone else, or we can make decisions that reinforce the illusion of our separateness from the Divine and from other people. The choice is always ours to make.

On a broader scale, we also choose the reality in which we live, for our individual reality is based on perception and choice. It is determined by what we choose to perceive and then by how we choose to interpret what we perceive. Do we look for the good or for the bad? Do we assume innocence first or guilt? Do we hope for the best or fear the worst? Do we choose to learn and grow wiser or do we choose to complain and grow bitter? Do we take something personally or do we realize that someone may be acting out of their own pain and sorrow? These are important questions and considerations by which we can change the reality in which we live by changing the choices we make.

Three of Swords

This card's numerological association with creativity, its suit's association with thought, and its traditional image of a suffering heart all conspire to suggest that this card addresses the lessons within our pain and suffering and the potential for growth that comes from learning those lessons.

Sticks and stones

"Sticks and stones will break my bones, but words will never hurt me." — *Traditional saying*

Do you remember that old saying from the playgrounds of our youth? In one sense it is true. The names someone calls you only hurt if you let them. But in another sense this isn't true; words *do* hurt. In fact, even negative thoughts hurt, but the person they actually hurt the most is the one speaking or thinking them.

The most common version of the Three of Swords shows three swords piercing a heart, which illustrates how hurtful thoughts and words can be. One piece of spiritual advice we can infer from this is to stop using derogatory labels for other people. Just stop totally. There really is no need for them, and using them stabs us in the heart a lot more than it does the other person. Go ahead and evaluate the other person if you must, but don't judge them and definitely don't condemn them, because that negative thought stabs your heart more truly than it does theirs.

For example, saying "John is usually late for our appointments," is an evaluation, but saying "That inconsiderate so-and-so is always late!" is a condemnation. The anger and animosity of that statement harms the person saying it, partly because they are making themselves a lesser person for doing it. Also, such thoughts bring more negative people and situations into their life through the Law of Attraction. In addition, any thought that reiterates our illusion of separateness takes us that much further from realization of our divine union.

So when you notice your mental chatter calling someone names, or when you hear yourself using epithets in your conversation, stop yourself. Remember that we are all in the same boat—this boat called "life"—and everyone is doing the best they can, even if we don't think the best they can do is very good. It is not up to us to judge. Also, doing this will decrease your tendency to dwell on negative thoughts and feelings, and that will improve your own psychological health.

Finally, keep in mind this quote from Henry David Thoreau: "The only way to speak the truth is to speak lovingly."

The pain of clinging to anger

When you feel that you are suffering because of what someone else has said or done in the past, ask yourself, "Who put those swords into my heart?" The common answer is that the other person stabbed you in the heart, but in reality, you are creating your own suffering by keeping the wound open, rather than removing the swords to let your heart heal.

Consider the following Zen parable which illustrates this point:

Two monks were returning to their monastery one day. Heavy rains the night before had left puddles all along the roadside, and at one point the monks came upon a young woman who was stopped, unable to continue because of an especially large pool of muddy water. The elder of the two monks lifted her and carried her across the puddle, and then the two men continued on their journey. However, the younger one walked along in quiet agitation.

That evening, he approached the elder monk and said, "Sir, as monks, we cannot touch a woman. Isn't that true?"

The elder monk answered "Yes, brother."

Tightlipped, the younger monk then stated, "But Sir, you lifted that woman!"

The elder monk smiled and said, "Ah, but I left her on the other side of the road. You are still carrying her."[47]

The thoughts of pain, anger, or resentment that we hold in our hearts hurt only us. Letting go of such thoughts is never easy, though, so what might help us do that? For a suggestion, consider the following quote from the book *The Sermon on the Mount According to Vedanta* by Swami Prabhavananda:

There is only one way to feel sincerely reconciled [with someone who has wronged you], and that is to try to see God in all beings, and to love Him in all. If you have been angry with your brother, pray for him as you pray for yourself—pray that both of you may grow in understanding and devotion to God.

Release painful myths

"We are not troubled by things, but by the opinions that we have of things."
— Epictetus

As noted in the previous section, thoughts of resentment hurt us far more than the original offending act does. Here is a similar take on this topic, but with a slightly different twist.

In her book *Who Would You Be Without Your Story?*, Byron Katie tells us that it is not the world that causes us suffering, and it is not other people either. It's our own beliefs about the world and about other people; it's our own stories about them that cause us suffering. Despite this, we hold on to those stories, and

---

[47] *For another version of this story (and many more such tales), see the book* Zen Flesh, Zen Bones.

we do so with a rather fierce tenacity. Why is that? If these thoughts cause us so much pain, why do we cling to them? There are a variety of reasons, such as the following:

- Holding on to them makes us feel superior. We like to keep in mind the errors of other people so that we may believe that we are better than they are.
- We want to believe that our problems are not our fault. "It's their fault."
- These thoughts are familiar territory. Letting go of them would take us into unknown territory, which is frightening.
- Thinking these thoughts is a habit that is hard to break. The dark stories we keep repeating are like a rut in a road that our minds fall back into easily.
- These stories are barriers that our ego sets up to keep us separate from other people. Without them, we would realize our oneness with everyone else, which is a threatening concept for the ego.
- Our egos hate to say "I was wrong." We have held on to these stories for a long time, so releasing them would force us to admit that we were wrong. Worse yet, it may force us to admit that we have been unfair to someone else, which means we are not superior after all. The suffering of our fear and anger is easier to take than the humiliation of admitting our error.
- Often these thoughts make us angry, which gives us an adrenaline rush, so holding on to them is like a drug addiction.

How can we discover where there is a dysfunctional story at work in our lives? A feeling like being stabbed in the heart is a sure sign, but essentially, wherever there is anger, hate, and fear, there is a dysfunctional story. Where there is peace, joy, and love, there is authentic vision.

Think about what story causes you suffering. For example, "My mother didn't love me," or "John treats me badly." Then try to understand why you hang on to that story. What do you get out of it, and what does it cost you in pain and suffering? When you see your story as both unhelpful and untrue, you can start living more in a way that comes from your soul and less in a way that is from your ego.

Finally, remember that we all behave badly sometimes because of our stories. Everyone has painful personal myths that they believe are true and that make them act from ego instead of from Spirit. So when other people act negatively and irrationally, keep that in mind. Of course, it is not up to us to judge them or to compel them to fix their stories—we have enough of our own to deal with—but it is up to us to have some sympathy, understanding, and compassion for them when they act badly.

The lessons of our mistakes

Our egos usually hate to admit mistakes, to say, "I was wrong." Such an admission can feel like a dagger in the heart, can't it! Since no one is right all the time, however, this tension between truth and our egoistic illusions is a perpetual cause of suffering. In an attempt to circumvent that conflict or to avoid our pain, we project blame and criticism onto others, and we cling to our erroneous beliefs and dismiss or justify our mistakes. This never solves anything though. In fact, it perpetuates and exacerbates the problem. Instead, we can improve our lives and relieve our suffering with a few simple steps. Here's how.

First and foremost, honestly assess your beliefs and actions. Then, when you see what might be a mistake, remember that you aren't perfect—no one is—and you deserve forgiveness, including your own. Also, realize that you can rectify your mistakes; they need not be a permanent blot on your character. So if your mistake caused a problem (and mistakes usually do), either for yourself or for someone else, consider how you might fix things or at least atone for your actions.

In addition, reevaluate your actions and beliefs to see how you may need to change them. For example, if someone says, "You always do such-and-such," instead of reacting with the typical "I do not!" (we all do this sometimes), stop and think about it. Say to yourself, "I wonder if there's some truth in that. Let me think about it." (It may help to also tell yourself, "I'm not a bad person, but I'm not perfect either.") Usually there will be some truth along with some exaggeration or misunderstanding in the accusation. When you think about it reasonably instead of emotionally, and objectively instead of reactively, you will be able to differentiate between what is true and what is false. (By the way, you will know when you have found a belief or action that you need to examine in this way when you feel a strong, visceral resistance to self-examination.)

Finally, take steps to avoid repeating your mistake in the future. Is there a lesson to learn or a habit to break? If so, commit to doing that. You might want to use affirmations to help you do this. (See my book, *Tarot Affirmations*.) Do not dwell on your mistakes, though; doing that only reinforces a flawed vision of yourself. Forgive yourself and move on.

This is how we can learn and grow without feeling like the truth is stabbing us in the heart. These steps are simple, but they require the courage to face the truth, which is not an easy thing to do. However, when we do that, a miracle happens: we uncover a new depth of peace in our lives. And with practice, this process becomes easier because we start to loosen the grip that our ego has on our lives, and we begin to rest in the loving—and forgiving—embrace of our divine Self.

Where the Light enters

"A wound is the place where the Light enters you." — Rumi

Once, while listening to an interview with Alice Walker, I heard her say, "There is no way to get the healing without knowing what the wound is." She was referring to the way that we don't want to hear or talk about some of the horrible wounds we have deep inside us. We consider them too shameful or too humiliating, so we want to shut them up in a dark attic and not examine them. Nevertheless, despite the pain involved, bringing our deep wounds into the light and talking about them is therapeutic and healing.

However, needing to examine and heal our wounds does not mean we need someone to rescue us. Sometimes the deepest suffering that darkens a heart is not something that can be solved; it can only be witnessed and shared. We have a tendency to try to explain or fix another person's sorrow, though, perhaps to stay at a safe distance from their pain, but often what is needed goes beyond worldly circumstances and into the spiritual realm. This is not to say that we should not try to help those who are in pain, but what may be needed most is the palliative balm of our tenderness, the restorative power of our silent witnessing, and the healing warmth of our soulful companionship. In that sharing, a sacred light enters us; the healing power of the Divine enters our hearts and begins to dissolve our sorrow.

Four of Swords

The Four of Swords represents rest and recuperation, and it may be about reflecting upon the past in order to prepare for a better future. On a deeper level, it also indicates meditation and introspection, which can lead to the discovery of your true Self.

Rest and recuperation

There is in everything a natural ebb and flow, cycles of activity and rest. In our fast paced modern world, however, we tend to place value on activity and discount the value of rest. But the Four of Swords advises us to give ourselves permission to rest sometimes, to disengage from life for a while. Similarly, it indicates letting go of conflict in our lives so that we may find a place of peace within ourselves.

When we try to do too much, we become rest-deprived (or worse, sleep-deprived), and consequently, we get cranky, we act irrationally, and we become less effective in everything we do. In other words, we act in ways that are not in alignment with our higher selves. So this card suggests that you carefully consider if you have been too rushed, too harried, too engaged in the rat race. If so, you may need to take some time to rest, to disengage from the conflicts of life. Or perhaps you need to take a vacation or, at least, to take up meditation.

In any case, it is good to take a break from work now and then, even if only to leave your desk and stretch your legs. Take a few deep breaths, go for a short walk and just observe the beauty of the world around you. It's amazing how much more centered and calm you will become from such simple acts of rest and recuperation. And then when you return to your worldly, everyday tasks, you will be better able to do them from a spiritual place in your heart.

Question your myths

"When you're asleep at night, when you're not dreaming, where is the world?" – Byron Katie

First of all, let's not get *too* existential here. I think what Katie means is "where is *your* world?" She tells us that our world begins with our thoughts about ourselves—all the thoughts about "me, myself, and I" that constantly go through our heads. Everyone we know and everything we experience, it is all incorporated into our world through our thoughts about how things affect us and through our distorted prism of taking everything personally.

For example, we don't really see other people as they are. In our private little world, they are just the story we tell ourselves about them, and those stories are our own personal invention. One result of this is that our generosity is conditional, our friendship is conditional, and our love is conditional. It all depends on how we think things affect us and how we judge them to be. And besides being erroneous, the "story world" in our heads is a constant source of conflict and sadness in our lives.

The Four of Swords addresses this situation by urging us to release those stories so that we may find new and better ones. Yes, this can be much harder to do than it sounds. Luckily, though, there is help. One thing you can do is this: Whenever your mind starts telling you its story about someone else (for example, "He's so thoughtless." "She's so mean.") stop for a moment and question that story. Is there another way of seeing this person or this situation? Then from there, try to change that story in your mind, and thereby change your world.[48]

The fourth state of consciousness

There are three well-known states of consciousness—deep-sleep, dreaming, and waking—and while we are immersed in any one of them, we think that it is the true reality. For example, a dreamer thinks her dream-self is real. Our authentic Self, however, is the pure consciousness that both encompasses and transcends the other three states. Some mystics call this fourth level of consciousness, which is characterized by serenity and bliss, "God consciousness," and our eternal yearning for peace and happiness reflects our deep-seated desire to return to this state of transcendent consciousness in which we can rediscover our true Self.

For help in understanding the transcendent fourth level of consciousness, consider this analogy: This fourth state of awareness is to our waking consciousness as our waking mind is to our dream mind. This is an ancient concept that has been around for millennia. For example, there is a thought in Hindu theology that the true reality is Brahma's consciousness and the manifest universe is merely His dream. Similarly, we may say that we are dreaming our own reality, and when that dream is not what our conscious minds want (which it usually isn't) we think we need a better dream. But really, what we need is to awaken to the true reality of transcendent consciousness. The sleeper needs to awaken.

On the face of it, this seems very esoteric, but science has also begun to discover a fourth state of consciousness. In the early 1970s, researchers at UCLA discovered that meditation shifted people into a state of consciousness where

---

[48] *If you want help doing this, Byron Katie's book* Who Would You Be Without Your Story? *is dedicated to exactly that work.*

brain activity is very different from that of waking, dreaming, or deep sleep. In mediation, brainwave scans reveal a state of restful alertness and integration of mental activity, which some meditation practitioners describe as pure consciousness or unbounded awareness. And so the Four of Swords tells us that there is a fourth level of consciousness that we may discover through the practice of meditation. In this way, we may find the serenity and bliss we so deeply desire and which is our true nature and birthright.

Five of Swords

This card can indicate arguments, bickering, personal attacks, chaotic or disordered thought, and an egoistic urge to prove yourself right.

Finding the truth in our "enemies"

"Let go of your attachment to being right, and suddenly your mind is more open. You're able to benefit from the unique viewpoints of others without being crippled by your own judgment." — *Ralph Marston*

When someone disagrees with us, we often consider them to be an enemy (at least, to some extent) because we take disagreement personally. What we hear is not "I disagree with your opinion;" we hear "*you* are wrong" and this bruises our sensitive egos. We feel a desperate need to perceive ourselves as being right, so other people *must* agree with us; they're either with us or against us. (Never mind that this is a false dichotomy.)

But what if those who disagree with us are not our enemies? What if they are teachers we are refusing to pay attention to? In truth, the disagreeable people we encounter in life are not *in* the way, they are *on* the way. In other words, they are not obstacles to our quest for enlightenment; they are part of the process. So if we listen to such "enemies" we can discover all sorts of valuable truths about ourselves. Of course, it's likely that not everything they say is true but some of it might be, so there usually is something important to be learned from them if we keep an open mind. Yes, it can be a painful process, but ultimately this is a process that will set us free.

Similarly, an insistence that we are right generally means that we are not listening to the other person. (Actually, in most arguments, it's typical that neither party is really listening to the other.) But how can we connect with someone if we refuse to listen to them? Also, consider the proverbial question: "Would you rather be right or happy?" Typically, when we insist on our correctness, an argument ensues in which someone leaves feeling unhappy or dissatisfied. (In fact, to some extent, everyone involved gets hurt.) This results from our egos wanting to protect themselves, for an ego does not care if anyone else is happy; it just wants to exalt itself.

We should also remember that on a spiritual level we are all One, so when we label someone as "wrong" or "adversary" we label ourselves as such too. And labels of right or wrong are of little consequence compared to understanding our Oneness with others.

Here is an exercise you might do to bring this message into your life. Think of someone you consider an "enemy" because they took an opposing side of an argument. Reflect on what you get out of this "us versus them" mentality, and consider what truth about yourself this situation may reveal. Perhaps you have some deep, hidden doubts about your position. Maybe you are projecting on to the other person some trait or characteristic that you dislike in yourself. Or is it just that your ego is defending itself at the expense of your happiness? In any case, try to think of this other person as a teacher rather than as an opponent.

In general, then, as you choose your responses to others, always keep in mind the question, "Would I rather be right or happy?"

Divinity in our "enemies"

As we begin to dedicate our attention to union with the Divine, we may begin to see a kindred divinity in the people around us who are kind, generous, and supportive. It is relatively easy to see this. What is not so easy, and thus more valuable, is to see the Divine in our "enemies" too, to see the Divine in people who disagree and argue with us, people who aggravate us, and people who wrong us. Deity is in them too, but it's harder to see that due to the superficial worldly conflicts that exist between us. The miracle is that as we open ourselves to the awareness of the Divine within difficult people, Spirit will begin to take over our relationships with them and those conflicts will fade.

Pulling ourselves up by pushing someone down

We sometimes see another person as being wrong, bad, or foolish—whether or not they actually are—in order to give ourselves the ego-satisfying illusion that we are better than they are. Instead of working on our own issues in order to pull ourselves up, we put other people down to provide the illusion that we have risen up. At such times, we need to ask ourselves if our lives are really so miserable that we have to deride other people in order to feel better about ourselves. Like all our self-delusions, this one is hard to see and to admit, and as a result, it is difficult to dispel. One way to work on this issue, though, is to take to heart something that Byron Katie says: "Every time you see someone as less than you, question it."

So ask yourself if there is someone who you think is not as good as you. Why do you think that? How valid is that thought? What do your negative thoughts about that person say about you? Since we often project our own shortcomings onto others, it's valuable to try the following exercise in understanding: Turn around your putdown of the other person to make it be about you instead. For example, if you condemn that person for being dishonest, say to yourself, "I am not as honest as I should be" and consider that possibility. If you have a strong visceral reaction to the inverted statement, that is a good sign that you do need to consider this possibility and do something about it.

In doing this exercise, you will not only experience an opportunity to burn away a bit of your own imperfection, but you may also find that you have brought that other person into your heart. And in so doing, you will come one step closer to discovering your oneness with everyone.

Six of Swords

This card indicates a search for peace, a desire to leave troubled waters, a change of perspective, and an effort to help others along the way. It also assures us that "we're all in the same boat."

Listen to your own advice

This card indicates providing support for each other, but, as Carl Jung said, "We can go with another only as far as we have gone with ourselves." One implication of this insight is that all the wisdom we offer other people—such as "You need to do this" or "You shouldn't do that"—is advice that we should listen to for ourselves as well.

It is helpful, therefore, to consider carefully the bits of wisdom we offer to others and then turn our suggestions around to see how they might help us. Amazingly, it turns out that there is much we can learn from ourselves when we listen to our own advice with an open mind, and in so doing, we will begin to discover our oneness with others. A consequence of this is that we will stop being so judgmental of other people, which is sometimes what is going on in our hearts when we offer advice.

Seeing with new eyes

"The real voyage of discovery consists not in seeking new landscapes but in having new eyes." — *Marcel Proust*

The Six of Swords, with its depiction of a somber voyage to a new and better land, can suggest gaining a new outlook on life in our quest for happiness and meaning. We usually think this will come from a change in our circumstances (such as a new job, relationship, or location)—and sometimes it may—but a change in our perspective is what's most effective because, as the saying goes, "happiness is an inside job."

Our search for happiness may entail learning to see the proverbial glass as half full instead of half empty, or it might involve looking for the good in other people instead of the bad. It may also take us on a journey of discovery where we find that the spiritual aspect of life is what's truly important and we stop measuring the value of things with a materialistic yardstick.

This choice of perspective is always ours to make, and as we arrive at this new consciousness, we will find that it is vital to improving our lives and bringing positive change to the world. As Albert Einstein said, "No problem can be solved from the same consciousness that created it. We must learn to see the world anew."

See the beauty, not the blemishes

As noted above, the Six of Swords indicates gaining a new perspective through a journey toward a more enlightened state, especially when that journey leads away from a place of suffering. Consequently, I was reminded of this card when I read the following in *The Book of Awakening* by Mark Nepo:

> *If peace comes from seeing the whole, then misery stems from a loss of perspective. ... [Misery] is a moment of suffering allowed to become everything.*

And so an important question to consider is this: "Do I focus on the petty problems that beset me every day, or do I see the sacred beauty of the world that is all around me?" The importance of this change of perspective may be obvious when we think about it (which we rarely do) but how can we make that change?

One way is to take a break. We know that we need to take a vacation once in a while, but sometimes it is important to just take a micro-vacation of a few minutes in order to gain a new perspective whenever we start to become mired in the unhappy illusion that our problems define us. For example, if you feel stressed at work, get up from your desk and take a walk outside. Listen to the breeze and smell the fresh air. Or maybe you can just gaze out a window at the trees and the birds outside. In any case, appreciate the beauty, the wonder, and the mystery of life. See the eternal Spirit in everything.

And whenever you are in pain, remind yourself that there is joy in your life too. "Count your blessings" is a cliché, but literally doing that is excellent therapeutic advice. It takes you away from your troubled waters and brings you to another, more peaceful shore where you can visit a beautiful landscape, if only for a short while.

Briefly, then, this card tells us to continually remind ourselves that there is more to life than its problems.

Don't let the destination obscure the journey

We often fail to see the beauty of our lives at this (and every) moment because we are too busy. We tell ourselves, "I can't stop now; I've got places to go, things to do, and people to see." But the Six of Swords tells us that it is important that we not let the destination obscure the journey. Yes, it's great to have goals, but we should not let them blind us to life's journey along the way or we will find life to be a dull voyage with only rare moments of fleeting satisfaction. Instead, we should always remember to love the people in our life, to keep a sense of curiosity about everything, and to stop and smell the proverbial flowers. We should also participate in life and contribute to it even if we don't see any guaranteed returns on that investment. It is the participation that really matters. So remember that your goals are not your life; *life* is your life.

You are where you need to be

"How can you follow the course of your life if you do not let it flow?" — Lao-tzu

Often when we are in a situation we don't like—a job, relationship, location, etcetera—we focus on the fact that we hate it and we want to get out of it, which is a perspective that creates even more suffering. However, the spiritual truth of the matter is that we are always where we need to be to learn the lessons we need and to effect the growth that will move us along our spiritual path. Yes, it may be a good idea to work on changing our situation too, but a change of attitude is probably what we need first. In any case, while we are in a difficult situation—in the "here and now" of it—we should love it because it gives us what we need right then.

We should also consider the old saying, "Wherever you go, there you are." This tells us that changing our situation without learning the lessons of where we are will solve little. Even in a new and "better" situation, we will re-manifest the problems that we brought with us. The most profound solutions are the ones that change us for the better, not the ones that change our external conditions.

Seven of Swords

This card has many pejorative associations, such as stealth, deceit, theft, and sabotage. It can also signify taking the easy way out, running away from something you do not want to face, or trying to get away with something you know you should not be doing. However, there are some positive messages in it as well. It can also indicate ingenuity, thinking outside of the box, and reclaiming what is yours.

Secrets

"There are some secrets that we think we're keeping, but those secrets are actually keeping us." — Frank Warren

The sneaky attitude of the figure on the Seven of Swords typically implies some sort of mischievous meaning, but I can also see it representing the secrets that we carry around with us. We think we benefit from keeping our secrets, but as the quote from Frank Warren reveals, our secrets often control us, and so the way to freedom includes finding a safe way to release them.

Of course, you do not have to go public with every secret you know. You need to be responsible about this, especially when the secrets you hold involve other people. There are some judicious guidelines about keeping secrets that are worth considering.

Some secrets are about harm we have done to someone else, and keeping those secrets may mean we do not trust the other person enough to handle the truth, which deprives them of the chance to prove that they may be more trustworthy than we expect. Also, jointly dealing with the chaos that can come up when such a secret is shared ultimately can be a valuable opportunity to grow closer together, depending on how the situation is handled. Everyone involved must be at a place where they are able to forgive, or at least willing to try to do so. Disclosure of this type of secret also enables us to atone for our mistakes.

Other secrets may involve the lies we tell about ourselves. These may range from our pitiable attempts to cover up perceived inadequacies to the self-aggrandizing fictions we hope will exalt us. We wish to benefit from these lies, but actually they shame us and they hold us back from living authentically. One way to deal with this type of secret is to change whatever it is about our lives that we feel we have to lie about. Another way is to examine the validity of our feelings of inadequacy so that we can overcome them. For example, gay and lesbian public figures who have come out after an extended stay in the closet invariably say that no longer living a lie is the biggest relief of their lives.

This discussion suggests the old adage, "Confession is good for the soul." Like lancing a boil, confession may be essential for the healing process to begin, especially if the secret is a haunting one. As Alcoholics Anonymous says, the foundation of a lasting sobriety comes from "the open and honest sharing of our terrible burden of guilt."[49] Also, when we admit our shameful secrets, we may discover that they were not so shameful after all. Even more importantly, keeping secrets keeps us separate from each other, while revealing them helps us realize our similarity and unity with other people.

---

[49] *Alcoholics Anonymous's Step 5 is:* "Admitted to God, to ourselves, and to another human being the exact nature of our wrongs."

Finally, within our romantic and familial relationships, secrets are particularly important to examine closely. In such a context, whenever we keep a secret we need to ask ourselves who or what are we trying to protect: the other person, our relationship, or ourselves? It makes a big difference. For a loving relationship to thrive and grow, we have to push the envelope of what secrets we are willing to share, but we should be wary of sharing a secret merely to assuage our guilty conscience if it might hurt the other person involved.

Getting away with it

"The measure of a man's real character is what he would do if he knew he would never be found out." — *Thomas Babington Macaulay*

What if you could get away with something—a lie, a petty theft, some unethical behavior that might benefit you? It may even be something as trivial as getting a little too much change from a cashier. If it's not a big deal and no one would find out, it can be tempting. So, would you do it?

The immediate answer from a spiritual point of view is that it would create bad karma, but that is only part of the problem with acting without integrity. A more important issue is that we create the person we are by the decisions we make and the actions we take. So the question when such temptations arise becomes, "Is this the person I want to be?" In other words, do you want to be a dishonest or unethical person? Is the material gain worth the spiritual loss? Considering the relative value of the spiritual world versus the material one, the answer to that last question should be obvious. Lying, cheating, and stealing—even in small, petty ways—diminish and debase a person. Dishonorable actions plant in your mind and in your life the illusion of the supremacy of material reality over that which is spiritual, which further mires you in the delusion of separateness from the Divine and from other people.

We do not have to be as monumentally ignoble as someone like Bernie Madoff (the perpetrator of a massive Ponzi scheme), for example, to pollute our souls. Even little drops of poison are noxious, and as they corrode our soul, a bit at a time, our ethics and integrity slowly degenerate, and it becomes easier for us to make other toxic decisions. The effects accumulate insidiously unless we choose to make a change. It is important to keep all this in mind when we wonder, "Can I get away with it?"

Finally, then, this card urges you to make a commitment to live your life with integrity. This will create a better world around you as it also helps you become a better person.

Eight of Swords

The common image on the Eight of Swords, which is of a woman bound, blindfolded, and fenced in by eight swords, is generally interpreted as meaning imprisonment, especially by thoughts and beliefs, and as having a victim mentality.

The happiness list

Here is an exercise to illustrate an important message of the Eight of Swords.

Make a list of the things you feel you need in order to find happiness. This list can include things like getting a job that pays some specific salary, finding and marrying your "soul mate," or having a beautiful home in a good neighborhood. Create that list now before reading the rest of this message. When you are done, return and continue reading.

Are you done?

Okay.

Now here is the message from the Eight of Swords. The list you just created is what's keeping you from being happy right now. It is your Prison of Discontent. Happiness is a choice we make and a skill we develop; it is not a condition we can only attain under the "right" circumstances. So if you make a commitment to release these requirements for happiness and instead find joy in your life right now, in the present moment, you will transform your life. This does not mean that you shouldn't have goals. It just means that you can and should experience joy right now regardless of whether or not you have reached those goals yet. That is the way to find and experience lasting joy and peace in your life.

The thoughts that bind us and blind us

"We are not troubled by things, but by the opinions we have of things." — Epictetus

The Eight of Swords says that reason can trap us in an illusion of materialism, walled off from the brilliant spiritual reality of our lives. Thus, it also says that our thoughts and beliefs can easily bind us and blind us. One of the most insidious of our misconceptions is the belief that our perceptions of the world are the total truth of it. Reality, however, is like a huge castle that has many, many rooms, but we peer into it through one particular window, and it is a very small, dingy window at that.

Consequently, we must realize that there is always more to any situation or relationship than what we see of it and what we think about it. When we do learn the rest of the story, we inevitably find more understanding and compassion for other people and perhaps for ourselves as well. This sort of discovery is freeing. Thus, a bit of encouragement in this card is that a change of attitude or point of view may allow us to relieve our suffering.

With this in mind, try this exercise: Consider a relationship that is causing you stress, sadness, or anxiety. (This can be either a romantic or a platonic relationship.) Remember that you do not know what this person's journey is all about since everyone has their own lessons to learn, and they have to learn them in their own way and in their own time. Consequently, it will help you to try to see things from the other person's point of view. You will probably resist doing this, but try anyway, for if you do, you will gain some degree of freedom due to the resulting expansion of your perceptions.

Similarly, consider that we do not really know other people; we know our perceptions and opinions of them based on their past actions. As George Bernard Shaw wrote in *Man and Superman*, "The only man I know who behaves sensibly is my tailor; he takes my measurements anew each time he sees me. The rest go on with their old measurements and expect me to fit them." So try to start with a clean slate every time. If you truly do this, you will be surprised at how your perceptions of the other person change, and you will see changes in your relationship with him or her as well.

Our imaginary fish tank

I once read a story about a man who filled up his bathtub to give his fish a place to swim while he cleaned out their small tank. After cleaning the tank, he returned to the bathtub to find that the fish were swimming around in an area the size of their tank even though they had much more room available in the bathtub. It was their conditioning, not their reality, that restricted the range of their movement.

Similarly, we limit our lives to the confines of what we think is real and what we think is possible. Like those fish in the bathtub, our conditioning rather than our reality restricts us. In addition, our five senses are very limited in what they can perceive, and every sensory input is mentally filtered and censored by our past conditioning. In fact, *A Course in Miracles* goes so far as to say, "No one really sees anything. [We] see only [our] thoughts projected outward."

Consequently, we should train our minds to be open to the realization that there is more to reality than what we can perceive with our senses and what we have been led to believe. With that dawning awareness we can begin to swim freely through the vastness of life instead of limiting ourselves to the confines of our imaginary fish tank.

Freedom from our beliefs

"Truth only reveals itself when one gives up all preconceived ideas." — *Shoseki*

In his book, *No Death, No Fear: Comforting Wisdom for Life*, Thich Nhat Hanh makes the point that freedom is, above all else, freedom from our own beliefs. To illustrate this point, he relates a parable about a man who believes that a charred body is that of his son killed in a fire. He cremates the body and carries it in an urn everywhere, so deep is his grief. However, unbeknownst to this man, his son is not dead. He had been kidnapped, but one day he escapes, returns and knocks desperately on the man's door, begging to be let in. The man cannot believe that the person banging at his door is his son. Has he not carried his son's ashes around with him all this time? So the man refuses to open the door, and eventually his son leaves, now lost to him forever.

When we are wedded to our beliefs and concepts, we become blinded and trapped by them. And so we should always entertain the possibility that we are wrong about something. Our egos hate this, of course, but it is the only way to find truth. And even more than that, each time we consider such a possibility, we weaken our ego's constraints on our ability to live an authentic life.

Nine of Swords

This card is traditionally interpreted in terms of worry, shame, and nightmares (literally and metaphorically). With its common depiction of a wretched soul awakened from a disturbed slumber, this card also indicates sleep disorders along with the problems and issues symbolized by that.

<u>Don't worry, be happy</u>

"Worrying is like praying for something you don't want to happen." — *Unknown*

"Don't worry, be happy" is a famous quote by an Indian mystic and sage named Meher Baba. On the surface, this may sound like a simplistic philosophy of denial, but that is not what Baba meant by it, as evidenced by more complex versions of his advice, such as "Do your best. Then, don't worry; be happy in my love. I will help you."[50] This expanded version combines elements of responsibility and faith with those of confidence and serenity. So, yes, we should plan for the future, but worrying about it is unproductive. After all, worrying never caused a single seed to sprout. Worse yet, it is counterproductive. As Corrie ten Boom said, "Worry does not empty tomorrow of its sorrow; it empties today of its strength." And so, contrary to popular belief, worry has more to do with our state of mind than with the state of our material circumstances.

In addition to the troubles it causes, worry also indicates the existence of other problems. It demonstrates an inability to live in the moment, a belief that our material existence is a truer reality than that of our soul, and a lack of trust in the existence of divine aid or a divine plan. Thus, this card may suggest that the most effective treatment for worry may be to learn to live in the "here and now" and to discover and trust in our divine nature.

<u>Why do we worry?</u>

Why do we worry so much? Why do we suffer so much anxiety in our lives? At its deepest level, the answer is pretty simple: It is because we forget that we are spiritual beings and think that we are material beings instead. For example,

---

[50] *This quote from Meher Baba should be interpreted within the context of the fact that he considered himself to be "the avatar of the age."*

we believe that the *things* in our lives are important (which they are not), we fear that they are beyond our reach when we need them, and we know that they are vulnerable and transient when we do have them. The truth, however, is that everything that is authentic and important in life is unassailable. Things like our realization of our sacred identity, our love of others, and our union with the Divine may be forgotten, but never lost. No one can take them from us. If we knew that and truly believed it, we would stop worrying.

Is it easy to make that switch of consciousness? Certainly not. If it were easy, everyone would do it. It is a radical shift in our consciousness, but is it vital? Absolutely. The stress of worry is self-destructive, not productive. If more people made this shift of consciousness, the stress level of the whole planet would drop. So to paraphrase Meher Baba, "Don't worry; be happy for you are a sacred child of the Divine."

Lucid dream therapy for our lives

Much of our suffering comes from buying into the false reality of our ego-dreams of fear and worry, blame and shame. In fact, these dreams are nightmares, which suggests that a way to overcome them is by considering a treatment for actual nightmares.

There is a psychological therapy called "lucid dreaming" that has been effective in helping people who suffer recurrent nightmares. In lucid dream therapy, the subject is trained to become aware that he or she is dreaming in order to gain equanimity during the nightmare and thereby diminish its fearful effect. Similarly, if we think of our material life as a dream, we can use a sort of spiritual "lucid dream therapy" to heal ourselves. The misfortunes of life will lose their distressing impact if we see them as happening in a dream that cannot harm our true spiritual Self.

Awaken from illusions about others

Much of the suffering in our lives arises from our illusions about other people—our dream-like thoughts about them and our ego projections onto them. We tend to believe those illusions without questioning, and we suffer the consequences. When we finally challenge those beliefs, however, we begin to awaken to an expanding reality about others. We begin to realize that the people we have had spiteful thoughts about are actually just like us.

Everyone has their own story, but when we dig deeply enough, we discover that all the stories are basically the same. We all have fears and desires, needs and problems, wounds and wisdom, virtues and vices. On one level, we all are damaged goods, but at a spiritual level, we all are exquisitely beautiful. Consequently our nightmare stories about other people are superficial, and generally they reflect more about our own perceptions, biases, hidden desires, and fears than they do about the reality of the other person's life.

When we finally dispel our belief in those illusions—when we spiritually wake up, so to speak—we may feel ashamed of what we have done to other people in our minds and hearts, and with our actions. The wonderful truth, however, is that there is no need for shame and guilt. Those are dysfunctional feelings, and they too are deceptions. Once we awaken from the nightmare of our condemnations of others, once we see through the illusions that we sincerely believed, we can move on with our lives in peace, truth, and freedom, which is the loving, compassionate way the Divine wants us to live.

The puppetry of our wounds

"In our sleep, pain which cannot forget falls drop by drop upon the heart until, in our own despair, against our will, comes wisdom through the awful grace of God." — Aeschylus

Our unacknowledged psychic wounds stay with us until we bring the light of our attention to dispel the darkness that hides them. We can tuck these wounds away in the musty attic of our unconscious minds, but we can't lock them in there. They peek out at us at night in our dreams and nightmares where they are disguised in symbolic masks, which makes it hard for us to recognize them.

The real problem, however, is that all too often those hidden wounds are pulling the strings that control our actions. They cause our dysfunctional behavior, and they bring disease and adversity into our lives. The way out of the pain they cause is to look at them honestly and courageously. We must be willing to look into the darkness in our lives and to ask for divine help and guidance in understanding and releasing it. When we do that, we awaken a bit more to our true, divine nature.

<u>For shame</u>

Our feelings of shame and guilt (which are often unconscious) are a denial of our divine nature and an affirmation of the illusion that the Divine is separate from the material world and from us. Consequently, such feelings keep us from a spiritual awakening.

The way out of this nightmare is through self-forgiveness. When we realize that we have made a mistake we should not use it as an opportunity to berate ourselves and to justify buying into the false reality of blame and suffering. When we do that, we hold ourselves back from spiritual growth by using our mistakes to define ourselves. Instead, we must acknowledge that in our material manifestation, we are all imperfect so we all make mistakes. Then we should try to learn from those mistakes so that we can grow in wisdom, and we should forgive ourselves so we may grow in compassion.

Ten of Swords

This card can signify taking logic to extremes, and so it also indicates those times when reasoning leads us to a dead end, either through overanalyzing things or by reaching beyond our limits of understanding. It also indicates the tyranny of the ego over Self. Through the deadly violence often depicted on this card, it has acquired a traditional meaning of brutality, although I generally see it more as the ideas, thoughts, and beliefs involved than the actual acts themselves.

<u>Boxes of labels</u>

The Ten of Swords says that we make life dull and lifeless when we force everything into tiny boxes of labels and explanations. Indeed, our world becomes a much smaller place when our perception of reality is limited by the illusions of naming and categorizing. We kill the magic of life when we make that mistake.

Of course, in order to understand things, our finite minds need to box them into frameworks and conceptual models. There is nothing inherently wrong with this. It is how we have to operate, since reality is infinite but our conscious faculties are not. The problem arises when we think (as we typically do) that our concepts *are* the reality. It is like thinking that human life can be defined by what is in a medical textbook.

Although the Ace of Swords says that we should try to understand life, the Ten of Swords says that we cannot, not completely. There are a great many things in life that we just have to feel and experience because they are beyond our ability to logically and rationally explain and comprehend.

Reasoning's dead end

"As soon as you see something, you already start to intellectualize it. As soon as you intellectualize something, it is no longer what you saw." — *Shunryu Suzuki*

We miss so much of life when we believe that if something cannot be explained, it cannot exist. In truth, there is much that cannot be seen and cannot be explained or described. For example, I have a friend who denies the existence of love. He thinks it is a delusion, because, as he says, "If love really exists, where does it go when two people fall out of love?" (Of course, one might use the same argument to say that life does not exist either.)

On the other end of the spectrum, we sometimes think that we can completely explain something and that our explanation of it is the sum total of its reality. But when we believe that, we essentially destroy our understanding of it, as explained in the Suzuki quote above.

In addition, this card may reveal the point at which we finally give up trying to understand life and begin to experience it instead. Thus, it indicates the end of analysis and the beginning of pure awareness and experience.

So the end of reasoning can be a good thing if it means that we stop needing to have explanations for everything and that we stop over-analyzing things. Then we can begin to listen to our intuition, trust that things are not always what they seem to be, realize that our thoughts about things are but one interpretation of reality, and live our lives fully.

And so an exercise that this card suggests is to contemplate something—anything—for a while without thinking about it and about what it means. Try to just see it, feel it, smell it, listen to it—anything but think about it. See if you can do that and just experience what happens.

Ruinous logic

Another way to consider this card is to see that a course of action based solely upon cold logic and analysis—without compassion or spiritual insight—is ruinous. Consider the way that people often justify inhumane actions based on soulless concepts of themselves, their work, or their world. For example, when taken to task for not considering the suffering caused by cold-hearted business decisions, a businessman might explain that his first responsibility is to his shareholders, since he is a businessmen first. In truth, however, we all are spiritual beings first, and the extent to which we have lost sight of that is the extent to which we have lost part of our own humanity

The fascination of violence

Our culture has a morbid fascination with war, violence, and cruelty to our fellow beings, and it is imperative that we reevaluate that fascination. When we succumb to that mindset and thereby become complicit in the actions associated with it, we further ingrain it in our cultural psyche, which in turn echoes it back upon us. Another way to consider this is first to consider that in numerology, the number ten reduces to the number one ($1 + 0 = 1$), which connects the concepts of Self and Community. In this case, we see that due to our essential Oneness with everything and everyone else, whatever we do to another person, we also do to ourselves. In the famous words of John Donne, "Any man's death diminishes me, because I am involved in mankind; and therefore never send to know for whom the bell tolls; it tolls for thee."

It is true that neither you nor I acting alone and individually can stop war or crime, or even diminish the popularity of gratuitous violence in our entertainment industry. However, we can, each one of us, make a bit of difference, which adds up. We can become more peaceful and thereby be the change we want to see in the world, as Gandhi advised. We can withhold our attention to and our patronization of violent-themed entertainment, and we can counter anger with compassion and meanness with kindness.

As an exercise in this shift in consciousness, try to do the following for a day: Be on the lookout for aggressive, violent thoughts. When they arise, acknowledge them, but then dismiss them, replacing them with peaceful ones.

Kill inhumanity through "death by a thousand cuts"

Sometimes it seems that there is so much inhumanity in the world—so many angry words, so many cruel actions—and there is so little that we, as individuals, can do. It can be easy for us to feel defeated by that, but there is a way to consider this issue that lends some consolation and hope, like the faint glow of dawn on the horizon.

The Ten of Swords suggests the expression "death by a thousand cuts." This term comes from an ancient Chinese form of torturous execution called *Ling chi* in which the victim is killed by a multitude of non-fatal cuts. Each cut is relatively small, but the cumulative effect is deadly. This term sounds rather dreadful, and in the context of the phrase's origin it is, but in general it says that a large number of small actions can have a great, synergistic effect. Something big can be whittled away slowly, a bit at a time.

We can use this concept to see how we can slowly "kill" the inhumanity that infects the world (or just the inhumanity that infects each of us personally) through repeated simple acts of kindness. Every day we can cut the beast of inhumanity in little ways. Each cut may seem minor, but the cumulative effect is large. So be kind, be loving, be compassionate, and be generous. You may do this in small ways, but if you do it often and consistently, the world around you will eventually change.

The ego's *coup d'état*

In his book *The Power of Now*, Eckhart Tolle defines his use of the word "ego" as "A false self created by unconscious identification with the mind." Indeed, it certainly seems as though the ego assumed dominion in our lives through a *coup d'état* in which the servant (the ego-mind) assumed control over the master (the authentic Self), and this has resulted in a world of suffering. The cure, of course, is to remember who we are, and thus to restore our authentic Self to the throne of our lives. But how can we subdue the ego? How can we restore the correct balance of power in our minds?

One very important tool is meditation, although at first this may not seem effective because the ego does not shut up easily or without a fight. But meditation works in the wonderfully subtle way of "death by a thousand cuts." Little by little, it will reinstall our deep, still Self as the rightful ruler of our lives.

It is also important that we strive to realize the truth about the ego. It is an illusion with no true reality of its own. It may be useful in some ways, especially in our childhood when we are weak and vulnerable, but it is only a tool. Of course, the ego tells us that it is essential for our survival, but actually it is only working to ensure its own survival. And so it creates the illusion of a fear-filled world of hazards, scarcity, and struggle in order to ensure its continued position of power in our lives, even if it means we have to stifle our true happiness and fulfillment as a result.

And so we can see how the ego is a parasite that we can learn to recognize by the masks it wears, such as fear, anxiety, and anger. As we gain this understanding and work toward rejecting the tyranny of the ego, we will develop a deep certainty that the true reality of our being is that of our divine nature instead. And as we realize this, our bondage to the ego will slip away.

The wonderful end of thought tyranny

This card's suggestion of an end to over-analysis points out a beautiful interpretation of it, which will surprise those who merely see it as a harbinger of failure and ruin. We must remember that this card is not in the suit of Pentacles, so it is not primarily about physical manifestations. Instead, it is in the suit of Swords, which is concerned with thought (among other things). Thus, we may view the fate of the man on this card (who is generally depicted as being stabbed multiple times) symbolically as the end of the tyranny of what is called "Monkey Mind."[51] As a result, this card says that when we finally put an end to the tyranny of our thoughts (which should be our servant, not our master as they usually are), we will find silence and stillness ... and bliss.

Page of Swords

This card is about learning new things, especially with an open mind. It also indicates innocence, curiosity, and vigilance.

The virtues of "I don't know"

"There's a lot of freedom in 'I don't know.'" — *Byron Katie*

Recently, while reading *Who Would You Be Without Your Story?* by Byron

---

[51] *For more about the monkey mind, see the section of the Five of Wands called "Cage your monkey mind".*

Katie, I came across the preceding quote, which brought to mind the Page of Swords. This short quote suggests some remarkable things, for indeed, "I don't know" can be quite a profound admission. Children are born with this brilliant open-mindedness, but it slips away from us as we grow up. We come to assume that our opinions are facts and that we know things we only think we know. As Josh Billings, a nineteenth century humorist, said, "The trouble with most folks isn't so much their ignorance. It's know'n so many things that ain't so." Consider also this quote from Confucius:

Real knowledge is to know the extent of one's ignorance.

"I don't know" is a wonderful place to start a journey of discovery since it is a prerequisite for having a "beginner's mind," which means being open-minded and free of preconceptions. To quote the Zen master, Shunryu Suzuki:

In the beginner's mind there are many possibilities; in the expert's mind there are few.

"I don't know" can also be the humbling and freeing realization that some things *can't* be known. Many things—especially things that are profoundly spiritual—can be felt or experienced but not known or rationally understood. Our ego minds don't want to admit this though. The ego hates to say in all sincerity, "I don't know," even though that is the best—the only, really—place to start a journey into wisdom.

In our fearful desire for security, we try to convince ourselves that we know everything—or at least that we know everything within the small circle in which we have circumscribed "reality"—because it's comforting to think so. But realizing that there is a lot of unknown out there can lead us to see how fascinating life and reality is, and it can make our own life more fulfilling too. It can be a bit scary, or it can be exciting. Which of those things we experience— the fear or the excitement—is up to us.

Naiveté

As mentioned in the previous section, keeping a "beginner's mind" is important when we embark upon any journey of discovery. After all, how can we make new discoveries if we think we already know the answers?

In addition, this innocent state of mind also lends us courage because sometimes naiveté means that we believe in miracles. Take, for example, the story of Joan of Arc. The Maid of Orléans certainly exemplified the strength and courage of the time in our youth when we believed in our dreams. Everyone else "knew" that this young girl could not possibly lead the dispirited French army to victory, but since she herself never once believed that, she went ahead and did it anyway. Thus, one could say that to some extent her success depended upon her naiveté. And so we can see in this card the advice to be naive enough to believe in your dreams.

An unexamined faith

An eagerness to learn is invaluable when traveling a spiritual path. We need to examine what we believe carefully and with an open mind, and not just accept unquestioningly what we have been taught by an established religion. This does not mean that we have to reject all that we have been taught. Indeed, our examinations may lead us to embrace the religious tradition in which we were raised. But it does mean that it is only through questioning and examining our spiritual beliefs that we will find our true path. After we have examined our beliefs, we can come to trust and hold fast to them, but even then, we should remain open-minded, realizing that our ideas, opinions, and beliefs can always develop and evolve further.

Knight of Swords

We may interpret the Knight of Swords as actions (which Knights represent) inspired by or based upon our beliefs (Swords). Consequently, it is about idealism, quixotic actions, and intellectual pursuits. This card also depicts chivalry and heroism.

Knowledge versus Wisdom

The Knight of Swords calls to mind the difference between knowledge and wisdom. He is on a quest for knowledge, but although knowledge may come from answers, wisdom lies in our capacity to evaluate those answers and to make proper use of them. It also comes with experience since we must act upon our knowledge in order to understand and absorb it.

A common pitfall in our quest for knowledge, though, is that, as Anaïs Nin famously said, "We don't see things as they are; we see them as we are." This indicates the common problem of bias, which taints the information we acquire, but perhaps a worse mistake in our pursuit of knowledge arises when we fail to realize that since we are finite and fallible beings, our perspective is limited and limiting. A wise man, on the other hand, knows that knowledge is relative and always subject to revision, and thus he remains humble about his learning.

And so a great part of our pursuit of wisdom is our pursuit of self-knowledge and self-improvement. To better understand the world, we must come to understand ourselves better, and we must also become better people. More specifically in terms of our spiritual quest, this message reminds us that what we may learn about spirituality is only knowledge. Acting upon that knowledge is what brings wisdom, and that is our true spiritual pursuit. So, for example, knowing the value of charity is meaningless unless we also act with true generosity.

As this knight—full of action as knights tend to be—sets out into the world, he may be on his way toward wisdom if he acts according to what he learns. And so it is for each of us as well.

The pursuit of spiritual knowledge

The knights in the Tarot deck are intrepid explorers in the realm of their suit, and they depict movement and discovery. Thus this one, the Knight of Swords, might urge us to explore various spiritual paths, discover new truths, and learn things about our own spirituality. Thus we see that it is important to learn about the journeys that others have taken and to study the teachings of leaders from spiritual traditions, even (or especially) ones other than the one we grew up with.

On the other hand, this card also warns of living too much in your head and thinking that mental explorations alone will bring enlightenment. We must remember that this is not the only knight in the deck. The other knights reveal other ways (such as charity, loving devotion, and passion for enlightenment) that are necessary to bring balance and wholeness to our journey. Thus, it is important to realize that although the path of intellect is an important part of our spiritual journey, it is only one component.

The "un-rewards" of the spirit

The Knight of Swords is associated with chivalry and heroism, and we may wonder how this relates to our spiritual pursuits. For one thing, it may suggest the question, "Is my assistance to others more about the credit or rewards than it is about helping other people?" In other words, are we doing it because it's the right thing to do, or are we doing it for the reward, even if that may be something as small as someone else's thanks or something as esoteric as good karma?

A sign of true kindness of spirit is a willingness to do a selfless act even if there were no reward, and in fact, even if no one would ever know. Ironically, though, such acts do bring rewards, but they are of the spirit, such as love, serenity, and divine union. Another perspective is to see that such selfless acts are themselves their own reward for they demonstrate our innate divinity, and what better "reward" is there than that?

Acting with purpose

A couple of pitfalls that people may encounter when they begin a spiritual pursuit are that they disengage from their worldly involvement or they separate their spiritual and mundane worlds, treating each one differently and acting differently in each.

While we may need (or at least benefit from) a meditative retreat from worldly life some times, for most of us, prolonged withdrawal denies our purpose for being here. People may disagree about what that purpose is. Perhaps we are here to learn to love and to forgive, or maybe we are here to teach others, or we may be here to explore an existence in the manifest world. There are many schools of thought on this topic. But in any case, here we are, and we must engage in life in order to learn, teach, or discover. We must fully participate in life in order to realize and live our purpose. There is a wonderful quote from William Arthur Ward that illustrates this advice for living fully:

Do more than belong: participate. Do more than care: help. Do more than believe: practice. Do more than be fair: be kind. Do more than forgive: forget. Do more than dream: work.

It is through our active participation in life that we learn and hone our spiritual skills, so to speak. Peace and clarity are relatively easy to accomplish while sitting quietly in meditation, but the true test is to be able to experience peace and clarity amid the distractions and obstacles of daily living. For example, can you maintain your balance and equanimity when your spouse yells at you? Experiencing that and learning from it is a spiritual practice. So consider this message as you go about your routines of life, and try to practice mindfulness in all your activities as you fully engage in life.

Knowing through doing

"We can only learn to love by loving." — Rumi

As noted in the preceding section, this card suggests that the best way to know something is by doing it. Nowhere is this more valid than in the esoteric and ineffable aspects of life, especially in our spiritual pursuit. Thus, for example, we learn charity through acts of generosity, we learn about love by acting compassionately, and we learn to live in the present moment by practicing mindfulness in all that we do. And through each of these, we also learn about our own divinity.

Queen of Swords

The Queen of Swords exemplifies self-respect and self-control, and she indicates "tough love." She also says that we gain wisdom from experience, even when that experience involves sorrow.

A warning against rigid dogma

This queen has learned the lessons of life from the proverbial school of hard knocks. Unfortunately, the grief and sorrow that are part of that school's curriculum can rob us of our compassion and tempt us to protect ourselves from the stinging vagaries of the world by clinging to strict rules of what is "right and wrong." We may do this because we want a rigid structure that will shield us from future pain, or maybe we just need something that will help us make sense of our misery. And sometimes we try to deal with our suffering through a sense that misery loves company, as in, "If I can't have what I want, neither can anyone else."

However, although a rigid dogma may seem to provide a safe haven from fate's slings and arrows, it may also make us emotionally barren. Thus this card serves as a warning against becoming moralistic, sanctimonious, and self-righteous—traits that lurk on the dark side of a spiritual path. If you find yourself falling prey to them, though, gently consider how you can temper your judgment with compassion and how you can act in a more understanding way toward others. Also consider the famous admonition "Know Thyself!" for we cannot begin to evaluate the lives of others until we have gazed unflinchingly into the dark corners of our own minds.

Learning from adversity

"To live is to suffer; to survive is to find some meaning in the suffering." — *Friedrich Nietzsche*

The Queen of Swords personifies our ability to learn and grow from adversity. Unfortunately, we do not always cultivate or use that ability. When faced with challenging circumstances, we need to commit ourselves to using our misfortune as an opportunity to become more insightful and to develop wisdom within the crucible of our pain. As an inspirational example of this, consider the early experiences of the 14th Dalai Lama.

In 1950, when the Dalai Lama was 15 years old, the Chinese army invaded Tibet. For several years the young Dalai Lama, who had assumed full political power in Tibet, attempted to negotiate a peaceful solution with Beijing, but to no avail. Then in 1959 when a Tibetan uprising was crushed by the Chinese army, the Dalai Lama fled to India where he presided over the Tibetan Government-in-exile until his retirement in 2011. Despite these experiences, when asked about Mao Zedong (the Chinese leader during the invasion of Tibet), the Dalai Lama said, "He was my greatest teacher. He taught me patience." Thus, what he learned from this difficult experience was patience, not bitterness, anger, or pessimism.

Nietzsche also said, "That which doesn't kill us makes us stronger," but there is more hope and advice in that saying than assurances or universal truth. Although hardship may encourage us to grow stronger and wiser, it does not guarantee it. The difference lies in the choices we make.

Besides encouraging personal development, adversity can impel us along our spiritual path too. In other words, when things go terribly wrong, our desperation can bring us to a state where we may "let go and let God," as the saying goes.

King of Swords

The King of Swords is confident in his beliefs and unflinching in his decisions. He symbolizes expertise and the wisdom of experience, and he urges us to find our own inner source of authority—the King of Swords that lives within each of us.

Expertise versus action

"Knowledge of the path cannot be substituted for putting one foot in front of the other." — M. C. Richards

It is a truism that we learn by doing, and nowhere is this truer than in the area of spirituality. What is even more important though is that we also create who we are by what we think, say, and do. For example, reading or talking about compassion and charity does not make you a compassionate and charitable person. It takes compassionate and charitable actions to do that, and this suggests a spiritual message in this card.

Reading books about spirituality and learning about spiritual practices like meditation are important activities. But then we need to get off our pedestal and go out into the world and help other people. That is how we become more spiritual people. We need not go so far as to follow Mother Teresa's path, but there are steps we can take in a similar direction. For example, this card might suggest that you think of a spiritual lesson you have learned and then commit to doing something that puts that knowledge into action. Not only will this improve your own spiritual pursuit, but through such actions, you can instruct and lead others as well.

Go beyond knowing

"[our] whole culture is based on the worship of ... the rational mind while other levels of knowing, like what we call intuition, have practically become dirty words." — Ram Dass

As noted in the previous section, there comes a time in our spiritual journey when it is no longer enough to engage in study about the path. Books, lectures, and workshops are great, but they function within the limited confines of the rational, analytic mind. At some point we have to do the work; we have to begin living and experiencing a spiritual path. As Ram Dass also says, "... to have what

Tarot and Your Spiritual Path

you seek, you have to go beyond knowing and become it."

Something that can help you "go beyond knowing and become it" is to create a list of everyday spiritual practices and then commit to doing them. I did that a while back, and although I don't always succeed in living up to those commitments, just having them explicitly stated reminds me to act in accordance with them, which does help me move toward them.

Here is my list of commitments as of this point in time:

To live with integrity

To act with mindfulness

To live in the present moment with no regrets or recriminations about the past and no fears or worries about the future

To focus on the good in other people and in the world instead of dwelling on what's "bad" or "wrong" with them

To live without complaining

To love everyone and to forgive everything

To live a life of generosity and service to others

To practice meditation daily

To see the Divine in everything and everyone

To turn my thoughts ever toward the Divine

A valuable exercise is to create your own list of commitments about your spiritual practice. Then, to help you act accordingly, review that list and recommit to it daily. (If this seems to be too daunting, start by making one commitment per day.) Also, this is an ongoing process so do not worry if the commitments you listed are "right." You can reevaluate and adjust them as you continue along your journey.

The dangers of expertise

As noted in the section for the Page of Swords titled "The virtues of 'I don't know'", Zen Master Shunryu Suzuki said, "In the beginner's mind there are many possibilities; in the expert's mind there are few." For the Page, this suggests advice, but for this King, it is a warning about pride, hubris, and inflexibility.

Thus this card says that it is okay for us to be an expert about something, but we should remain humble and open-minded too.

Another danger of acquiring expertise is described as follows by A. Parthasarathy in his book *Vedanta Treatise: The Eternities.*

> *[When we] do not assimilate, absorb the knowledge taken in, ... accumulated knowledge becomes a burden rather than a blessing.*

One interpretation of this is that a danger of acquiring knowledge without assimilating it (i.e., without "becoming it" as Ram Dass says) is that as a "learned expert," all that knowledge merely feeds the ego and creates vanity. In addition, when we think we know it all, we may think we do not have to listen to others and so we do not learn from them. We close our eyes to new possibilities and our minds to new ideas. In short, we lose our humility, which is an important aspect of a truly spiritual person.

PENTACLES

Many New Age pundits talk about how to bring abundance into our lives, which is great in and of itself. The problem arises when we move from creating abundance to desiring and depending upon it. A fundamental characteristic of a spiritual path is movement toward a state where our sense of wellbeing is no longer dependent on the conditions of the world around us. When we are finally able to release our attachment to the things of the material world, our sense of joy and serenity will become stabilized by our focused attention on our connection to the Divine, and it will be unaffected by pleasure or pain, success or failure. In accordance with that, the spiritual messages of the cards in the suit of Pentacles tend toward helping us transcend materialism rather than indulge in it. Indeed, the path to the Divine indicated by the suit of pentacles is the way of generosity, service, and gratitude.

One way to remember the spiritual message of this suit is to consider the wonderful relevance of a pentacle as the icon for this suit as used in many Tarot decks. A pentacle consists of a star (spirit or divinity) within a coin (the material world) or a circle (as in "the circle of life"). This says that this suit is not just about physical manifestation; it is also about using our journey through this physical plane to find sacred meaning in life. This way of looking at the cards in this suit lends them a subtlety of meaning that can bring new life and an uplifting spirit to our Tarot readings whenever a Pentacle card arises.

Ace of Pentacles

The Ace of Pentacles indicates an opportunity or boon, and it can signal the advent of abundance and prosperity. A common image on this card is that of a divine hand offering a pentacle, which says that seeing the divine within the manifest world is one of the essential aspects of a spiritual path.

Basic, primary needs

"Without food ... all other components of social justice are meaningless." — *Norman Borlaug*

Sometimes when I engage in a conversation about the supreme importance of our quest for reunion with the Divine I encounter a question like this: "So, do you think we should just tell children starving in Third World countries that they shouldn't worry about food; their spirituality is all that matters?" Although it sounds a bit snarky, this is a valid question to consider, and certainly a discussion about our primary physical needs is relevant to the Ace of Pentacles.

We are intensely motivated by our basic needs when they are unsatisfied, but when they have been met, they cease to be compelling. (If you want proof of this, hold your breath and see how quickly and powerfully your thoughts turn to your need to inhale.) It is also true that the more basic the unsatisfied need, the stronger and more persistent the motivation.

When primary human needs are not being met, they dominate a person's life and drown out other concerns and desires, including motivation for spiritual enlightenment. Thus it is important to work to relieve suffering in the world instead of just telling people that their hunger (for example) is an illusion and they can achieve bliss if they would just focus on seeking reunion with the Divine. That may be true, but in such circumstances, it is a doomed (and callous) argument.

All this is not to say, however, that people who are poor cannot (or will not) follow a spiritual path. Indeed, if their most basic needs are met, they may be better at following a spiritual path than those who are rich, since the wealthy easily become addicted to their materialism. This is the basis of the biblical warning: "It is easier for a camel to go through the eye of a needle, than for a rich man to enter into the kingdom of God."[52]

Returning to the question about hungry children, of course we must first address their basic needs, since living in a human incarnation means that those needs are the prime motivator as long as they are unmet. In addition, though, we should also consider the following quote from Ram Dass:

Do what you can on this [material] plane to relieve suffering by constantly working on yourself to be an instrument for the cessation of suffering.

Postscript: There is a difference between a need and a want, and it is a difference that we often choose to forget. For example, adequate nutrition is a need, but filet mignon and chocolate cake are wants.

---

[52] *Matthew 19:24*

Appreciation and gratitude

The Tarot Aces embody the essence, epitome, and ideal of their suit. In the case of the Ace of Pentacles, this ideal includes appreciation and gratitude for what we have, as opposed to an obsession to gain the things we do not have. This is what, in truth, defines the word "abundance," as the following quotes beautifully illustrate:

"If the only prayer you said in your whole life was, 'thank you,' that would suffice." — *Meister Eckhart*

"It is when you become grateful for what you have that you become an abundant person." — *Marianne Williamson*

"Acknowledging the good that is already in your life is the foundation for all abundance." — *Eckhart Tolle*

There are many ways to cultivate this sense of appreciation and gratitude. It can be as simple as saying a silent "Thank you" whenever something nice happens. Another way is demonstrated in a beautiful story I once read about a man named John Kralik who started writing thank you notes and thereby changed his life. At a time when his life was in the dumps, Kralik had an epiphany: Instead of focusing on what he didn't have, he would find a way to be grateful for what he did have, and that way was to write "Thank You" notes.[53] The following quote states this process succinctly:

"When you appreciate something, it comes again. If I was thankful for clients paying their bills, they seemed to pay faster. If I was thankful for cases, they seemed to come more." — *John Kralik*

To put this into practice in your own life, surprise someone today with a note of thanks. It will make their day as well as set the foundation for your own abundant life. You may also want to start a Gratitude Journal, which serves a similar purpose.

Opportunities

The Universe is constantly sending us valuable opportunities to learn and grow, but we must be open to them, even though they often come disguised as

---

[53] *If you're interested to learn how this process changed Kralik's life, see his book called* 365 Thank Yous: The Year a Simple Act of Daily Gratitude Changed My Life.

problems. And when we do avail ourselves of an opportunity, we must remember that the secret to true happiness is to avoid attachment to the results of our efforts.

To expand upon this message, consider the fact that sometimes we succeed and sometimes we don't for various reasons. This doesn't mean that when we fail, it was not a good opportunity. Thomas Edison, for example, failed "10,000" times before he made a functioning electric light, but his failures did not discourage him. Instead, along the way, he said: "I have not failed. I've just found 10,000 ways that won't work." Thus, one lesson in this card is to focus on those efforts that do succeed and to persist despite the failure of others. Another lesson, one that delves deeper into our spiritual life, is that it's always important to do the right thing, but then it's also important to release our attachment to the results of that "right action" and allow the Divine to work through our efforts as appropriate.

Create a beautiful life

"What you are is God's gift to you; what you make of yourself is your gift to God." — George Washington Carver

The Divine gives us tools and offers us opportunities, but ultimately, we create our own lives, and it is up to us to create beautiful and meaningful ones. This exquisite truth has been relayed to us by many sages throughout history, but it is difficult for many of us to acknowledge it. Perhaps the responsibility of it weighs heavily upon us, and we may not think we are up to the challenge. But as we come to realize our oneness with the Divine, we begin to see that we are indeed co-creators of our world, whether we like it or not. When we approach life with negativity, selfishness, and fear, that is what we create for ourselves. In other words, those are the types of opportunities (i.e., "problems") we create. But when we envision passion, generosity, and love, then we manifest that light instead.

Spiritualize your life

"Matter emanates from and encases the soul." — Robert Place and Rosemary Guiley[54]

---

[54] *This quote is from the description of the Ace of Coins in the book* The Alchemical Tarot *by Place and Guiley.*

The Tarot's Aces are numerologically related to the Magician card, so we can find meaning for this card in that association. Just as the Magician represents the dictum "As above, so below," this card also says that we can draw down the creative power of the Divine when we realize and utilize our connection to that power. But the message that the manifestation of our material lives arises from our thoughts and desires (both conscious and, unfortunately, unconscious)[55] is only half of this vital truth. The other half is that we can make our material lives and the material world in which we live more sacred by cultivating spiritual intention in our every thought, word, and deed. So remember this old saying, "It's not just what you do; it's also how you do it that counts."

Two of Pentacles

"It takes no more time to see the good side of life than to see the bad." — *Jimmy Buffett*

There is a sense of balance in this card, such as juggling tasks and responsibilities. Also, there is a sense of whimsy in many versions of it, so it can indicate playfulness, or even the play of change in our lives.

Balancing the secular and the spiritual

"Most people struggle with life balance simply because they haven't paid the price to decide what is really important to them." — *Stephen Covey*

Balance on the physical and material plane is a fundamental meaning for this card. It can have mundane implications such as balancing tasks, finances, or responsibilities, or it can imply the more sacred meaning of balancing the mundane and the spiritual aspects of life. In order to find a balance between those two, we choose which is truly important to us and then give more weight to that one. It is important to note, however, that since our materialistic culture has shaped our consciousness, if we have not made an explicit choice to emphasize the spiritual aspect of life, then we have made an implicit one for the material side because that's the default setting, so to speak.

---

[55] *This is sometimes referred to as the Law of Attraction.*

Unfortunately, most of us avoid choosing to give primacy to our spirituality. Perhaps this is because we fear the stereotypical image of an ascetic living in abject poverty. But choosing a spiritual life does not mean you have to reject a material life. You don't have to choose between earthly pursuits and spiritual ones; you just have to choose your actions in the material world based on a spiritual perspective instead of a materialistic one. In fact, the true choice involves seeing the spiritual meaning in all of your decisions, activities, and circumstances. Deeper still, it means choosing to create spiritual meaning in every part of your everyday life.

These insights are reflected in the Zen proverb, "Before enlightenment, chop wood, carry water. After enlightenment, chop wood, carry water," which means that enlightenment does not result in doing different things but in doing the same things differently—with a different attitude, heart, and consciousness. Although we may do the same old things when enlightened, we will do them with a new understanding, we will do them compassionately and mindfully, and we will be fully engaged in them. Then when we are fully present in our work, it becomes a joy instead of a burden. Thus, the spiritual choice is not the dour, joyless drudgery that the popular notion of it would have us think. Instead it is, ultimately, light, fun, and joyful.

The spirit of joy

"In singing and dancing is the voice of the Law." — Hakuin Ekaku

On many versions of the Two of Pentacles there is a person who seems to be having fun. Indeed, this is generally the most playful, fun-filled card in the whole deck, and it offers a spiritual message to go out and have fun in life. That does not mean we should fritter away our lives; it just means that we are meant to enjoy life. We should choose to find joy in what we do instead of approaching our tasks with a begrudging attitude. It also means that if our work brings us true joy, we can be pretty sure that we have made the right career choice.

There is a keenly transformative power in having fun. Finding and expressing joy is a wonderful way to experience our spirituality and to realize the Divine in the world around us. In fact, if an activity does not bring joy, it probably does not come from the soul, or it may indicate that you are doing it "wrong"—perhaps with uncertainty, fear, or reservations.

In her book, *Seventy-Eight Degrees of Wisdom*, Rachel Pollack says, "Unless we truly believe that the process of self-discovery is a joyous one we will never follow it through." This is as true of the spiritual component of self-discovery as it is of the mundane aspects.

Laughter is the best medicine

"What soap is to the body, laughter is to the soul." — Yiddish Proverb

We have all heard the saying "Laughter is the best medicine," and that's as true for the soul as it is for the body. Thus, a bit of advice in this card is to find more humor and laughter in your life and stop taking yourself so seriously. Do not be afraid to take an irreverent look at life (and at yourself) now and then. Laugh at our human foibles. This does not mean it's okay to laugh at specific people, or at their specific problems or failures. That is derision, not real humor, and it is the ego's attempt to feel better about itself by putting down some other person or group. Instead, laugh about things that we all do. And while you are at it, find a way to laugh from delight, for the sheer joy of life. One way to do that is to play with children. *They* know all about that sort of laughter. Or play with your dog or cat. They too know how to have fun in life. There are many ways to rediscover the precious art of fun and laughter. Try one!

Three of Pentacles

A common interpretation of this card is that of people working together on a large creative venture. This has obvious spiritual implications if we consider our spiritual quest to be that sort of endeavor. It is larger than life, and in fact, it is the ultimate creative venture.

Working together on our spiritual journey

A wonderful message that came to me once when I contemplated this card was this: "We are all working together to return to the Divine." Indeed, our spiritual journey is a group effort. Every individual's path is unique, but every individual's movement back to Spirit brings us all that much closer to the Divine since we are all One. We are all a part of something greater than our individual selves.

This card also indicates a few pitfalls for us to beware of. There is a tendency of religions to anthropomorphize the Divine (which is severely limiting), to carve in stone their specific interpretation of the Divine, and to see divinity as something apart from us. All of these things have a tendency to inhibit rather than nurture spiritual growth, and it is important to see beyond them, to see that "God" is not a large and powerful version of a man, does not belong to one particular sect, and is not separate from us. Those are concepts that can keep us from returning to Spirit.

Working together within our diversity

"Snowflakes are one of nature's most fragile things, but just look what they can do when they stick together." — Vista M. Kelly

Snowflakes are eternally the same despite their infinite diversity. They all share a common essence—they all are made of frozen water crystals—yet no two are alike. It's the same with us. We are all "frozen souls"—Spirit manifested in a material body—so we are all the same in our essential spiritual nature, yet we are all unique. No two people are identical.

We marvel at the distinctiveness of individual snowflakes, and we are enchanted by their intricately unique forms. Unfortunately, we fail to extend that sense of wonder and delight to the infinite variety of humankind. We adopt a tribal "us versus them" attitude. Instead of celebrating our diversity so that we can all work together, we try to make other people conform to our patterns of behavior, belief, and appearance, or we just plain condemn theirs.

Perhaps we should try to be more like snowflakes. They don't judge each other or try to change each other. Instead, they stick together, and it can be rather awe-inspiring to see the incredible results when they do. (Consider, for example, the irresistible power of an avalanche.) So if we stick together instead of judging and condemning, if we all work together and use the powerful synergy of our differences, we can do anything. Perhaps we can even create a wonderful new world of peace, joy, and harmony.

Creativity and spirituality in ordinary labor

"[Our] challenge ... is to live in such a way that there is no duality, no separation between the spiritual path and its manifestation in everyday life." — Rick Fields

The Three of Pentacles suggests that there is a spiritual aspect to ordinary labor when we express our creativity in our work. We all have divinely creative potential, and manifesting it is part of our spiritual practice. But it is not the grandeur of what we do that defines us. We need not build a castle, discover a cure for cancer, or compose a symphony in order for our lives to have value. Rather, it is the sincerity of our efforts, the care we take in them, and the spirit we put into them that creates worth and greatness in anything we do.

Just as the Magician card assures us that we can express our divine creative potential, this card says that we can manifest that potential in whatever work we undertake. Our spirituality can be discovered and expressed through even the simplest labor; it is all in how we approach it. In fact, there are many spiritual traditions that maintain that work done as devotion to the Divine (rather than for selfish reasons) is an essential form of spirituality. Consider, for example, the following quote from *Religion in Practice* by Swami Prabhavananda:

> *Whatever work you do, whether you like it or not, know that it is the Lord's work, and adjust yourself accordingly. Remember this, all work must be done as worship of God ... The true karma yogi does not work to gain publicity. No matter how insignificant his work may be, he throws himself wholeheartedly into the task, because, for him, his work has become worship of God.*

Another perspective on this message of the Three of Pentacles can be seen in the following story about three masons, which is attributed to a writer named Margaret M. Stevens:

> *When the first man was asked what he was building, he answered gruffly, without even raising his eyes from his work, "I'm laying bricks." The second man replied, "I'm building a wall." But the third man said enthusiastically and with obvious pride, "I'm building a cathedral."*

So a question to keep in mind is this: Which man are you? Are you merely laying bricks or are you building a cathedral?

Four of Pentacles

While material security and stability are indicated by the Four of Pentacles, there is a dark side to this card as well. It warns us of possessiveness, of becoming dependent upon material things, and of clinging to our possessions as if they, in and of themselves, are important. In short, there is a risk of letting our possessions separate us from our humanity.

True wealth

I sometimes call the Four of Pentacles the Scrooge card because it tells us that our material possessions are worthless if we merely grasp and hoard them and if we worry about losing them rather than enjoy sharing them with others. True wealth lies not in what we possess, but in our ability to give, and this is determined more by how big our heart is than by how big our bank account is. Indeed, if we do not share what we have with others, financial security has no deep and lasting meaning. Ultimately, then, the value of our material possessions is determined by how we use them and what we make of them.

The root of all evil

"It isn't a question of whether or not one makes money, but of how one makes it, and how one uses it." — Kriyananda (James Donald Walters)

This card can indicate the sadness or emptiness of a life spent in the pursuit of wealth, so its obvious spiritual implication is a warning against materialism. However, although this statement is true, it can benefit from a deeper examination.

We sometimes cast a critical eye on anyone who is affluent, considering that they must be bad in some way—perhaps greedy, superficial, or materialistic. In fact, there is a common saying that "money is the root of all evil." However, the original quote is "The love of money is the root of all evil."[56] That is an important distinction, and with it in mind, what we see is not an admonition against wealth, per se, but an admonition against the obsessive pursuit of it and fixation on it. On the other hand, a life spent in poverty is not necessarily more virtuous or spiritual than a life spent in affluence. Just as a millionaire can be altruistic, a pauper can be materialistic. It is our relationship to money, not our possession of it (or lack of it) that is important. Do we find money to be incidental to living a fulfilling life, or is it crucial? Do we possess it, or does it possess us? Do we constantly want and need more money, or are we able to find happiness in what we already have? These are all vital questions that this card

---

[56] *1 Timothy 6:10*

suggests we consider.

The value of stability

While this card is a warning against greed and possessiveness, it does not go to the other extreme and extol the virtues of poverty. In order to develop spiritually, it helps to have stability in our lives since we easily get anxious and agitated when our health or finances are unstable. Since anxiety is not very conducive to a spiritual practice, there is value to gaining material security in your life. However, the question then becomes, "How much do we have to have in order to find peace and happiness?" and the problem is that for many of us, the answer is generally "More!" But if you have your basic needs met so that you do not have to worry about them, then you do not need more money to become happy; you need more stability within. Through practices like meditation, mindful living, and spiritual devotion, you can create inner stability and find a place of refuge within where you will find peace and security in times of turbulence and anxiety. So a spiritual practice is like putting money into a savings account when times are good so that it will be there to carry you through when times get tough.

Filling the imaginary void

Sometimes it seems that we are desperate to collect as many things as we can. It's like we are all living according to that old humorous quote: "Whoever dies with the most toys wins." But we do not need a lot of possessions in order to be complete or secure, and the accumulation of things does not even accomplish that goal.

The problem is that since we don't remember our perfect, divine Self, we feel defective or incomplete. To fill that void—which actually is imaginary—we seek fulfillment in external things, such as rich food, superficial relationships, and extravagant possessions. These things may give us a temporary sense of completion, but that feeling is doomed to be fleeting because it too is an illusion since none of those things are permanent.

For example, we may discover that what we thought was a great relationship does not complete us after all, so we start looking for another one. Or perhaps we decide that we need more toys, so we go into debt to buy a fancy new car, which we hope will help us keep up with the proverbial Joneses. Or we try drowning our sorrows in alcohol, or we plan another vacation, and so on.

We each have our own dysfunctional ways of filling the void that is not really there, when the real solution is to work on rediscovering our true, divine nature, which *does* make us whole. When we begin to remember our oneness with the Divine, the things of the world—possessions, relationships, etcetera—actually become more satisfying in ways they never were before. As we lose our unreasonable expectation that they will complete or fulfill us, we will be able to enjoy them just as they are, without expectations about them, attachments to them, or dependencies on them.

This is one reason that spiritual enlightenment is always said to be blissful. When we stop believing the illusion of an insatiable void in our lives, we become free to enjoy the sensual world in its fullness, and we live without the sad disappointments that inevitably come from an attachment to things that are transient.

How other people affect our needs

It is a sadly unfortunate fact that we often look at people merely in terms of how well they can serve or support our needs and desires. Would he be a good boyfriend? Can I make money off of those people? Similarly, we often see people in terms of how they may be blocking our needs. This might cause a reaction as simple as cursing someone who cuts in front of us in traffic because Heaven forbid we should get where we are going ten seconds later as a result of this affront. It can involve withholding our congratulations for a coworker who gets a promotion out of the belief that this diminishes our own opportunities. And it can make us resentful toward someone who broke up with us if we staked our happiness on that relationship.

In any case, as long as we view and define other people in terms of how they affect our wants and desires, we block our perception of them as they truly are: people with hopes and fears (just like us), people struggling to recover their spiritual identity (just like us), and people who are physical manifestations of the Divine (just like us). In having such a distorted view of other people, we adopt a miserly view of life that is grounded in a belief in our material needs and our separateness from each other. But relinquishing this illusion unlocks the infinite source of bliss that gives us the deep happiness which is the joy of living.

Five of Pentacles

> *"People are like stained-glass windows. They sparkle and shine when the sun is out, but when the darkness sets in, their true beauty is revealed only if there is a light from within." — Elizabeth Kubler-Ross*

The common, surface interpretations of this card concern poverty and misfortune, but there are deeper connotations, such as alienation (being cast out into the cold), simplicity, austerity, and the steadfastness of sticking with someone through thick and thin, "for richer or for poorer." And then there are the spiritual implications inherent in those earthly interpretations.

Abundance birthright

> *"But strive first for the kingdom of God and his righteousness, and all these things will be given to you as well." — Matthew 6:33*

This is going to sound heretical to some people in light of what a lot of New Age pundits seem to say about deserving and manifesting wealth, but here goes anyway: It is your birthright to have abundant love, joy, and fulfillment, but it is not your birthright to be wealthy. Why? Because that's not what's important.

As long as we think that bringing more and more wealth into our lives is important, we keep ourselves from being joyful and at peace. Now, this does not mean that scarcity and suffering are desirable or even okay. It does not mean that anyone should be poor, homeless, or starving. Not at all. The idea that there is not enough to go around and that as a consequence some people have to be poor is a materialistic illusion too.

The message here is that having a life filled with love, joy, and fulfillment is what's truly important. Furthermore, the point is that true wealth comes from the simplification of desires, not from the multiplication of them, for that buys into the illusion of materialism. Abundance is just a side effect of our true mission of bringing love and joy into the world and of relieving suffering in others. Part of the trick, however, is to understand what abundance means. Does abundance mean acquiring everything we *want* or is it having all that we *need*?

What do we value?

> *"People weep rivers of tears because ... they cannot gain riches. But who sheds even one teardrop because he has not seen God?" — Sri Ramakrishna*

We try so hard to fill the existential void in our lives with material things and physical pleasures. These things are neither fulfilling nor lasting, however, so this effort leaves us with an emptiness that we can never fill, a constant craving that we never truly satisfy. But we keep filling the void with *things*, all the while wondering why they are never enough.

Similarly, we spend so much time and effort protecting our "valuables." We put alarms on our cars and locks on our doors. We put our money in vaults or search for the safest investments for it. We value our material possessions so much that the very thought of losing them causes us anxiety. But do we value our higher, spiritual selves nearly as much? Do we even consider—much less fear—spiritual poverty?

As Howard Thurmond said, "When property becomes sacred, personality becomes secular." It then becomes hard to realize that what is fulfilling and enduring lies outside the material realm. For example, an ability to appreciate what we have is an enduring treasure. Most of us bemoan the things we don't have, but an abiding sense of gratitude and appreciation for what we *do* have is the eternal medicine that heals the wounds of our unfulfilled cravings.

Of course, the ultimate rock upon which we may build a stable and secure life is our unfolding realization of our true, divine nature. When we rediscover our oneness with the Divine, the winds of change lose their power to blow us off course, and neither poverty nor wealth on a material plane can shake the foundation of our serenity. That is the proverbial house built on rock and not on shifting sand.

Clutter of possessions

"The ability to simplify means to eliminate the unnecessary so that the necessary may speak." — Hans Hofmann

It is a sad truth that the clutter in our lives impedes our spiritual progress. It's not just about having an attachment to material things, as in the proverbial case of a rich man having less chance of entering the Kingdom of Heaven than a camel has of going through the eye of a needle. Material possessions can anchor us in the material world, and they can easily come to possess us more than we possess them, especially considering all their demands for maintenance and protection. This does not necessarily happen, but it is easier to focus on our soul's needs when we do not have so many mundane concerns vying for our attention. This is not an admonition to embrace poverty, but it is advice is to simplify your life and to avoid attachment to your possessions.

In addition, "clutter" can also refer to mundane pursuits as well as material possessions. So much of our culture is based on attraction to that which is external and impermanent, typically by distracting us from that which is essential and deep. In fact, we have an entire industry dedicated to this. It's called "advertising," and it is expert in the art of distraction, keeping us from being mindful and serene as it seeks to convince us that we need things that we don't. And so we have an ADHD[57] culture of rampant consumerism, with the resulting problems of war, crime, and pollution. Simplification is the key here too. Focus on what is essential and recognize the unnecessary complications that you have allowed into your life.

For example, you might want to make an honest assessment of what you need and don't need in your life. Include in that consideration habits, responsibilities, and hobbies as well as material possessions. Then see how much of all that you can eliminate. You will find that when you clear the clutter from your home, your car, and your desk, fresh, new energy will flow into your life.

Gratitude

This card emphasizes the importance of gratitude (especially gratitude to the Divine) during hard times, the times when it is both most difficult and most important to do so. This is true for a few reasons. First, if we can cultivate the ability to have gratitude for our lives under such circumstances, we will always be able to do so. Second, gratitude and appreciation lead to abundance, and hard times are when we need it the most. Finally, doing this will lead us to a realization of what is important in life (life itself, our relationships, and so on) and help us understand that the things in life—our material possessions—are not what are really important.

Misfortune's blessings

"Grant that I may be given appropriate difficulties and sufferings on this journey so that my heart may be truly awakened and my practice of liberation and universal compassion may be truly fulfilled." — Tibetan prayer

---

[57] *Attention deficit-hyperactivity disorder*

The cards that are numbered Five in the Minor Arcana reflect the Hierophant (also numbered V), especially in its aspect of a teacher, and so the Five of Pentacles urges us to learn from misfortune, because adversity is not here merely to cause us suffering. It is here to help us learn lessons of appreciation, forgiveness, and non-attachment. In fact, even our attachment to things (which, ultimately, we need to release) is a source of learning, so before letting go of an attachment, we might examine it to see why it is there. What is its lesson? Why did it bring us to this place in life?

In addition, misfortune can be a blessing in disguise because our hardships can make us more conscious of our need for spirituality. When things are going well, we don't usually bother to wonder about the eternal, unchanging world of Spirit. When we are cast down into misfortune, however, we are much more open to considering it. As Marianne Williamson says, "A certain amount of desperation is usually necessary before we're ready for God." When we hit rock bottom, we are in a place where we are willing to look "up" toward the Divine, and that new perception is a blessing hidden in misfortune. For example, in his book, *Man's Search for Meaning*, Viktor Frankl tells a story about a young woman he encountered in the concentration camp who was dying. He was surprised to find her in good cheer despite her impending death, which she explained in this way: "I am grateful that fate has hit me so hard. In my former life I was spoiled and did not take spiritual accomplishments seriously." If this woman could find this blessing in her horrific circumstances, perhaps we can too.

Six of Pentacles

"The poor, the illiterate, the ignorant, the afflicted—let these be your God. Know that service to these is the highest religion." — Swami Akhandananda

The Six of Pentacles is often interpreted as charity, which is a quality that is easily seen as being spiritual. This seems simple, yet there is a surprising amount that can be said about generosity and its important role in our spiritual journey.

Random acts of kindness

"Inasmuch as ye have done it unto one of the least of these my brethren, ye have done it unto me." — Matthew 25: 40

As we care for people in need and focus less on ourselves, we integrate spirituality into our lives. Thus it is through simple, everyday acts of charity and generosity—proverbial "random acts of kindness"—that we make our mundane lives and our spiritual practice one and the same. Indeed, compassionately helping a beggar can be a far more spiritual practice than going to church on Sunday.

Through repeatedly practicing simple acts of kindness, we wear away the dross of our ego-self to reveal the gold of our divine Self. As Aristotle said almost two and a half millennia ago, "We do not act rightly because we have virtue or excellence, but rather we have those because we have acted rightly. We are what we repeatedly do." So every day, perform at least one random act of kindness, one work of charity that no one else will ever know you did, and little by little, your life will become more spiritually aligned.

What hampers our charity?

"What you do for yourself, you're doing for others, and what you do for others, you're doing for yourself." — Pema Chödrön

There are homeless people all around us (which is a very sad comment on the state of our society) and we, as individuals, so rarely reach out to help them, at least not directly. Why is that? What would it hurt us to give something to a homeless person once in a while? A dollar? A quarter, even? If you have ever done this, you've probably seen that the unfortunate person also appreciates your acknowledgement of their humanity—maybe as much as the money itself—and that does not cost us anything to give.

Unfortunately, we make all sorts of excuses for not giving money to the homeless. We tell ourselves, "He'll just spend it on wine anyway," or, "I give money to a local charitable organization and that's enough," or, "They're all just crazy (or lazy)." The truth, however, is that these excuses are, in the main, insincere and disingenuous.

So again, why do we so rarely reach out in charity toward homeless people? Are we afraid that their poverty and misery are infectious, or do we fear that someone will see us interacting with a filthy person and judge us as being filthy too? Maybe we realize that a dollar is not going to fix this person's life, so dealing with this issue in such a small way makes us feel inadequate. Better to just ignore it and hope it goes away, right? We also find the pain in the eyes of a homeless person to be too immediate and heartrending to confront directly. It scratches a tender part of us. We may think, "There but for the grace of God go I," but contrary to our protestations of devout faith, it seems we must have but a tenuous belief in the grace of God. After all, if He could let this happen to that poor wretch begging on the street corner, then He might just let it happen to me too some day. Maybe if we ignore the problem in front of us, we can ignore that frightening possibility.

We tell ourselves that we are too wise, too busy, or too broke to give a homeless person some spare change, but the truth is that we are just too afraid. Perhaps the wisdom of Pema Chödrön's words can help us confront and overcome our fears, though. Then, in the vanquishing of them, we can begin to be the generous and charitable person that our soul knows us to be.

Why bother with charity?

"And though I have the gift of prophecy, and understand all mysteries, and all knowledge; and though I have all faith, so that I could remove mountains, but have not charity, I am nothing." — 1 Corinthians 13:2

It can be tempting to wonder if we really should give to the poor. If the material world is a mere shadow of spiritual reality, and if enlightenment comes from transcending our attachment to material things, then does it make sense that we should just tell people who are indigent not to worry about their problems since it's all an illusion anyway? We may think that the best thing we can do for them is to tell them to use their poverty as a means to release their attachment to materialism. Of course this isn't true, but why not?

A visual clue may be found on many versions of the Six of Pentacles card: the balance scales. We need to evaluate where people are in their lives and on their spiritual journey, and take that into account. For many people, the simple necessities of life are what they need in the here and now to relieve their suffering. In fact, for someone whose basic, physical needs are being easily met to tell someone whose needs are not that they should release their attachment to material things would be callous and cruel. So in such cases, relieving the physical suffering of the needy is the true spiritual exercise and expression of our oneness with them. We can advise them to release materialism when they have surplus material to release.

On a deeper level, the answer to this conundrum is that thinking of charity as a service to other people is only the beginning of the story. The profound truth comes when we see that it is a service to the Divine out of love for the Divine. This is the awareness that allows us—impels us even—to do things for people who will never even know of our generosity, much less repay us.

Charity of the Spirit

"'Giving to get' is an inescapable law of the ego." — *A Course in Miracles*

When charity comes from the ego, it is not truly charity. It is tainted for it has strings attached, or it comes with hopes of reward, even if that reward is as non-materialistic as an expectation of going to heaven. When charity is of the Spirit, however, it comes from a sense of our oneness with others and with the Divine. For example, if the other person were your child, would you think twice about giving them what they need? Would you expect anything in return? When charity is of the Spirit, that is how it feels, for then we realize that everyone is our child, our lover, our self. Also, charity of the Spirit blossoms forth as an act of devotion to the Divine with no expectations about the results.

So consider your acts of charity when they arise to see where they come from: ego or Spirit. If there are strings attached or hopes of reward, release those strings or expectations. Try to act with a generous heart toward a stranger as you would with your child. Another way to cultivate charity of the Spirit is to act according to the biblical advice that whatever you do for the least of God's children, you do it for Him.[58]

Charity and our divinity

"I slept and dreamt that life was joy. I awoke and saw that life was service. I acted and behold! Service was joy." — *Rabindranath Tagore*

I have discussed charity with regards to the message of this card, and in particular, I have talked about why we practice charity if the material world is an illusion anyway. The answer—to relieve suffering at the level on which it exists—is true on one plane of our existence, but we also can examine this issue at an even deeper level.

While it is true that we should exercise charity to relieve the suffering of

---

[58] *This paraphrases Mathew 25: 40*

others, we also need to be generous for the sake of our own spiritual evolution, our own progress toward divine union. In other words, we practice charity in order to manifest our charitable Self, which is a part of our innate but perhaps forgotten divine nature.

A similar point was made thousands of years ago in the Bhagavad Gita (9.27):

> *Whatever you do, whatever you eat,*
> *whatever sacrifice you undertake,*
> *whatever charity you give, whatever efforts you make,*
> *do all that as an offering to Me.*

It was also made by Swami Vivekananda more than a century ago as follows:

> *It is sheer nonsense on the part of any man to think that he is born to help the world... We must ... constantly do good because ... that is the only way we can become perfect... Be grateful to the man you help, think of him as God. Is it not a great privilege to be allowed to worship God by helping our fellow man? ... Give up all results to the Lord, then neither good nor evil will affect you.*

So consider the question, "Does the world need us to be charitable, or do we need the world to give us the opportunity to learn how to be compassionate through acts of generosity and charity?"

Seven of Pentacles

This card is often seen as a test of our patience as we wait for the results of our efforts. It also indicates making a reassessment of what we are working for and a test of our sense of satisfaction with what we have.

Reassessment of life

There is a saying to the effect that as we climb the ladder of success, we should check now and then to be sure it is propped up against the right wall. A spiritual take on this saying is the advice to pause for a moment to reassess our path in life. Are we spending enough time on the things that are truly important, like being with the ones we love or working to help those in need? Or are we merely going through the motions of making money? After all, there is also an old saying that no one, at the end of their life, ever regrets not spending more time at the office. These are the kinds of assessments that this card suggests we would do well to consider from time to time.

Re-examination of our spirituality

In addition to reassessing how we are living our lives, this card also suggests a re-examination of our spiritual progress and a rededication to that path. It is normal to have doubts and confusion occasionally about something as ineffable as our spiritual journey. Mother Teresa's struggles with her religious beliefs are a famous example of this, which proves that it can happen to anyone. Such concerns should not be suppressed, though, or they will fester deep inside. Also, they should not stimulate self-criticism about our level of faith because actually it is an unwillingness to subject our beliefs to scrutiny that shows a lack of faith. This is because a reluctance to reevaluate our convictions indicates that we fear that our faith will not stand up to careful examination. Of course, we have to realize that spirituality is by definition something that cannot be proved or disproved by the scientific methods applicable to the phenomena of the material world. Ultimately, it is within our own hearts that we should look for evidence of the Divine.

Thomas Edison said, "Genius is 1% inspiration and 99% perspiration," and spirituality is much the same. Our faith is that 1% part, and perseverance and a steady practice are the other 99% of what makes up our spiritual genius. Spirituality may also be compared to our love of another person. Even when we encounter a dry spell in which we may question the love in a relationship, we remain faithful and keep working on it, trusting that the feeling will return.

There are a variety of things that can help at such times along our spiritual path. One is the support of like-minded people, or at least of open-minded people. Another is a consistent spiritual practice which may include meditation, charity, and reading inspirational texts. These can carry us along as long we rededicate ourselves to this path.

Eight of Pentacles

This card indicates the everyday tasks of life and the spiritual quality that such mundane activities can reflect if we are open to seeing it. It also advises us to pay attention to details, and it illustrates the old saying that "practice makes perfect."

Be the task

This card reminds me of a saying that is related to the spiritual practice of mindfulness:

When there is a task to do, be *the task.*

This means that we should totally engage in our every activity, that we should approach each task in our day-to-day life with focused concentration and a quiet mind. Meditation can help us achieve this sort of concentration, but it also improves with practice, and that practice can involve any sort of task. As an example, when you do something as simple as peel a potato, focus on that, and only that. Do not think about what you are going to do with that potato after you peel it, and certainly don't think about an argument you just had with someone or worry about a future event. Just be with the experience of peeling the potato. Focus your attention on it. Watch the peelings curl away. Feel the texture of the potato in your hand. Be mindfully present as you work on this task. In short, be the task. In this way, even something as simple as peeling a potato can be a spiritual practice.

Chop wood, carry water

"Before Enlightenment, chop wood, carry water. After Enlightenment, chop wood, carry water." — Zen proverb

I've mentioned this proverb before, but it bears repeating in a discussion of the Eight of Pentacles, which can indicate repetitive tasks and doing a job mechanically.

Back when I used to work in the 9-to-5 world, I would often hear people disdainfully refer to their work day with the old saying, "Same shit, different day." But as the Zen proverb cited above tells us, the mark of a spiritual person is not that he does different things, but that he continues to do the same ones with a new consciousness and a different perspective. With a more enlightened outlook, we also realize the importance of doing our work with focused attention (i.e., with mindfulness as we stay "in the moment") and of working without complaints since life is exquisite however it unfolds. In this way, any job can be a spiritual practice.

When I left the 9-to-5, work-a-day world over a decade ago, I did so with great relief. As I put it at the time, I was very happy to get out of "that soul-sucking job." I certainly have no regrets about making that change, but I see that prior career differently now. Had I known then what I do now, I would have realized that a job is only soul-sucking if we let it be. Instead, we can use any job as grist for the mill in our spiritual journey, and we can approach any task from a perspective that arises from our realization of our divine nature. When we do that, our job becomes "chop wood, carry water" in the second sense of the Zen proverb: it becomes a part of our spiritual journey.

Nine of Pentacles

This card is about appreciating what you have accomplished and having appreciation for the world around you. It also has a traditional connotation of a comfortable home life.

Feng Shui

Many of the spiritual messages in this book are about our "inner space," meaning our heart and mind and soul. But this card, the Nine of Pentacles, reminds us that our "outer space"—the world around us—plays a part in our spiritual progress too.

Our inner selves are both reflected in and affected by how we arrange our environment. Accordingly, a message from this card is to make your home a place of peace, comfort, and renewal. No matter how modest your home is, it can be all that, for the size and budget of your home are not important. A small cottage can be a warm, soothing environment, while a mansion can seem cold and sterile.

So this card asks us to consider questions like these: Do you need to put your home into better order? Do you need to spend some time cleaning house? Do you need to add a touch of warmth to your décor? It is also important to remember that there are always little things you can do to bring a touch of beauty into your home. For example, perhaps there are a few wildflowers growing nearby that you can bring home to set in a cup of water on a windowsill. Finally, this card suggests learning about Feng shui to see how altering your external conditions can support your inner growth and transformation.

Create both a better world *and* a better you

Although Mahatma Gandhi said, "Be the change you want to see in the world," this card suggests that such a transformation can work in the other direction as well—you become the change you work for in the world. For example, when you do charitable works, you bring more generosity into the world while also becoming a charitable person. So as we strive to create a better world, we also improve ourselves, just as our efforts to improve ourselves also create a better world. The two efforts are intertwined and synergistic.

Similarly, this card advises us to live in harmony with nature and the world around us. There is a magical connection between us and the world we live in, but most people don't realize that. Consequently, they don't see any problem with living in disharmony with the world. Even if they discover material gain that way, they create disharmony within themselves as well as within the world. But if we understand our innate oneness with everything, acting in harmony with the world comes naturally. As Alan Watts said, "... there is no separate 'you' to get something out of [life], as if [it] were a bank to be robbed."

Prosperity consciousness

There is a fragile, ephemeral nature to all material things, but this seems especially true of things of physical beauty that we treasure the most. Thus, this card urges us to appreciate and enjoy what we have now while we still have it. Although this may sound like a recommendation to be pessimistic or defeatist about our future fortunes, it actually is advice to live in the present moment—the proverbial "Now"—and to always be thankful for all that we have. Consequently, although this card is of the suit of Pentacles (which represents material manifestations) it has profound implications for our mental state too in that it encourages us to develop a "prosperity consciousness" through a persistent sense of appreciation.

Riches versus abundance

"Most of the luxuries, and many of the so-called comforts of life, are not only not indispensable, but positive hindrances to the elevation of mankind." — Thoreau

In New Age philosophy there is a lot of talk about creating abundance and bringing prosperity into your life. This seems quite materialistic, but that is only if we confuse abundance with riches, the latter being a matter of material things while the former is not necessarily so.

Recently, this card reminded me of Thoreau's experiences at Walden Pond, a discussion of which can reveal a lot about the difference between riches and abundance. Thoreau spent two years at Walden Pond living a very simple life, but his account of that time in his book, *Walden*, indicates that he never felt poor there; he always felt abundant. In fact, his experiences there illustrate that what we need materially are just the necessities of life such as sustenance (food and water), shelter, clothing, and fuel. His writing also says that returning to such simplicity and being self-sufficient in it allows us to find a deep serenity that an attachment to material wealth usually does not. After all, is it not true that people of great wealth go to extraordinary lengths to guard, maintain, and increase their material wealth, almost as if they are experiencing a delusional fear of scarcity and poverty? Where is the peace and serenity in that?

Thus we see that abundance is having what you need versus everything you want. It is a state of mind more than the state of your bank account. And it is about creating things for the world rather than about hoarding things for yourself.

Ten of Pentacles

The Ten of Pentacles illustrates abundance, but while the previous card may indicate personal prosperity, this one is about the good fortune we create for and with other people. This card is also suffused with a very spiritual energy by virtue of the common placement of its ten pentacle icons in the pattern of the Kabalistic Tree of Life, which reveals the sacred reality that lies above this material plane.

We all create abundance together

"[Your life's] purpose has nothing to do with what you get out of [life] but everything to do with what you put into it." — Neale Donald Walsch

This card, with its traditional depiction of a marketplace, is often interpreted as a sign of abundance in our lives, and certainly this is an important message. But beyond that, since the number ten may be considered a higher order of the number one (which represents the individual self), this card has implications about our community or society (the collective self). Thus this card says that it is important to remember that we create abundance together; no one does it alone.

This message reminds me of a fable about a man who died and was given a tour of both heaven and hell. (I'm not sure why he was given this tour since I doubt he was going to be offered a choice between these two options, but that's beside the point.)

First he was taken into a room with a big table around which sat a lot of sad and hungry looking people. There was a large tureen in the center of the table filled with a wonderful smelling soup and everyone had a spoon. But the handles of the spoons were too long—longer than a human arm—so the people could not use them to get the soup into their mouths. This eternally frustrating scene, the man was told, was hell.

Next he was taken into a room that was set up exactly the same way, with the people, soup tureen, and long-handled spoons, but this time the people were happy and looked very well fed. The difference was that they were feeding each other with those long spoons. This, of course, was heaven.

The sacred reality above the material one

In many versions of this card, we see ten pentacles in an esoteric pattern called the *Tree of Life* superimposed over a scene depicting a marketplace. This says that there is a sacred reality above the material one we typically perceive, depend upon, and live in. This implication, along with the marketplace often depicted on this card, suggests an interesting analogy that can help explain the spiritual reality of our existence.

We may consider life to be a huge game that we are all playing, or rather, that the Divine is playing with Itself. The problem arises when we humans think that this game is the ultimate reality. Also, we think that we, the players in this game, are real too, which is why we take it all so personally and why we invest so deeply in the events of life. This is why we suffer so much.

To make this analogy a bit more specific, consider what it would be like if the little tokens in a game of Monopoly were conscious and thought they were real. For them, being sent to jail would be dreadful, building a hotel on one's property would feel like a big success, going past GO and collecting $200 would seem like a windfall, and the roll of the dice would be like the capriciousness of fate.

Next, consider what would happen if one of the tokens were to realize that none of this purported reality—itself included—is the ultimate reality and that it is just a token on the Monopoly board (i.e., the material plane), which belongs to Deity. Perhaps this little token would continue to go round and round on the board, but its anxiety and worry and suffering would disappear as it becomes conscious of its true self, which is a component of the Divine. This little token will now be able to observe the game with equanimity, i.e., without emotional attachment to what happens. It can enjoy the process of the game without obsessing about which token owns the most property or has the most money, without resenting how much it has to pay when it lands on Boardwalk, and without worrying about what will happen with the next roll of the dice. And it will no longer fear the end of the game, for this little token knows that it is "in the game, but not of the game" (to paraphrase the popular saying, "be in the world, but not of the world.")

Just like that little monopoly token, we too can realize that there is a true, sacred reality above the material one. And in that realization, we will begin to escape the suffering of this earthly plane.

Spirit and abundance

Many people consider spirituality to be a sort of afterlife retirement plan. Really, though, it is a guide to living joyfully and vibrantly right here and now. Without traveling a spiritual path, we may find financial prosperity, but with it we can also achieve peace of mind and abiding joy along with those things, or without them too. It won't matter either way. And so spirituality is not about the material things we have (or don't have). It leads to abundance and fulfillment on a higher level than the material plane, which is symbolized on this card by the *Tree of Life* pattern superimposed above a scene of material wealth.

Another way to view this symbolism is to see that Spirit is the source of all abundance, although we misunderstand what abundance is. It is not the possession of a lot of things. It is having everything without needing to possess anything. This comes when we see our oneness with all and realize our transcendence beyond things of the material world.

Page of Pentacles

The youthful innocence typical of the Tarot's Pages is, in this case, directed toward worldly things. At its best, it turns to awe, wonder, and excitement such as what a child feels on Christmas morning.

A kid at Christmas

A while ago I came across some pictures of my young nephew taken at Christmas. In one of them he had just opened a present that he had hoped for, and the look of joy and excitement on his face is so vivid you can almost hear his squeal of delight. As I looked at that picture I thought, "Wouldn't it be great if we, as adults, still got that excited and found that much joy when we got a gift?" But we usually don't. We smile politely and say, "Oh, how nice. Thank you." Instead, maybe we can try to see that everything in our lives is precious, which starts with acknowledging the value of the things we have and expressing appreciation for them.

Here is a suggestion, then: Make a list of several things in your life that mean something to you, that bring you joy. (Do not hesitate to include items of purely sentimental value.) Then think of a way to express your appreciation for each one, even if you just say a silent "Thank you!" to the Divine. Perhaps as a result, the next time someone gives you a gift, you will find a bit more joy welling up inside your heart. And considering what it is like to be around a kid at Christmas, rest assured that your joy will be contagious.

Seven million wonders of the world

"There are no seven wonders of the world in the eyes of a child. There are seven million." — Walt Streightiff

The Page of Pentacles expresses a childlike curiosity, awe, and enjoyment of the wonders of the physical world, which urges us to see everything through the inquisitive and wondering eyes of a child. When we examine things without preconceived notions like a child does, we retain our sense of wonder, we appreciate things more deeply and joyfully, and we find new possibilities in all that we encounter. As a consequence, this card urges us to recall and regain that sense of wonder and curiosity about the world. As a way to practice that, keep in mind the old saying, "Take time to stop and smell the flowers." If you can do that, you will never truly grow old.

The magical world

"To me every hour of the light and dark is a miracle. Every cubic inch of space is a miracle." — Walt Whitman

Children see so much magic in the world around them, but we adults see everything as being ordinary. We think that we are smarter than they are, but could it be that we are just jaded? Have we gained knowledge about the world at the price of our sense of the miraculous? It is not an inevitable or necessary trade off, but it seems to be almost universal.

Perhaps we lost our fascination with magic through the disappointment we felt when we discovered that the more obvious examples of it (such as Santa Claus) turned out not to be true. Or it may have been that the adults around us scoffed at our dreams and imagination, squelching our perception of the miraculous. And so, like little Jackie Paper in the song *"Puff the Magic Dragon,"* we grow up and lose interest in a miraculous life, leaving the magic to languish, deprived of our love.

But maybe if we let our children hold onto magic as long as possible, they will be able to bring more of it into our world. Or perhaps if we start looking for it again we will find it on our own. After all, there is magic in the touch of a loved one, enchantment in a beautiful song, mystical beauty in a forest, and a miracle in a smile we may bring to someone who is sad. You may wonder if any of that is really magic, though. The answer is both yes and no. It's all in your perspective.

Knight of Pentacles

This knight is dependable, hard working, and enterprising, and he exemplifies loyalty, patience, and prudence. In the RWS Tarot deck, he is the only one of the four knights who is stationary, which indicates his grounding and his careful, measured approach to life.

Spiritual wisdom in everyday tasks

"Put your heart, mind, intellect and soul into even your smallest acts. This is the secret of success." — Swami Sivananda

The Knight of Pentacles is often interpreted as being about making a living and working hard to provide for the welfare of yourself and your family— seemingly mundane, secular activities. They are important for our earthly lives, but how might they apply to living spiritually?

As I have mentioned before, enlightenment does not mean you do different things in your life; it means that you do the same things, but differently. It means realizing that there can be spiritual fulfillment in doing the laundry, cleaning house, and driving to work—everyday tasks that most people think of as dull and tedious. Before enlightenment, you may feel bored, stressed, or resentful as you do them. After enlightenment, you feel a sense of bliss and oneness with the world as you do them. The activities remain the same, but with a world of difference.

So how do you get there? One way is to integrate your spiritual wisdom into the mundane tasks of your daily life. Whenever you learn a new spiritual truth, try to apply it to one (or more) of your daily activities. As practice, take a moment right now to think of a spiritual truth and write down how it may apply to how you should approach or perform some ordinary task in your daily life. Then keep that in mind for the rest of the day, reminding yourself of this spiritual truth whenever you perform that task.

Another way is to practice being totally present in all of your activities. Indeed, perhaps an esoteric reason for work is to lead us to practice mindfulness in all that we do. It may be relatively easy to achieve some level of calm, clarity, and serenity during meditation or while practicing religious devotion, but can we cultivate those qualities while performing our daily tasks, including the more onerous ones? It's not nearly as easy, but it is much more valuable for the effort.

And so we see that this card urges us to practice mindfulness in our work. To achieve this, it is advisable to begin with simple, repetitive tasks like washing the car, folding the laundry, or brushing your hair. Focus on the movements you make and any sensory inputs you perceive, including minor ones you might otherwise overlook such as the textures you feel or odors you smell. Just notice it all, and whenever any thoughts about the task (or about anything else) arise, notice them and dismiss them, then return your attention to the activity. Take it slow and steady. Focus on what you are doing. Stay grounded in your body and your task. And as you learn to do this and apply it to everything you do, you will begin to live your life with a sense of peace and harmony with the world.

One step at a time

When traveling a spiritual path, it is easy to get discouraged sometimes. The goals seem so lofty that we wonder if we will ever get there, and we doubt ourselves since it is easy to see our flaws and shortcomings in stark contrast to where we want to be. Then, just when we think we have a handle on our spiritual development, something happens to show us that we don't, at least not yet.

We know we should view life with equanimity, but when someone comes along and pushes our buttons, we get angry. We think we know how to love one another, but when someone hurts us, we find ourselves viewing them with a decided lack of compassion. We think we've learned to put judgment and superficial views of other people behind us, but then we see someone doing something stupid, unethical, or deceitful, and we have a knee-jerk reaction to judge that person. We think we love ourselves and recognize our innate divinity, and yet when we do the things mentioned above, we berate ourselves.

The Knight of Pentacles has a message for us at such times, for he is like Aesop's proverbial tortoise, as opposed to the hare. He reminds us that a journey of a thousand miles not only begins with one step but also is traveled one step at a time. His message is to be mindful of what we are doing and to be aware of both our mistakes and our successes so that we can note them, learn from them, and move on. We live within the material world, and we are fallible physical beings. We try to be spiritual, but of course we sometimes fall short of our goals and ideals. Instead of self-reproach, though, we should remember that it is in the doing that we truly learn. So don't get discouraged. Trust in the support of the Divine and know that if we stick with it, it does get better.

Queen of Pentacles

This queen is like a caring and nurturing mother. And like most mothers, she is also of necessity creative, generous, practical, and resourceful.

The Universe will nurture us

The Queen of Pentacles indicates the nurturing that a mother gives her child. She cares about her child unconditionally, giving of herself without hesitation or reservation. Thus, we may infer from this card an ideal for how we treat other people. The mother-child relationship comes closest to realizing our oneness with everyone, and so it is a model for how, in spiritual enlightenment, we should treat other people. Another spiritual message that we may infer from this aspect of the Queen of Pentacles is the advice to believe that the Universe (in its Mother Goddess aspect) will take care of us in the way that a loving, caring mother treats her children.

Generosity does not deplete us

This card depicts love's generosity, and it suggests a quiet inner strength that is supportive of the well-being of others. While we may exhibit a giving nature toward people close to us, such as our family members, we are typically much less charitable with people with whom we do not share an intimate bond. Why, we may ask, should we give to someone with whom we have no immediate connection? Of course, this perceived lack of connection is an illusion since we are all connected to each other. But more than that, we need to understand that our generosity does not deplete us. Instead, we create a more generous environment by being charitable. So through the seeming paradox that abundance is born of charity, our generosity makes way for the wealth that the Divine sends into our lives with each new opportunity. Indeed, this card says that the bounty of the Universe flows through our lives to the extent that we give of ourselves to others.

Generosity without strings

A profound sense of trust may be necessary when we practice generosity. When we give to someone, we must trust that our charity is helping them, that they are growing even when we cannot see it. In fact, every bit of that person's growth may be invisible to our earthly eyes, but that should be okay. Even if we don't see the growth, that does not mean that it isn't there, at least at a deep, spiritual level.

As an illustration of this, consider a gardener who has planted seeds. For a time, she will not see anything happening, but she can't dig up the seeds to check on them. She has to trust that they are growing. So it is with us when we give to others. Do they appreciate what we have done for them? Are they using our generosity wisely? Is our charity doing any good? Be wary of questions like that, because they may indicate that we are attaching strings to our generosity, and that tarnishes it, converting it from spiritual love to a materialistic transaction. On a more profound level, it is irrelevant if the other person matures or evolves. We give of ourselves out of loving service to the Divine, which has manifested in the other person, just as a mother nurses her child out of the love she feels in the moment. There are no strings attached to that generosity, and neither should there be to ours if it is to be a sacred practice.

King of Pentacles

This king is adept and enterprising. Having the easy generosity that comes from wealth (or at least financial security), he typically becomes a benefactor or philanthropist.

The flow of wealth

As noted above, this king has "the easy generosity that comes from wealth," but the riches of this king do not necessarily come from a large bank account, they may also arise out of his profound realization of his oneness with the Divine. And so a spiritual message of this card is that when we finally arrive at this awareness, we see that true wealth is a matter of our generosity, not our possessions. In fact, this card says that the abundance of the Universe flows through us when we exhibit sincere generosity. To suppose otherwise is like expecting water to flow through a hose that is plugged up at the end. Water may be able to flow into it, but only up to its limited capacity. Then, since it can't flow out, the water will eventually stagnate within the hose. Using that analogy, we may say that realizing our connection to the Divine is like hooking the hose up to the faucet, and generosity is like unclogging a hose that is stopped up from long disuse.

A spiritually successful businessman

This king is often seen as representing a successful businessman. This seems like a very worldly (i.e., non-spiritual) interpretation, but it need not be restricted to our mundane life. This is because what you do for a living can have a spiritual component if you do it from your heart and if you use it as a means of serving the Divine through serving other people. If you can do that, you will find that you have become successful in your career no matter what the monetary results are.

A material "what" and a spiritual "how"

A spiritual message for this card that is similar to the one in the section above is that it's not *what* you do so much as it is *how* you do it that matters. Spiritual endeavors are more defined by the generous and compassionate intent and manner with which we approach them than by their outward trappings. Of course, doing something harmful to others is not going to become spiritual merely by thinking that you are doing something nice. What this actually means is that you do not have to start a soup kitchen for the poor in order to travel a spiritual path. Starting a "mundane" business can be a spiritual endeavor too if you do it in a way that has integrity, fairness, and a spirit of generosity at its core. For example you might start a business that has a policy of paying a fair wage to its employees and a mission to produce products that are eco-friendly. In fact, you might want to keep this message in mind as you go about your daily business doing everything you normally do, but now doing it all with a sense of compassion and with a generosity of spirit.

෴ ෴

Part 3: Spreads for Spiritual Readings

In this part of this book, you will find spreads that bring more spiritual content to your readings. Of course, you can use the card meanings presented in this book to bring depth to any Tarot reading, no matter the spread. However, you may want to use these or other spreads that are specifically designed to bring more spiritual meaning into your readings.

One card readings

The simplest spread consists of one card. You can use that one card to comment on your situation generally, or you can assign a specific question to it. The following are a few examples of questions you may use that will address secular issues—financial difficulties, relationship problems, career decisions, etcetera—yet also incorporate a spiritual dimension that will provide a soulful component to your readings.

- What is my divine purpose in my current circumstances?
- What spiritual guidance does the Divine have for me at this time?
- What profound lesson can I learn from the situation I am in?
- What is the spiritual component of my problem that I need to understand?
- What is the soulful purpose of my relationship with [*insert name here*]?
- How can I address the problem I am facing in a way that is spiritually awakened?

Alternatively, instead of questions that address specific problems, more general questions may be used for readings of a more purely spiritual nature. For example:

- How is my life currently helping me become more spiritually enlightened?
- Where is my soul leading me at this time?
- What is the most important spiritual lesson I need to learn at this time in my life?
- How can I strengthen my relationship with the Divine?
- What is one step I can take along my spiritual path today?

Readings using questions like these are especially effective when you are (or want to be) in a reflective mood, and they can lift you out of ennui or depression when you are feeling mired in the drudgery of the mundane world.

Also, the use of one card to address this kind of question provides an excellent technique for doing a daily reading for a Tarot journal. To do this, begin each day by formulating a question of the type noted above (either a specific one or a general one) and then use it for a one-card reading. You may then let the resulting reading, which you can record in a journal, set the tone for the day. Besides the guidance and insights that such readings provide, this practice will also help you attain a higher level of spirituality as you begin to see all aspects of your daily life from a more soulful perspective.

Modified spreads

You can add a spiritually-oriented position to any existing spread to ask a question like one posed in the prior section or like one of the following:

- What is the spiritual lesson that I need to learn from this situation?
- What guidance is my Higher Self offering me in this situation?
- How can I cope with this situation in a soulful manner?

For example, you might add a card to indicate your spiritual lesson in a simple three-card *Background / Problem / Outcome* spread as follows:

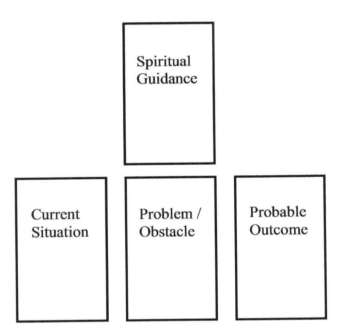

Or you can modify a position in a spread to have a more spiritual slant. For example, you might change the final card in a *Background / Problem / Advice* spread to be "Spiritual Guidance." Or in the Celtic Cross spread (see the spread layout on the next page), you might redefine the seventh and eighth positions (which are generally labeled as "You" and "Your environment" respectively) to be "The worldly aspect of this situation" and "The spiritual aspect of this situation."

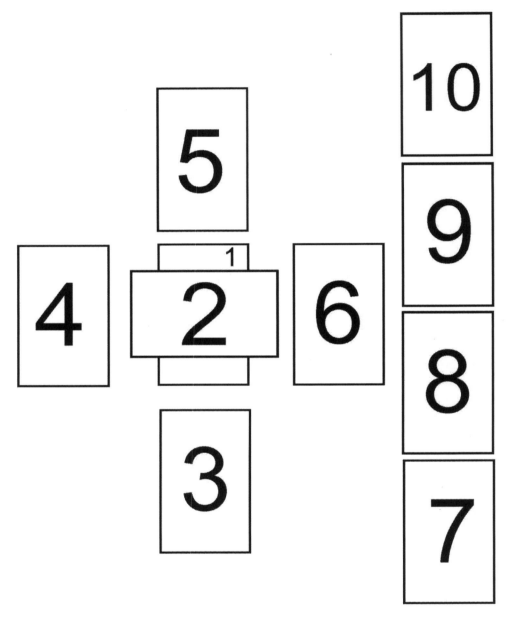

Celtic Cross layout

New Spreads

The following are some spiritually oriented spreads that I have created which you may find useful in your spiritual development.

The Spiritual Triangle Spread

My creation of the *Spiritual Triangle Spread* was inspired by a workshop presented by Alexandra Genetti[59] at the Fall 1999 *Los Angeles Tarot Symposium* titled, "The Magical Triangle."

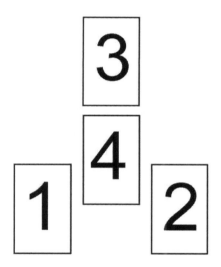

Interpret these cards using the following positional meanings:

1. Your current situation
2. The problem you are facing in this situation
3. Divine guidance for resolving this problem
4. The spiritual lesson to be learned

---

[59] *Alexandra Genetti is the creator and author of the* Wheel of Change Tarot *deck and book.*

Gratitude and Forgiveness Spread

At first glance, this relationship spread may not seem particularly spiritual. However, incorporating appreciation, atonement, and forgiveness in our relationships and in our everyday lives truly is an important step along a journey of enlightenment.

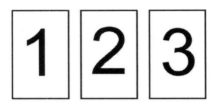

Interpret these cards using the following positional meanings:

1. What should you express gratitude for in this relationship?
2. What do you need to apologize or atone for?
3. What should you forgive? (Or, what do you need to forgive yourself for?)

The Fleeting vs. Eternal Spread

Whether it involves shifting circumstances or perspectives, change of some sort is what often draws a person to a Tarot reading. The spread described here deals specifically with change, and it does so by addressing it from two very different perspectives: the sacred and the secular.

We generally consider our bodies, minds, and emotions—the ephemeral and ever-changing aspects of ourselves—to be who we really are, but of course it is our eternal soul that is our true Self. Remembering the truth about this dual nature of our being can be a source of strength, serenity, and comfort in a world filled with pain, adversity, and loss, and it is an essential step toward dealing with our problems in a soulful manner. A reading with the following spread will shine the light of our soul's purpose on the mundane issues of our lives.

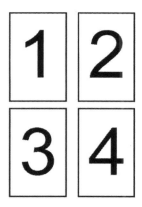

Interpret these cards using the following positional meanings:

1. What is changing in your life right now?
2. What do you need to know about this change?
3. What is the eternal, spiritual truth underlying this transitory part of your life?
4. What do you need to understand about this eternal truth?

Life's Lessons Spread

As we go through life, we encounter innumerable spiritual lessons. In fact, every problem, obstacle, and hardship that we face presents us with another opportunity to learn such lessons, and the spread described below was designed with this in mind.

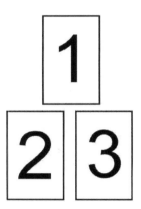

Interpret these cards using the following positional meanings:

1. The lesson your soul wants you to learn in your current situation
2. The qualities that you need to cultivate to help you learn this lesson
3. A specific action you can take that will allow you to practice the wisdom that comes from this lesson

Spiritual Journey Spread

This spread is a modification of the classic Past, Present Future spread where the positional meanings are oriented toward spiritual issues rather than worldly ones.

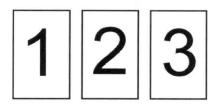

Interpret these cards using the following positional meanings:

1. What spiritual lesson have you recently confronted?
   How did you deal with it?
2. What important spiritual lesson are you facing now?
3. What lies ahead on your spiritual path?

The Divine Purpose Pentagram

This spread describes the divine purpose you are meant to fulfill at this time and provides guidance about how you can do that. Lay out the five cards of this spread as if they form the points of a pentagram.

Interpret the cards using the following positional meanings:

1. The divine purpose you are meant to fulfill at this time
2. Spiritual guidance that you need right now
3. The main source of support currently available to you in pursuit of your purpose
4. Thoughts, ideas, and concepts that are affecting (either supporting or blocking) your attainment of your divine purpose
5. Passions or desires that are affecting (either supporting or blocking) your attainment of this purpose

Spiritual Truth Spread

There are those who say that the purpose of human life is to seek truth and to bring a higher consciousness into the world. With that in mind, I created the next spread to examine the specific spiritual truths that one might be seeking and trying to bring into the world at this time.

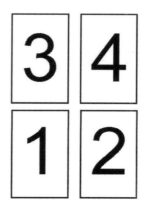

Interpret these cards using the following positional meanings:

1. What truth are you seeking at this point in your life?
2. How can you find that truth?
3. What truth are you bringing into the world?
4. How can you be a vehicle for bringing this higher consciousness into the world?

Serenity Spread

The Serenity Spread was inspired by the well-known Serenity Prayer:

God, grant me the serenity to accept the things I cannot change; the courage to change the things I can; and the wisdom to know the difference.

A reading with this spread will provide spiritual guidance during a difficult situation through its advice for finding serenity, courage, and wisdom.

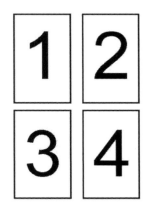

Interpret these cards using the following positional meanings:

1. What do you need to accept in this situation?
2. How can you find the serenity to do that?
3. What can you change?
4. How can you find the courage to make that change in a spiritual way?

Love and Compassion Spread

This spread will support a reading about how love and compassion support your spiritual journey. You can tailor the spread to make it more specific to your life, but here is an example of what you can use:

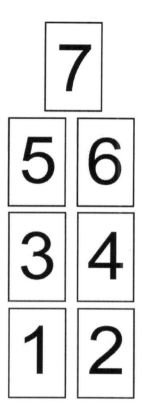

1. Where do you need to express more love in your life?
2. To whom do you need to express more compassion?
3. How does your love for other people differ from your compassion toward them?
4. How are they similar?
5. How do love and compassion enrich your life?
6. How do they heal and transform you?
7. How do they contribute to your spiritual growth?

Tarot and Your Spiritual Path

To help you better understand positions 3 and 4, consider what the dictionary says about these two words. It tells us that love is a profound feeling of attachment and affection for another person, as well as concern for their well-being. The definition of compassion is a bit more complex. This word is derived from the Latin word *compati*, "to suffer with," so literally, it means "suffering with another person." It is not that simple, of course. Compassion is defined as a profound awareness of and sympathy for the suffering and misfortune of another person which is accompanied by a desire to ease their pain and help them with their adversity. So the two words are similar, but with important differences.

Keys to Happiness Spread

A few years ago I read about a study at the University of California at Riverside that showed that the path to a happier, more meaningful life is built upon several factors:

1. Gratitude
2. Kindness
3. Forgiveness
4. Appreciation of small pleasures
5. Good health
6. Positive thinking
7. Supportive relationships

None of these factors should be very surprising, but we often overlook them. So I created a couple of spreads to examine these keys to happiness and to encourage their use. Here is the layout for the first version of this spread:

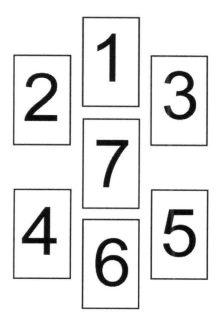

Interpret these cards using the following positional meanings:

1. What is something that you should be grateful for?
   (Commit to expressing that gratitude today.)
2. Who do you need to forgive?
   (Send thoughts of love and forgiveness to that person.)
3. What "random act of kindness" can you do today?
4. What small pleasure should you take notice of today?
5. What is one concrete action (or resolution) that you can take today to improve your health?
6. How can you cultivate positive expectations in life?
7. In what way(s) can you devote more quality time to your relationships (family and/or friends) today?

What follows is an alternative version of this spread (abbreviated to 6 cards) that removes the "small pleasure to notice today" card and handles the final three cards a bit differently.

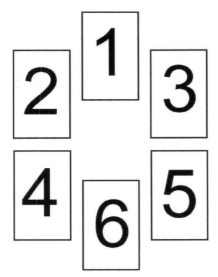

In this case, you will read the first three cards as before. The final three cards, however, should be read somewhat differently. Think of a health issue you are having before laying down Card Four, an upsetting situation before laying down Card Five, and a troublesome relationship before laying down Card Six. Those three cards will then provide guidance for those specific issues, as indicated in the following list of positional definitions.

1. What is something that you should be grateful for?
   (Commit to expressing that gratitude today.)
2. Who do you need to forgive?
   (Send thoughts of love and forgiveness to that person.)
3. What "random act of kindness" can you do today?
4. What is one concrete action (or resolution) that you can take today to improve your health issue?
5. How can you cultivate positive expectations about the upsetting situation that you face?
6. In what way(s) can you devote more quality time to the troubled relationship?

Mysticism Spread

The numbers three and seven have magical associations in most mystical traditions. Therefore, I created this spread with a layout composed of three cards in a triangle surrounded by seven cards positioned at the points of a septagram (a seven pointed star).

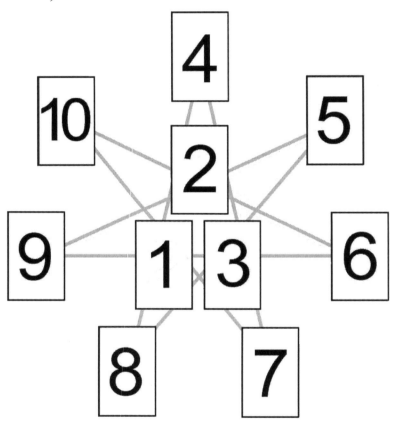

In the spread's positional meanings, I gave the three central cards a "Past, Present, and Future" orientation, and I associated the seven cards at the points of the star with the seven classical planets along with abbreviated astrological meanings for them.[60] There are other associations you may make, however, using

---

[60] *These abbreviated meanings should be seen as examples that work well for me. Feel free to adjust them to suit your own astrological understanding.*

different arcane traditions. For example, you might want to relate the seven outer cards to the seven Chakras or to the seven classical virtues: Prudence, Temperance, Strength, Justice, Faith, Hope, and Charity. For the central three cards, there are various correspondences in mystical traditions which you might use instead of Past, Present, and Future. Here are a few examples: Hinduism's trinity of Brahma, Vishnu, and Shiva suggest Creation, Protection, and Elimination; the three pillars of the Kabalistic Tree of Life suggest Mercy, Balance, and Severity; or you might use the "three greatest treasures" that Lao Tzu describes in the Tao Te Ching: Simplicity, Patience, and Compassion.

Using the correspondences I first mentioned, you would interpret these ten cards using the following positional meanings:

Triangle:

1. Past – the path you have traveled so far

2. Present – your Higher Self's advice for today

3. Future – the spiritual path ahead of you

Seven Planets:

4. Moon – Emotions, unconscious, mystery

5. Mercury – Communication, reasoning, travel

6. Venus – Love, harmony, beauty

7. Sun – Soul vs. ego, Karma

8. Mars – Energy, conflict

9. Jupiter – Growth, joy, expansion and opportunity

10. Saturn – Lessons, limitations, duty, dharma

Cଓ ଓ

Appendix 1:
Spiritual Commitments

As a result of writing this book, I have developed the following set of Spiritual Commitments which succinctly distill the sacred truths I have discovered along the way. By this I mean that these are things to which I periodically reaffirm a commitment as a way of keeping on track along my spiritual path. I present them here as suggestions for you to consider so that you may create your own set of commitments and thus work toward transforming your life.

To transform my thoughts, I commit:

> To practice meditation daily

> To live mindfully in the present moment:
>
>> without regrets or recriminations about the past
>> without attachments to things or to the anticipated results of my current actions
>> without fears and worries about the future

> To live without complaining (See the Serenity Prayer, page 71)

> To focus on the good in other people and in the world instead of dwelling on what is "bad" or "wrong" and to list several things every day for which I am grateful

> To love everyone as myself and to forgive all

> To see the Divine in everything and everyone (including myself) and to turn my thoughts ever toward the Divine

To transform my actions, I commit:

> To dedicate my efforts in all things to the Divine

> To act with integrity at all times and in all ways

> To practice kindness, generosity and service

CB ❧

Appendix 2:
Glossary

There are terms used in this book that the reader might interpret in ways that differ from how I have used them. Consequently, I decided that it would be useful to include a short glossary to explain my usage of them.

Divine
Throughout this book I have used the general term "the Divine" instead a specific one like "God." One reason for this is that I want this book to be accessible to spiritual aspirants of all traditions. Another reason may be understood based on this quote from *The Yoga of Jesus* by Paramahansa Yogananda:

> *God as Spirit has no circumscribing name. Whether one refers to the Absolute as God or Jehovah or Brahman or Allah, that does not express Him.*

Ego
The ego refers to our illusory sense that we are separate from our spiritual Self. The ego believes that it is the totality of our identity and our being and that we are the center of the universe (figuratively speaking). It also may be seen as the antithesis to our soul. For a lengthier discussion about the ego, see the section "What is the Ego?" (See page 145).

Evil
I do not believe in the popular notion of evil, which is that there are people who, under the influence of something (such as "Satan"), go around doing bad things just for the sake of doing bad things. People take wrong action (hate, violence, greed, etcetera) as a result of their wounds, their suffering, and their misunderstanding. To dismiss them as "evil" causes us to mistake where they are coming from, which then cripples our ability to deal with them in an effective and responsible fashion. Thus, I generally use this word to mean dysfunctional actions perpetrated by wounded, unenlightened people as they act out of ignorance. I would refer the reader to the section of the Devil card titled "Resist not evil" (see page 75) where this definition of "evil" is presented: "a veil of ignorance [that] covers the truth of God."

Judgment
This word (and the related term "to judge") is perhaps the one most misunderstood by other people of any that I use, and it seems to

invite contentious debate. It is important to explain that I use it differently in my spiritual discussions from its synonym *evaluation*. As discussed in the section titled "Misunderstanding *judgment*" (page 97) this word can mean an objective evaluation of a situation and the formulation of an educated opinion about it, but I generally use it to mean a moralistic condemnation of other people and a presumption to determine their worthiness.

Kabbalah   Kabbalah refers to an esoteric system that originated with a mystical branch of Judaism. Its esoteric teachings describe the nature and purpose of the universe and human beings as well as the relationship between the Divine and the manifest universe, all with the goal of helping the adherent live an enlightened life.

Mundane   I use this word to indicate the material realm of existence as opposed to the world of our spiritual self. Thus, I rarely use it in the pejorative sense of dull, banal, or unimaginative.

RWS   RWS (Rider-Waite-Smith) refers to the Tarot deck designed by A.E. Waite, illustrated by Pamela Colman Smith, and originally published in 1909 by William Rider & Son.

Self   It should be understood that there are several distinct meanings for this word. One is our mortal self, meaning our physical body and earthly personality. Then there is the ego-self, which is defensive and devoted to the illusion that we are separate from other people and from the Divine. Finally, there is our true, divine Self. This is our eternal soul, which is at one with the Divine, and I have capitalized it in this book, as opposed to the other two (the mortal versions of self).

Soul and Spirit   These two words are commonly used as synonyms, but in this book, I generally use them distinctly. I consider our soul to be our eternal essence. It is what continues after the death of our physical body. I define spirit as the ineffable, non-material essence of our mortal life in this material world.

☾ ☽

Appendix 3:
Bibliography

In addition to obvious and well-known spiritual texts such as the Bible, the Quran, the Tao Te Ching, and the Bhagavad Gita, the following are some valuable resources to supplement your exploration of spirituality. Books that I have referenced in this text are included in this list.

Albom, Mitch. *Tuesdays with Morrie*; Doubleday, New York, NY, 1997

Allen, Marc. *The Greatest Secret of All: Simple Steps to Abundance, Fulfillment, and a Life Well Lived*; New World Library, Novato, CA, 2011

Aurelius, Marcus. *Meditations*; Penguin Classics, New York, NY, 2006

Bentov, Itzhak. *A Brief Tour of Higher Consciousness*; Destiny Books, Rochester, VT, 2000

Buscaglia, Leo. *Celebrate Life!;* Nightingale-Conant, Niles, IL, 1995

Byrne, Rhonda. *The Secret*; Beyond Words Publishing, Hillsboro, OR, 2006

Campbell, Joseph. *Hero with a Thousand Faces*; Princeton University Press, Princeton, NJ, 1949

———. *Pathways to Bliss: Mythology and Personal Transformation*; New World Library, Novato, CA, 2004

Case, Paul Foster. *The Tarot: A Key to the Wisdom of the Ages*; Macoy Publishing Company, Richmond, VA, 1947

Chödrön, Pema. *Start Where You Are: A Guide to Compassionate Living;* Shambhala, Boston, MA, 2001

Chopra, Deepak. *A Path to Love: Renewing the Power of Spirit in Your Life*; Harmony, New York, NY, 1996

Deikman, Arthur. *The Observing Self*; Beacon Press, Boston, MA, 1983

DuQuette, Lon Milo. *Book of Ordinary Oracles*; Weiser Books, Newburyport, MA, 2005

Dyer, Wayne. *The Awakened Life*; Nightingale-Conant Corporation, New York, NY, 1990

Fields, Rick, et. al. *Chop Wood, Carry Water: A Guide to Finding Spiritual Fulfillment in Everyday Life*. J.P. Tarcher, Inc., New York, NY, 1984

Frankl, Viktor. *Man's Search for Meaning*; Beacon Press, Boston, MA, 2006

Greer, Mary K. *Mary K. Greer's 21 Ways to Read a Tarot Card*; Llewellyn Publications, Woodbury, MN, 2006

Hicks, Esther and Jerry. *The Law of Attraction*; Hay House, Inc., Carlsbad, CA, 2006

Housden, Roger. *Ten Poems to Change Your Life*; Harmony, New York, NY, 2001

Kabir. *The Kabir Book: Forty-Four of the Ecstatic Poems of Kabir*, Trans. Robert Bly; Beacon Press, Boston, MA, 1993

Katie, Byron. *Who Would You Be Without Your Story?*; Hay House, Inc., Carlsbad, CA, 2008

Keyes, Ken Jr. *Handbook to Higher Consciousness*; Living Love Publications, Coos Bay, OR, 1975

Kralik, John. *365 Thank Yous: The Year a Simple Act of Daily Gratitude Changed My Life*; Hyperion Books, New York, NY, 2010

Kübler-Ross, Elisabeth. *On Death and Dying*; Scribner, New York, NY, 1997

Macbeth, Jessica. *Moon over Water: The Path of Meditation*; Gateway Books, Dublin, Ireland, 1990

Malachi, Tau. *The Gnostic Gospel of St. Thomas: Meditations on the Mystical Teachings*; Llewellyn Publications, Woodbury, MN, 2004

Millman, Dan. *Way of the Peaceful Warrior*; HJ Kramer, Inc., Tiburon, CA, 2006

Mirabai. *Ecstatic Poems*, Trans. Robert Bly and Jane Hirshfield; Beacon Press, Boston, MA, 2009

Moore, Thomas. *Care of the Soul*; HarperCollins, New York, NY, 1992

————. *Soul Mates*; Harper Perennial, New York, NY, 1994

Moody, Raymond, Jr. *Life After Life*; HarperOne, New York, NY, 2001

Nepo, Mark. *The Book of Awakening*; Conari Press, San Francisco, CA, 2000

Nhat Hanh, Thich. *Call Me by My True Names*; Parallax Press, Berkeley, CA, 1999

————. *No Death, No Fear: Comforting Wisdom for Life*; Riverhead, New York, NY, 2003

————. *Peace Is Every Breath: A Practice for Our Busy Lives*; HarperCollins, New York, NY, 2011

Nouwen, Henri. *The Wounded Healer: Ministry in Contemporary Society*; Doubleday, New York, NY, 1979

Paramahansa Yogananda. *The Yoga of Jesus*; Self-Realization Fellowship, Los Angeles, CA, 2007

Parthasarathy, A. *Vedanta Treatise: The Eternities*; A. Parthasarathy, Mumbai, India, 2009

Place, Robert Michael and Guiley, Rosemary Ellen. *The Alchemical Tarot*; Thorsons, London, England, 1995

Plato. *The Republic;* Trans. Allan Bloom; Basic Books, New York, NY, 1968

Pollack, Rachel. *Seventy-Eight Degrees of Wisdom*; Thorsons, London, England, 1997

Rumi. *The Soul of Rumi: A New Collection of Ecstatic Poems*. Trans. Coleman Barks. HarperOne, New York, NY, 2002

————. *The Rumi Collection;* Trans. Various; Shambhala, Boston, MA, 2000

Ram Dass. *Be Here Now*; Hanuman Foundation, Boulder, CO, 1978

————. *Grist for the Mill*; Bantam Books, New York, NY, 1979

Reps, Paul and Senzaki, Nyogen. *Zen Flesh, Zen Bones*; Tuttle Publishing, Boston, MA, 1998

Ricklef, James. *Tarot Affirmations*; CreateSpace, Charleston, SC, 2009

Salzberg, Sharon. *Lovingkindness: The Revolutionary Art of Happiness*; Shambhala, Boston, MA, 2002

Saint Teresa of Ávila. *The Interior Castle*; Trans. E. Allison Peers. Dover Publications, Mineola, NY, 2007

Schucman, Helen. *A Course in Miracles*; Foundation for Inner Peace, Tiburon, CA, 2007

Sri Ramakrishna. *Sayings of Sri Ramakrishna*; Vedanta Press, Hollywood, CA, 2004

Suzuki, Shunryu. *Zen Mind, Beginner's Mind*; Random House Inc., New York, NY, 1972

Swami Prabhavananda. *The Sermon on the Mount According to Vedanta*; Vedanta Press, Hollywood, CA, 1963

————. *Religion in Practice*; Vedanta Press, Hollywood, CA, 1969

Thoreau, Henry David. *Thoreau: Walden and Other Writings*; Bantam Books, Inc., New York, NY, 1962

Tolle, Eckhart. *A New Earth: Awakening to Your Life's Purpose*; Penguin Group, Inc., New York, NY, 2005

————. *The Power of Now: A Guide to Spiritual Enlightenment*; New World Library, Novato, CA, 2004

Tolstoy, Leo. *Leo Tolstoy: Spiritual Writings*; Orbis Books, Maryknoll, NY, 2006

Walsch, Neale Donald. *The Complete Conversations with God*; Putnam Adult, New York, NY, 2005

————. *Friendship with God: An Uncommon Dialogue*; Berkley Trade, New York, NY, 2002

Williamson, Marianne. *A Return to Love*; Harper Perennial, New York, NY, 1996

Zukav, Gary and Francis, Linda. *The Heart of the Soul: Emotional Awareness*; Free Press, New York, NY, 2002

℘ ℘

Made in the USA
San Bernardino, CA
05 January 2014